JN055310

人形演劇の現在
モノ、モノ遣い、アクター

ボイド眞理子【著】

Japanese Contemporary Objects, Manipulators, and Actors in Performance

Mari Boyd

上智大学出版
Sophia University Press

Fig. 2.1. Nori Sawa, *King Lear*, 2005, Studio
Rubin, Prague. Courtesy of ArtPrometheus.

Fig. 2.2. Miyako Kurotani, *Half-Moon, Kurosolo Series No. 1*, 2013, Sengawa Theatre, Tokyo.
Photo © kino asa. Courtesy of genre:Gray.

Fig. 2.3. Tengai Amano, *Heitaro's Yokai Diary*, 2004, Shizuoka Performing Arts Center. Courtesy of I.T.O. Project.

Fig. 2.5. Jo Taira, *La Marie-Vison*, New National Theatre, Tokyo, 2012. Photo © Daisuke Omori. Courtesy of Jo's Group.

Fig. 2.4. Shigeru Kimura (dir.), Asako Fukunaga (art dir.), *Twilight Dream—Selected from Ranpo Edogawa's Short Stories*, 2016, Aichi Puppet Theatre Center (Himawari Hall), Nagoya. Photo © Takashi Horikawa. Courtesy of Object Performance Theatre.

Fig. 2.6. ARICA, *On the Island*, 2019, BUoY, Tokyo. Photo © Katsu Miyauchi.

Fig. 2.7. Niwa Gekidan Penino, *Avidya—The Dark Inn*, 2016, ROHM Theatre Kyoto. Photo © Yoshikazu Inoue. Courtesy of Kyoto Experiment.

Fig. 3.1. Kiyokazu Yamamoto, *Choan and the Ripped Umbrella: Heisei Trick Peep Show*, 2008, Theatre Tram, Tokyo. Courtesy of Youkiza.

Fig. 4.1. Youkiza and Wishing Chong, *Doll Town*, 2017, The Suzunari, Tokyo. Courtesy of Youkiza.

Fig. 4.2. Ryudo Uzaki and the New ☆ Ryudo Group, *Sonezaki Shinju Rock*, 2002, Sogetsu Hall, Tokyo. Courtesy of New ☆ Ryudo Group.

Fig. 4.3. Hiroshi Sugimoto, *Sonezaki Love Suicides Kannon Pilgrimage*, 2014, Kanagawa Arts Theatre, Yokohama. Photo © Hajime Watanabe. Courtesy of Odawara Art Foundation.

Fig. 4.4. Koki Mitani, *Much Ado About Love Suicides*, 2012, Parco Theater, Tokyo. Photo © Futoshi Osako. Courtesy of PARCO CO., LTD.

Fig. 4.5. Hitomiza, *King Lear*, 2008, Haiyuza, Tokyo. Photo © Yamazaki Kazuo. Courtesy of Hitomiza.

Fig. 4.6. Marionette Company Isshiza, *Artaud 24 Heures*, 2011, Akasaka Red Theater, Tokyo. Photo © Yasushi Yaginuma. Courtesy of Isshiza.

Fig. 4.7. Setagaya Public Theatre and Complicité, *Shun-kin*, 2013, Setagaya Public Theatre, Tokyo. Photo © Tsukasa Aoki. Courtesy of Setagaya Public Theatre.

Fig. 4.8. Youkiza international collaboration with French artists, *Descendants of the Eunuch Admiral*, 2010, Theatre Tram, Tokyo. Photo © Jun Ishikawa & So Kuramochi. Courtesy of Youkiza.

Fig. 5.1. Geminoid HI-2. Courtesy of Hiroshi Ishiguro Laboratory ATR.

Fig. 5.2. Seinendan + Osaka University Robot Theatre Project, *Three Sisters Android Version*, 2012, Kichijoji Theatre, Tokyo. Photo © Tsukasa Aoki. Courtesy of Seinendan.

Fig. 6.1. Youkiza and Théâtre du Rêve Expérimental, *As the Sparrows Wended in a Windless Winter*, 2017, Za-Koenji Public Theatre, Tokyo. Courtesy of Youkiza.

Japanese Contemporary Objects, Manipulators, and Actors in Performance

人形演劇の現在
モノ、モノ遣い、アクター

Mari Boyd

Sophia University Press, Tokyo

Sophia University Press

One of the fundamental ideals of Sophia University is "to embody the university's special characteristics by offering opportunities to study Christianity and Christian culture. At the same time, recognizing the diversity of thought, the university encourages academic research on a wide variety of world views."

The Sophia University Press was established to provide an independent base for the publication of scholarly research. The publications of our press are a guide to the level of research at Sophia, and one of the factors in the public evaluation of our activities.

Sophia University Press publishes books that (1) meet high academic standards; (2) are related to our university's founding spirit of Christian humanism; (3) are on important issues of interest to a broad general public; and (4) textbooks and introductions to the various academic disciplines. We publish works by individual scholars as well as the results of collaborative research projects that contribute to general cultural development and the advancement of the university.

Japanese Contemporary Objects, Manipulators, and Actors in Performance
© Mari Boyd, 2020
Published by Sophia University Press

Printed and distributed by GYOSEI Corporation, Tokyo
ISBN 978-4-324-10829-1
Inquiries: https://gyosei.jp

To Elizabeth and Laura Boyd, who love to read

Acknowledgments

I would like to express my gratitude to the many Japanese and foreign performing-object theatre artists and companies, playwrights and actors, as well as organizations like UNIMA-Japan and the Japan Puppet Theater Conference (Zenninkyo) for their cooperation, information, and permission to translate as well as reproduce copyrighted material.

Special thanks go to Edo Marionette Theatre Youkiza for allowing me the delight of attending their rehearsals and to Kathy Foley, Distinguished Professor of Theatre Arts at the University of California, Santa Cruz, for her invaluable comments and advice.

Of particular support also have been Sophia University Press, Gyosei Corporation, and copyeditor William Andrews. Any errors or omissions are my own.

Note on Names and Translations

1. With the exception of historical figures, Japanese names are presented in the order of given name followed by family name.
2. The translations of quoted material from Japanese publications are mine unless indicated otherwise.

CONTENTS

PART TWO Japanese Material Performance in Translation

Illustrations

Color plates

2.1. Nori Sawa, *King Lear*, 2005, Studio Rubin, Prague. Courtesy of ArtPrometheus.

2.2. Miyako Kurotani, *Half-Moon, Kurosolo Series No. 1*, 2013, Sengawa Theatre, Tokyo. Photo © kino asa. Courtesy of genre:Gray.

2.3. Tengai Amano, *Heitaro's Yokai Diary*, 2004, Shizuoka Performing Arts Center. Courtesy of I.T.O. Project.

2.4. Shigeru Kimura (dir.), Asako Fukunaga (art dir.), *Twilight Dream—Selected from Ranpo Edogawa's Short Stories*, 2016, Aichi Puppet Theatre Center (Himawari Hall), Nagoya. Photo © Takashi Horikawa. Courtesy of Object Performance Theatre.

2.5. Jo Taira, *La Marie-Vison*, New National Theatre, Tokyo, 2012. Photo © Daisuke Omori. Courtesy of Jo's Group.

2.6. ARICA, *On the Island*, 2019, BUoY, Tokyo. Photo © Katsu Miyauchi.

2.7. Niwa Gekidan Penino, *Avidya—The Dark Inn*, 2016, ROHM Theatre Kyoto. Photo © Yoshikazu Inoue. Courtesy of Kyoto Experiment.

3.1. Kiyokazu Yamamoto, *Choan and the Ripped Umbrella: Heisei Trick Peep Show*, 2008, Theatre Tram, Tokyo. Courtesy of Youkiza.

4.1. Youkiza and Wishing Chong, *Doll Town*, 2017, The Suzunari, Tokyo. Courtesy of Youkiza.

4.2. Ryudo Uzaki and the New ☆ Ryudo Group, *Sonezaki Shinju Rock*, 2002, Sogetsu Hall, Tokyo. Courtesy of New ☆ Ryudo Group.

4.3. Hiroshi Sugimoto, *Sonezaki Love Suicides Kannon Pilgrimage*, 2014, Kanagawa Arts Theatre, Yokohama. Photo © Hajime Watanabe. Courtesy of Odawara Art Foundation.

4.4. Koki Mitani, *Much Ado About Love Suicides*, 2012, Parco Theater, Tokyo. Photo © Futoshi Osako. Courtesy of PARCO CO., LTD.

4.5. Hitomiza, *King Lear*, 2008, Haiyuza, Tokyo. Photo © Yamazaki Kazuo. Courtesy of Hitomiza.

4.6. Marionette Company Isshiza, *Artaud 24 Heures*, 2011, Akasaka Red Theater, Tokyo. Photo © Yasushi Yaginuma. Courtesy of Isshiza.

4.7. Setagaya Public Theatre and Complicité, *Shun-kin*, 2013, Setagaya Public Theatre, Tokyo. Photo © Tsukasa Aoki. Courtesy of Setagaya Public Theatre.

4.8. Youkiza international collaboration with French artists, *Descendants of the Eunuch Admiral*, 2010, Theatre Tram, Tokyo. Photo © Jun Ishikawa & So Kuramochi. Courtesy of Youkiza.

Charts

Black and white figures

Cover figures

1. Jo Taira, *La Marie-Vison*, New National Theatre, 2012. Photo © Daisuke Omori. Courtesy of Jo's Group.
2. ARICA, *On the Island*, 2019, BUoY, Tokyo. Photo © Katsu Miyauchi.
3. Niwa Gekidan Penino, *Avidya—The Dark Inn*, 2016, ROHM Theatre Kyoto. Photo © Yoshikazu Inoue. Courtesy of Kyoto Experiment.
4. Miyako Kurotani, *Half-Moon, Kurosolo Series No. 1*, 2013, Sengawa Theatre, Tokyo. Photo © kino asa. Courtesy of genre:Gray.
5. Shigeru Kimura (dir.), Asako Fukunaga (art dir.), *Lakai*, 2004, Toga Festival. Photo © Takashi Horikawa. Courtesy of Object Performance Theatre.
6. Youkiza and Wishing Chong, *Doll Town*, 2017, The Suzunari, Tokyo. Courtesy of Youkiza.
7. Ryudo Uzaki and the New ☆ Ryudo Group, *Sonezaki Shinju Rock*, 2002, Sogetsu Hall, Tokyo. Courtesy of New ☆ Ryudo Group.
8. Hiroshi Sugimoto, *Sonezaki Love Suicides Kannon Pilgrimage*, 2014, Kanagawa Arts Theatre. Photo © Hajime Watanabe. Courtesy of Odawara Art Foundation.
9. Koki Mitani, *Much Ado about Love Suicides*, 2012, Parco Theater, Tokyo. Photo © Futoshi Osako. Courtesy of PARCO CO., LTD.
10. Nori Sawa, *King Lear*, 2005, Aoyama Round Theatre, Tokyo. Courtesy of Aoyama Round Theatre.
11. Marionette Company Isshiza, *Artaud 24 Heures++Encore*, 2014, Tokyo Metropolitan Theatre (Theatre East). Photo © Yasushi Yaginuma. Courtesy of Isshiza.
12. Setagaya Public Theatre and Complicité, *Shun-kin*, 2013, Setagaya Public Theatre, Tokyo. Photo © Tsukasa Aoki. Courtesy of Setagaya Public Theatre.
13. Youkiza's international collaboration with French artists, *Descendants of the Eunuch Admiral*, 2010, Theatre Tram, Tokyo. Photo © Jun Ishikawa & So Kuramochi. Courtesy of Youkiza.
14. Seinendan + Osaka University Robot Theatre Project, *Three Sisters, Android Version*, 2012, Kichijoji Theatre, Tokyo. Photo © Tsukasa Aoki. Courtesy of Seinendan.
15. Youkiza and Théâtre du Rêve Expérimental, *As the Sparrows Wended in a Windless Winter*, 2017, Za-Koenji Public Theatre, Tokyo. Courtesy of Youkiza.
16. Tengai Amano, *The Voyage of Imperial Prince Takaoka*, 2018, The Suzunari, Tokyo. Photo © Takeshi Yamada. Courtesy of I.T.O. Project.

17. Kiyokazu Yamamoto, *Choan and the Ripped Umbrella: Heisei Trick Peep Show*, 2008, Theatre Tram, Tokyo. Courtesy of Youkiza.

Cover figures

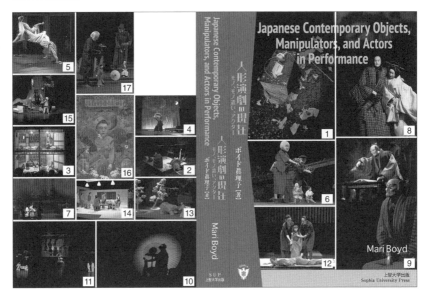

Objective

To disassemble the preconceptions held both at home and abroad that Japanese puppetry is limited to traditional *bunraku* (*ningyo joruri*) and to "child's play," I will argue that the stimulus of object theatre, imported from the West, has been fundamental to opening the floodgates for the growth of artistic, adult material performance that reflects the posthuman turn of our contemporary society. This endeavor will include discussion of the significance of the visibility/invisibility binary, the reinvention of dramatic and literary masterpieces via material performance, and investigation of technological advances enabling new forms of collaboration such as robot/android theatre and New Media Theatre. Detailed play analyses are provided to indicate that performing-object plays can be uncompromising explorations of sociocultural issues and posthuman concerns appropriate for adults and as such can serve to enhance the value and enjoyment of the performing arts.

Introduction

The resurgence of objects in performance in the West began in the late 1880s, became theorized in the 1990s, and had a direct and profound effect on Japanese material practitioners and their productions.

Today, performing-objects comprise a vast category of material images, including first, conventional puppets and masks purposely made for performance, and second, found-objects, human-made or otherwise, that act according to their inherent nature, like a bag blowing in the wind, or to agency given them by humans. Puppets and performing-objects are overlapping terms both commonly in currency; the older term puppet(ry) will continue to be used in this study, but in a limited way.

A puppet is usually considered to have the following characteristics. It has two levels of corporeality: the design of its physical structure (material, weight, joints, center of gravity, etc.) that determines its potentiality for movement; and its actual movement, which comes from the manipulator's expressive work (kinetic, gestural, or emotive). As Basil Jones, co-founder of Handspring Puppetry Company (f. 1981), notes, through being manipulated, the puppet becomes the "site of the signification of life" (2014, 61–69). It also offers what material performance theorist Steve Tillis calls the "double vision of perception and imagination" by which the puppet "pleasurably challenges the audience's understanding of the relationship between object and life" (1992, xx). Lastly, the conventional puppet usually requires real-time control by a manipulator in a shared space.

As material performance scholar John Bell points out, the new generic term "performing-object" has a broader range than "puppet" and includes performative techniques not normally categorized as puppetry while sharing the same basic approach (1997, 29–30). In this regard, computer graphics and digital technology have greatly broadened our concept of a "puppet," although some kind of human management is still in effect. In this book, terms like "puppet" and "puppetry" will be reserved as far as possible for premodern performance, conventional puppetry, and quotations whose sources use those terms. "Performing-figures" will sometimes be used to indicate that the objects are humanoid figures.

In Japan, a paradigm shift occurred in the 1990s to 2000s, due to both a culmination of gradual sociocultural changes since the 1980s, especially in pop culture and the new wave of material performance practice and theory from the West concerning the nature of performing-objects and the manipulator's relations with them. The three main, overlapping characteristics of Japanese material performance from the end of the twentieth century are as follows.

The first characteristic is that an upsurge in Japanese material performance moved the creative focus from children-centered education and entertainment to adult-centered art; or conceptually, from magical illusionism to alternative puppet-performer theatre that envisions the Real. Different artists subscribe to different interpretations of the Real; this writer's interest lies in Lacan's interpretation that the Real refers to the part of oneself repressed in order for one to become a subject.[1] The second characteristic is the rapid growth of intertextuality, hybridity, and intra- and interculturalism (or interweaving) borne of diversity and resourceful production acumen in an increasingly borderless and globalized world. The third is the application of new technologies, digital and otherwise, to performing-objects to illustrate or experiment with perceptions of the Real.

This book is a "not-*bunraku*" study of material performance. *Bunraku* or *ningyo joruri*, which has certainly been inspirational for practitioners and aficionados, is already well researched by Western academics and will be treated lightly here. In fact, it was a comment on the *World Encyclopedia of Puppetry Arts* (WEPA, f. 2013) website about the scarcity of their information on the contemporary period of Japan that motivated this researcher to write this book.[2]

Despite its emphasis of revealing the process of manipulation, object theatre does challenge the *bunraku* concept, if not the practice, of having manipulators always in full view of the audience—some discussion will be included in a section in Chapter 4 titled "Three intracultural productions featuring *bunraku*."

The "betwixt-and-between" quality of contemporary performance can be demanding and disorienting for the audience. While to take viewers by surprise is a legitimate strategy, preparing them for something different is also valid. In this respect, applying the concept of framing (Sone 2017, 82) helps the viewer understand by clarifying how hybridity, diversity, and collaboration function in general and in specific productions.

"To frame" commonly means to draw up plans like an outline. Or a frame can be an open structure that gives shape and support to or enclos-es something. Yuji Sone, author of *Japanese Robot Culture*, uses it in an abstract way to mean "creating an imaginary space where a robot, a so-cial issue, etc. can be experimented with" (ibid.). The success of a pro-duction depends heavily not only on how it is framed onstage but also through the various kinds of outlying media. For example, in the case of robotics and robot theatre, research projects have received immense pub-licity together with financial aid in recent years from prominent sourc-es—like the Agency for Cultural Affairs (ACA), Grant-in-Aid for Scien-tific Research from the Ministry of Education, Culture, Sports, Science, and Technology (MEXT) and the Japan Society for the Promotion of Science (JSPS), major corporations, and academic institutions—which frame Japan as a brand, i.e., the "next-generation robot and human col-laborative society."

This book is divided into two parts and nine chapters. Part One pro-vides an overview of the development of contemporary Japanese materi-al performance and its strong connections with the West.

Chapter 1 Overview presents three aspects of modern Japanese mate-rial performance: the growth of modern Western-derived puppetry and audiences; the relations between the old and new animisms and perform-ing-objects; and a statistical assessment of contemporary Japanese mate-rial performance.

Chapter 2 The Rise of Object Theatre focuses on how Western object theatre triggered the 1990s paradigm shift from "puppetry" to the more inclusive "performing-objects" and "material performance," which ena-bled Japanese artists to loosen ties with a secular and humanistic per-spective on life and draw strength from other relationalities bringing their concept of material performance to what it is today.

Chapter 3 Rupture and the "Real" addresses the major theories rele-vant to comprehending modern material performance in Japan. This is followed by a discussion of how the rupture of standard Western stylistic form was first attempted through genre-breaking. This process eventually extended to collaboration in co-creating dramaturgical strategies with di-verse practitioners.

Chapter 4 Collaborative Productions addresses the variety of drama-turgical strategies deployed in domestic and international/global collabo-rations that now abound in the artistic pursuit of diversity. Encounters with the immense range of sociocultural diversity in the world have led to the rise of three perspectives on cultural globalization: cultural differentiation, cultural convergence, and hybridization, which also manifest in theatre.

Chapter 5 Robot and Android Theatre and Chapter 6 New Media Theatre and Intermedial Theatre address two aspects of technological development in relation to performing-objects: first, robot theatre in the context of aggressive national branding of robotics as the forefront of technological and societal innovation; second, the concept of intermediality as used in New Media Theatre.

Part Two contains translations of three plays that feature performing-objects. Chapter 7 presents Tengai Amano's *Heitaro's Yokai Diary* (2004), a work brimful of *yokai* monsters zealously testing the spirit of a young samurai; Chapter 8 offers Kiyokazu Yamamoto's *Choan and the Ripped Umbrella: Heisei Trick Peep Show* (2011), a play about a villainous doctor who stops at nothing to satisfy his greed for money; and finally, Chapter 9 presents Kuro Tanino's *Avidya—The Dark Inn* (2015), which is about two puppeteers at an old, hot-spring inn, where their bizarre homunculus dance draws out the inner darkness of the residents.

1   Cf. Chapter 2, p. 51 and Chapter 3-1.
2   This is not to denigrate the WEPA or writers and translators for the contemporary period (since 1945), i.e., Kathy Foley, Jean-Jacques Tschudin (d. 2013), Koshiro Uno (d. 2015), and Masao Yoshikawa, who have all conducted excellent research for their entries.

PART ONE

Contemporary Japanese Performing-objects and Material Performance

Chapter 1

Overview

1-1 The growth of modern Western-derived puppetry and audiences

First, an overview of the changing sociocultural and political uses of material performance and their targeted audiences of the past century in Japan will be presented with identification of the major pivotal changes that have arisen from the influx of Western practice, theory, and policy.

It is important to remember that premodern Japanese puppetry, such as ritual puppets, automata, stick puppets, *ningyo joruri*, and string puppetry, was fashioned for adults though children could also enjoy some of the fare at festivals, sideshows to *rakugo* (comedic storytelling), and on other occasions.

While domestic changes and developments were taking place, Western puppetry was introduced to Japan in a series of waves that made a lasting impact on local puppetry. In the late nineteenth century, the first wave introduced the new idea of a dedicated children's puppet performance based on magical, illusionist theatre that was not considered to contradict or challenge the indigenous animistic culture. The visits of the English D'Arc Marionette Theatre company between 1894 and 1900 drove this development (Kato 2007, 31). Their typical illusionist puppet shows in which puppeteers stayed hidden to promote a magical belief in autonomous puppets were showcased at Hanayashiki, an upscale amusement park in Asakusa, Tokyo. Based on slapstick, comedy, and an omniscient narrator, the D'Arc style was geared to children and their specialty was a European trick skeleton figure. These Western marionettes won such public adulation that *kabuki* actor Onoe Kikugoro V capitalized on their popularity and included similar marionette characters played by *kabuki* actors in his program (ibid., 31). Local followers of this illusionist style based on invisible manipulation also formed their own groups.

However, some professionals like Edo Marionette Theatre Youkiza (hereafter Youkiza; Edo ito-ayatsuri ningyo Youkiza),[1] were not impressed by the clumsy *papier mâché* dolls nor the "premodern" skills and attitude of these Western puppeteers. The specific D'Arcy style faded out in the 1930s when its novelty had worn off, but the notions of magical illusionism and targeting young children as the main audience of a show took hold for a very long time.

The second wave rose in the 1920s, when Japanese avant-garde artists, enthralled by Western performance theory and methods, actively imported Western avant-garde theory about the significance of string-objects in the arts and raised the artistic value of material performance. Poets and painters such as Hakushu Kitahara (1885–1942), Kanae Yamamoto (1882–1946), Mokutaro Kinoshita (1885–1945), and Frits Rumpf (1888–1949), all connected with the Circle of Pan (Pan no kai, 1908–1913), shared a fascination with *commedia dell'arte*, Gordon Craig's uber-marionettes, and Henrich von Kleist's marionette theory. The new modern Japanese string-object theatre diverged from the traditional in its rejection of the transmission of *kata*, or form; it attended as much to the total artwork involved in the scenography as to the string-object's expressiveness or the narrator's style and technique.

Professional manipulators also became involved. A private string-object performance of Maeterlinck's *Agravaine and Sélysette* in 1923 led to the founding of the Tsukiji Puppet Theatre (Tsukiji ningyoza). Kitahara and Yoshiro Nagase (1891–1978) formed the Teatro Marionette in 1924. A couple of years later, the famous producer and critic Toji Kawajiri (1908–1932) began the Dana Puppet Theatre (Dana ningyoza) with string-objects. In 1929, this group transformed into PUK Puppet Theatre (PUK PUPA TEATRO; hereafter PUK),[2] the most renowned of all modern performing-object companies in Japan today and noted for its dedication to the freedom of artistic expression and antiwar activities. PUK began as a string-object company but later expanded its repertory to include a large variety of styles, such as Guignol figures and black light performance.

This movement also reflected a modern concern with freedom and social issues. In 1926, Isshi Youki I (later Magosaburo X) collaborated with Gentaro Koito, a Western-style painter, and Yohei Fujinami IV, a *kabuki* stage property specialist, and performed at the Imperial Hotel entertainment hall. Five years later, Isshi mounted a string-puppet adaptation of the expressionist *The Cabinet of Dr. Caligari*. Although these shows won critical acclaim, lavish expenditures plunged them deep into debt both times and effectively put a damper on further experimental endeavors. Nonetheless, it was in the 1920s, when stimulated by European marionette performance and theory, modern Japanese string-object theatre secured a high reputation as a novel contemporary art form while other modern performing-object styles were considered less sophisticated. In the field of children's early education, Sozo Kurahashi (1882–1955), a kindergarten principal and notable proponent of children's education through performing-objects and arts, opened the Ochanomizu Puppet Company (Ochanomizu ningyoza) in 1923 for children (Kato 2007, 91).

During this period, the first wave concepts of magical illusionism and children-centered audiences spread and took root in public children's entertainment and preschool programs for the very young. In addition, domestic sociopolitical circumstances opened up different courses of activity.

The third wave set in from the 1930s, turning material performance into a useful propaganda tool for celebrating patriotism and militarism, and ended with Japan's defeat in World War II. For instance, in the 1932 Shanghai Incident, three Japanese officers conducted self-immolation when breaking through the enemy lines. This patriotic self-sacrifice riveted public attention and became the topic of songs, films, plays, and puppet shows entitled *Three Heroic Human Bombs* (Bakudan sanyushi, 1932). The earliest children's puppet play to overtly depict contemporary warfare and death, the material version using *mezashi*[3] string-puppets was produced as part of an event hosted by the Asahi Children's Association (Asahi kodomo no kai) in 1932.

During World War II, the Imperial Rule Assistance Association (Taiseiyokusan-kai), newly established in 1941 by then Prime Minister Fumimaro Konoe, adopted Nazi cultural policy for disseminating jingoism and supporting the war effort. They noted that "puppetry's mobility, facility of operation, facility in construction, and its recycling of used materials rendered it an ideal communicative medium in the daily life of the people" (Kato 2007, 231). This statement suggests that string-objects were no longer the coveted type; easy-to-manipulate hand puppets were utilized instead.

Mobilized puppetry companies dedicated to promoting the war effort traveled around the country offering such plays as an idealized three-generation *yamato* family with seven children, all hand-puppets, to drive home the "doctrine of Japanese nativist *yamato* fighting spirit, national and family unity, and an attitude of persevering until victory day" (ibid., 107). The war years ironically provided an excellent opportunity for the development of material performance.

By the postwar period, both children and adults had acquired much viewing experience, and amateur puppetry circles were popular in companies and schools. As this generation had learned that material performance could be deployed as a political tool, many company puppet circles were operated by labor union members with leftist leanings. By this time, modern Japanese material performance had become thoroughly modernist and illusionist; puppeteers stayed concealed to promote a magical belief in the independent life of puppets.

The fourth wave arrived as part of the Allied Occupation (1945–1952). Under the guidance of General McArthur and the GHQ, the Ministry of Education relegated puppetry to preschool educational activities and up to third graders in compulsory school curriculum to communicate democratic principles in an enjoyable manner. The attitude that puppetry was officially for children quickly became ingrained so that even when superior productions were held publicly, they did not receive critical reviews as art. This attitude persisted well into the 1990s until other trends in entertainment gradually began to include character toys and mobile puppet-like figures.

From the 1960s to the mid-1970s, *angura* (underground) theatrical experimentation, including *buto* dance, appropriated material performance techniques, such as masks, painted-face, doppelgängers, and ventriloquists, as well as premodern manipulation style and staging methods—and instigated the process of genre-breaking and transcending borders with other arts and disciplines. For instance, playwright-director Juro Kara included a ventriloquist and his dummy in his well-known play *The Virgin's Mask* (1969); playwright-director Shuji Terayama

(1935–1983) freely adapted traditional recitation and puppet-like acting (*ningyoburi*) in *Hunchback of Aomori* (1967) and *Heretics Gate* (1971). As far as puppetry was concerned, the underground movement included enthusiastic professional manipulators like the present Youki Magosaburo XII[4] but did not transform the field of puppetry to any discernable extent.

In mainstream material performance, PUK became a major contributor to the activities of Nihon-UNIMA, commonly known as UNIMA-Japan (the Japan chapter of the Union Internationale de la Marionnette, f. 1967). Together with the Foundation Modern Puppet Center (Gendai ningyogeki senta, f. 1969) and the Puppet Theatre Hitomiza Theatre (Ningyo gekidan Hitomiza, f. 1948) collective, which includes Deaf Puppet Theatre and Woman Bunraku, PUK has been instrumental in spearheading international projects and collaborative exchange with material performance organizations globally. These companies target children and youth with an eye to raising their social awareness. Thus, while catering to family audiences, their performances provide socially thematic content that is often satisfyingly relevant and complex for adults as well. Hitomiza will be discussed further in the intercultural section of Chapter 4.

The most recent wave of international influx came in the late twentieth century. European object theatre and material performance were proactively introduced by practitioners associated with UNIMA-Japan and eventually enabled co-creative interdisciplinary collaborations to take place. The nature and ramifications of this wave are the main focus of this book and the discussion will begin from Chapter 2. This overview will proceed to the second aspect of animism as change and growth in material performance is stimulated by both domestic circumstances and importation from abroad.

1-2   Animisms, Shinto, and material performance

The Japanese brand of performing-object theatre, unlike that in most parts of the West, retains an animistic view of the world. Some background on this point is called for. A revisionist approach to the old anthropomorphic animism arose among Western anthropologists in the mid-twentieth century. Around the same time, fans of Japanese *anime* became aware of the pervasiveness of animism in animation narratives and imagery. Called techno-animism, this practice refers to the integration of technology, humanity, and spirituality, which enables humans to develop stronger ties with objects.[5] This section will address the old and new animisms together with two kinds of Shinto beliefs, and link them with changing views on material performance.

Animisms and Shinto

Today there are two versions of animism: the so-called "primitive" belief named so by Edward Tylor (1832–1917) in the latter half of the nineteenth century; and the new concept based on anthropologist Irving Hallowell's mid-twentieth-century research on the Ojibwe communities in Canada.

The term animism is a derivative of the word "anima," which means breath, vital principle, life, or soul. Tylor promoted its use in his 1871 seminal work *Primitive Culture* to refer to the indigenous and naive belief of various primitive peoples in the presence of spirits and souls in both living and nonliving entities. The popular indigenous Japanese belief in Shinto was a much-cited case in Tylor's discussion. In its time, Tylor's notion was widely accepted without much question. The well-known Japanologist W. G. Aston applied Tylor's approach in his study *Shinto: The Way of the Gods* (1905), although he did not actually use the term animism.

Premodern Japanese puppetry was permeated with assumptions, associations, references to Shinto beliefs based on animism. Performances were offerings of entertainment for the *kami*, who were believed to inhabit many natural things, and children were expected to have affectionate ties with nature.

Ethnologist Josef A. Kyburz, notes that after all "nature is not external to culture and society but is an imminent component or symbiotic constituent of them; moreover, the reality of nature is contingent upon human artifice and mediation."[6] What complicates the discussion of animism and Shinto is that from the Meiji period (1868–1912), besides popular Shinto, State Shinto was cultivated as a hyper-nationalistic rallying point around the emperor and his alleged divinity, becoming a driving force in times of imperialistic expansion and war. After World War II, the 1945 Shinto Directive, which had given instruction on Shinto in public education with special attention to the emperor's ancestry, was annulled. This created a lacuna that continued well beyond the 1970s. By the early twenty-first century, descriptions of Shinto returned, with major school text publishers like Daiichi Gakushusha and Tokyo Shoseki including descriptions of Shinto as a long-living animistic belief system in their ethics texts published in the 2010s.

As Akiyoshi Yamamura, a Shinto researcher, notes (2018, 281), this is somewhat ironic as in the West, religious studies experts contend that the old spirit-possessed animism "began as an expression of a nest of insulting approaches to indigenous peoples and the earliest putatively religious humans. It was, and sometimes remains, a colonialist slur" (Harvey 2013, xx).

The new animism

Many anthropologists have developed a postmodern view of animism. Among the revisionist views of animism today, the general agreement is that the new animism is neither a formal philosophy nor a symbolic representation of society, but local, specific, and pragmatic. Graham Harvey, for instance, looks for it "in-between" in the relating together of beings (often of different species) rather than "within" in the possession of or by "spirits." Thus, he emphasizes a meta-communicability that involves all animate and non-animate beings (2013, 2–3). Nurit Bird-David calls this aspect of the new animism a relational epistemology.

Bird-David's view sheds light on the animism practiced by object artist Miyako Kurotani and many others in their artistic endeavors. What they understand or believe is that spiritual connections that nourish their creativity could also be interpreted as a healthy and developed relational epistemology.

Actor-manipulator Michiko Iida of the company Hyakki Yumehina (f. 2010), and a disciple of Hoichi Okamoto (1947–2010) of Hyakki Dondoro (1974–2010), says that one must find one's *kami*, or spirit guide, in one's own locality.[7] Such a statement connects well with the attitude required to foster relatedness.

> Knowledge [...] is developing the skills of being-in-the-world with other things, making one's awareness of one's environment and one's self finer, broader, deeper, richer, etc. Knowing [...] involves "dividuating" the environment, rather than dichotomizing it, and turning attention to "we-ness." (Bird-David 1999, 77–78)

"Dividuating" in this context means being conscious of how something/someone relates to oneself rather than "individuating," i.e., being conscious of something/someone as a separate entity.

At the same time, this is not to say that emotional projection or anthropomorphism is encouraged. The secularized conceptualization of neo-animism avoids both, and, in this respect, anthropologist Bruno Latour's concept of actant is useful. While it refers to anything that modifies other actors/actants through a series of actions (Latour 2004, 75), the focus here will be on nonhuman/material actants. These entities have characteristics, tendencies, and even (quasi-)agency, but not spiritual aspirations as humans may. The testing question would be whether the entity modifies other entities, thus contributing something new to an assemblage.

An example that allows easy verification would be a catalyst that enables a chemical reaction between two or more substances. But there are also many examples that are difficult to verify due to the limits of human sensory capacity, like actants indiscernible to the human eye. For instance, the lyrics of the Japanese national anthem comprise a prayer that the emperor's reign may last the eternity it takes for pebbles to transform into a huge rock on which moss grows. In this case, each material entity could be said to be an actant that modifies the other organic entities in its assemblage over thousands of years to eventually become an immense rock. The geological time is so extensive that no one is equipped to see the process completed and the lyrics are presumed to be metaphoric.

Political theorist Jane Bennett's concept of vibrant matter echoes the view of Latour and neo-animists.

> By vitality I mean the capacity of things—edibles, commodities, storms, metal—not only to impede or block the will and designs of humans but also to act as quasi-agents or forces with trajectories, propensities, or tendencies of their own. (2010, vii)

The vibrancy of matter implies that the relations between the human and nonhuman are equal and mutual. In the case of the manipulator, he cannot be the one who simply dominates an object for a certain effect but must find how to respond to its predispositions arising from its design and inherent nature. Humans must bring a different consciousness to relating to nonhuman matter. Thus, material performance advocate Penny Francis distinguishes between "material performance," which generates a creative exchange among actants, and "performance with materials," which employs objects and figures decoratively without reaching a flashpoint (Posner et al., eds. 2014, 6). The objects in this study, the homunculus in *Avidya—The Dark Inn*, the child figure that matures in *Shun-kin*, and androids in robot theatre are some examples of Francis' concept of "material performance."

According to Posner, commentary frequent among practicing manipulators is that "the puppet is unruly, that it wants to do things that differ from what we would impose upon it, and that we can best bring out its life if we listen to it" (ibid.). Playwright-director Tanino, for example, feels the close relational power of things to humans as a conduit to eroticism, the uncanny, and a sense of psychic power.

At the same time, some manipulators in Japan, like Magosaburo XII of Youkiza, say that a puppet is a lifeless object, and it is sufficient to make it perform by pulling the right strings based on the manipulator's expert knowledge of the object's center of gravity and design features without complicating the art with talk of vibrancy.

To reiterate, the new animism is not a formal philosophy but local and pragmatic. It looks "in-between" in the relating together of beings instead of possession by "spirits." The relations between human and nonhuman are egalitarian and reciprocal. Thus, a meta-communicability that involves all animate and non-animate beings can be pursued.

Summary

The shift from puppet figures manipulated by an invisible manipulator to open staging with the visible onstage presence of the manipulator has released an explosion of creativity in theatricality and dramaturgy. It has also raised a philosophical issue concerning the relations between the human and nonhuman. Japanese neo-animists emphasize the search for communal spirituality as well as an equal relationship with the nonhuman. Western neo-animists prefer to emphasize the need for respect for the nonhuman, especially their transformative abilities as actants in a dynamic relational assemblage.

1-3 A statistical survey of contemporary Japanese material theatre

The term "material theatre" in Ric Knowles's sense (2004) is preferred in this section as the questions extend beyond the performance aspects to include the socio-theatrical activity surrounding the production to reception process, so that funding sources, relations with local governments and art associations, location of venues, etc., are to a certain measure taken into account.

It is not easy to gain a comprehensive survey of professional Japanese material theatre at the present time. However, some helpful information is available from a number of sources covering the period from 1997 to 2015.

According to the WEPA website managed by UNIMA, there are:

> approximately 130 professional puppetry companies and over 2,000 active amateur groups. [...] Japanese puppet companies [...] mainly perform in nurseries, kindergartens, and primary schools. Most prefectures [...] have a non-governmental department that arranges performances throughout the year, known as Association for Organizing Family Audiences (Zenkoku oyako gekijo kodomo gekijo renrakukai) [...] [E]ach year approximately 100 puppet festivals are held locally.

The older 1999 survey by the Japan Council of Performers Rights & Performing Arts Organizations (CPRA, or Geidankyo, f. 1965) indicated that material artists had the lowest average annual income of all the various types of traditional performers, even when income from TV material performances was included, although actual figures were not provided. Akiko Kato states in her *History of Japan's Material Performance 1867– 2007* (Nihon no ningyo engeki 1867–2007, 2007) that "a performing-object artist's private income averaged ¥2,500,000 in 1997" (2007, xx).

According to CPRA, in the 1970s to 1980s, children's material performance was a profession one could live by, but it was never recognized as art that theatre critics would take seriously. It was education/entertainment for young children and their accompanying caregivers. In local government, puppetry comes under children's culture or welfare and is mainly under the jurisdiction of the Ministry of Health, Labor and Welfare. During the Occupation period, Japanese Ministry of Education incorporated puppetry into the school curriculum for first to third graders and recommended it as nurturing material for preschoolers. Today, 70 percent to 80 percent of its audience is in the two-to-eight-year-olds bracket.

In 2014, the Japan Puppet Theater Conference (JPTC; Zenninkyo) compiled its Puppet Production Report with the cooperation of the Japan Union of Theatrical Companies for Children and Young People (Jienkyo). JPTC also included in the report the results from a separate questionnaire it had conducted on its own.

The following is a translation of the findings, revealing the great extent of the children-centered emphasis of modern material theatre.[8] Comparisons with their 2002 report are provided except in the case of new questions, which make comparison impossible.

All the puppet companies belonging to JPTC and other non-member professional puppet companies, totaling fifty-two, were invited to provide information on their productions held between April 1, 2013 and March 31, 2014 (i.e., the Japanese 2013 fiscal year). Thirty-four companies joined, bringing the participation rate to 65 percent. As the total number of modern professional puppet companies in Japan is 130, it is unfortunate that the pool of participants was limited.

Part I Questionnaire Results on Puppet Productions

(1) Puppet productions

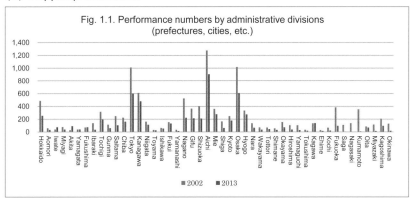

Fig. 1.1. Performance numbers by administrative divisions (prefectures, cities, etc.)

Comment: Osaka, Aichi, and Tokyo are the major performing-object centers of Japan. However, a decrease was noted in the total number of production stages compared to the earlier 2002 survey, with those three centers losing the largest numbers—about 400 productions in total.

In contrast, productions increased in Iwate, Fukushima, and Akita, the prefectures devastated by the 2011 Great East Japan Earthquake, where many puppeteers nationwide have contributed to reviving local puppetry and performing-object activities.

(2) Types of production

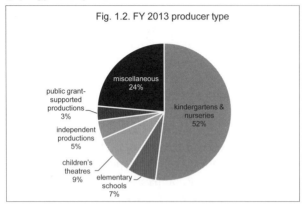

Fig. 1.2. FY 2013 producer type

Comment: Little change in ratio is evident since 2002, though there is a general decrease in numbers. Small puppet companies with small-scale productions are having difficulty maintaining financial solvency.

(3) Kindergarten and nursery productions by administrative divisions

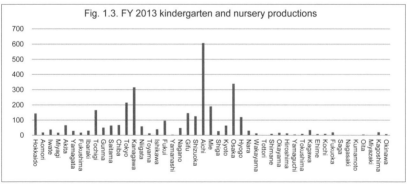

Fig. 1.3. FY 2013 kindergarten and nursery productions

Comment: With over 600 shows a year, Aichi Prefecture has the highest level of activity. This indicates that Aichi puppet companies perform locally the most.

(4) Elementary school productions by administrative divisions

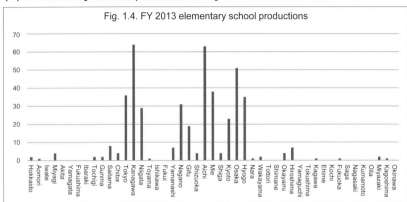

Fig. 1.4. FY 2013 elementary school productions

Comment: Performances at elementary schools are one-tenth the number of those for preschoolers; Kanagawa and Aichi prefectures lead with over sixty shows a year.

(5) Children's theatre for parents and children by administrative divisions

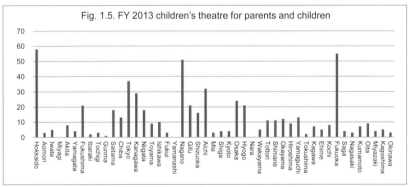

Fig. 1.5. FY 2013 children's theatre for parents and children

Comment: The distribution of children's theatre differs greatly from that of kindergarten, nurseries, and elementary school productions. Value can be seen in producing children's theatre in dedicated theatre buildings.

(6) Independent productions

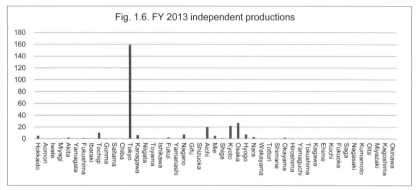

Fig. 1.6. FY 2013 independent productions

Comment: Tokyo, with 160 performances, ranks highest for independent productions, well ahead of Osaka by 140. The JPTC analysis is that the activities of PUK (with a membership of seventy) increase the overall numbers.

Part II Questionnaire Results on Puppet Companies

A. Concerning the Companies

(1) Gender ratio

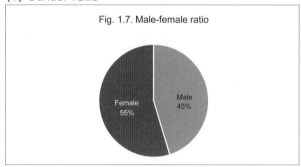

Fig. 1.7. Male-female ratio

Comment: No earlier data exists.

(2) Age distribution among puppet company members

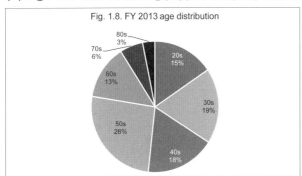

Fig. 1.8. FY 2013 age distribution

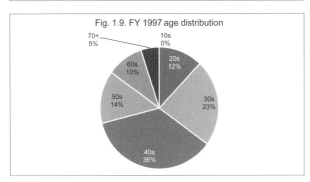

Fig. 1.9. FY 1997 age distribution

Comment: The above reveals the reality of an aging society. It is evident what will happen in a decade.

(3) Duration of membership

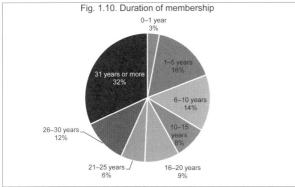

Fig. 1.10. Duration of membership

Comment: Veteran company members are plentiful in this industry.

(4) Member turnover in the past decade

Fig. 1.11. Member turnover in the past decade

Attrition of members

New members

0   20   40   60   80   100   120   140

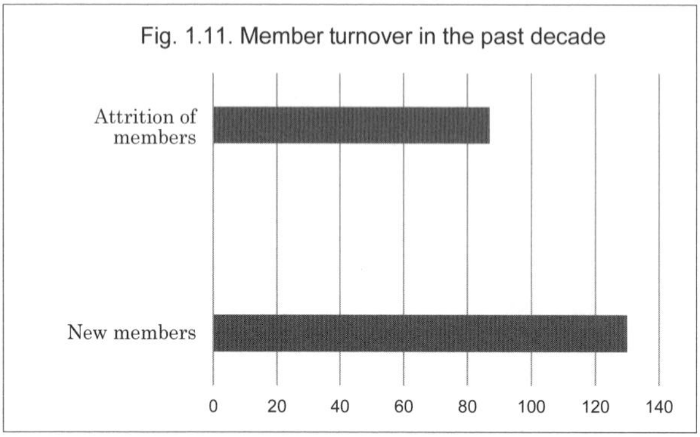

Comment: The numbers seem to indicate that the overall number of members is increasing. It is necessary to factor in the rise in new puppet companies, rather than assume an increase in the size of the puppet companies. At the same time, it is true that the total number of people entering this industry is increasing.

B. Productions

(1) Production size

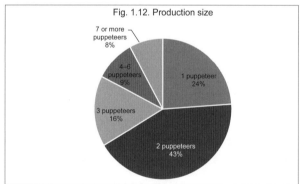

Fig. 1.12. Production size

7 or more puppeteers 8%

4–6 puppeteers 9%

1 puppeteer 24%

3 puppeteers 16%

2 puppeteers 43%

Comment: Eighty-three percent of the productions are performed by three or fewer puppeteers. In addition to the increase of small puppet companies with a maximum of three puppeteers, large companies prefer to produce small-scale performances by three puppeteers as well. Such performances tend to have a longer life in the repertory. It would be mistaken, however, to conclude that large-scale productions are decreasing.

(2) Authorship

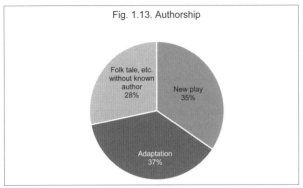

Fig. 1.13. Authorship

Folk tale, etc. without known author
28%

New play
35%

Adaptation
37%

(3) Target audience age

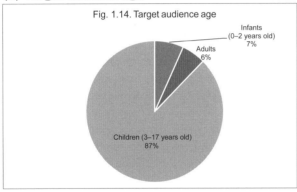

Fig. 1.14. Target audience age

Infants (0–2 years old)
7%

Adults
6%

Children (3–17 years old)
87%

To sum up, the yield of this survey is that modern material theatre continues to be designed for preschool and elementary school children and thus is a guaranteed performance category. Material performance is a low-income occupation, performance companies are small-scale in membership and finances, and the number of public performances is on the decrease. Despite the buzz of activity, the professionals are in a situation of slowly diminishing returns. The future is not necessarily bright as they are in competition with a growing variety of new, mediated info-entertainment. As the adult-geared part of this genre is not large but nonetheless high in artistic quality, diversifying would help these artists survive and excel at their work.

1   Founded in 1635, Edo Marionette Theatre Youkiza has performed string puppetry for 385 years. It has inherited the traditional practice of its predecessors and the spirit of premodern culture. Magosaburo XII, the current head of Youkiza, started a training program in 2004 to promote the transmission of the marionette tradition and to foster the growth of new talent. Historically, Youkiza is noted for its innovative contributions to marionette theatre and the performing arts. Magosaburo IX (1872–1947) made daring experiments, which by 1903 crystallized into a performance style called "new *kabuki* string puppetry." Under the leadership of Magosaburo X (later Sessai, 1907–1997), Youkiza was also part of the 1920s avant-garde movement. For their outstanding artistic activities, Youkiza and Sessai received the ACA National Arts Festival MEXT Award; Governor of Tokyo Award; Medal with Purple Ribbon; Order of the Sacred Treasure, Gold Rays with Rosette; Person of Cultural Merit, and other accolades. For further information on the contemporary activities of Youkiza, see n. 4 on Youki Magosaburo XII.

2   Cf. Entry on PUK Puppet Theatre in WEPA. It engages mainly in children's puppet theatre. https://wepa.unima.org/en/puk-teatro-de-titeres/.

3   *Mezashi* refers to a number of similar puppets lined up and held together by a horizontal bar and manipulated so that their movement is generally coordinated.

4   Magosaburo XII is a traditional puppeteer, actor, and the head of the 385-year-old Youkiza. His specialization is female impersonation (*onnagata)*. His actor training included the major traditional styles with the best masters—he learned *no* acting from Hideo Kanze and *kyogen* from Sennojo Shigeyama, and attended Tetsuji Takechi's Takechi Kabukiza. He also trained in magic lantern performance and received the title of the Senyu Ryokawa III. His major roles are Lady Masaoka in *The Precious Incense and Autumn Flowers of Sendai* and Princess Yaegaki in *Twenty-four Examples of Filial Piety.* The reason his activities are indispensable for this book is that he has become a major presence in intra/intercultural collaborations. Carrying on Youkiza's indomitable spirit for innovation, he has conducted invaluable experimental work with diverse contemporary artists, such as director Makoto Satoh and international directors from France and China.

5   Cf. Wikipedia, s.v. "techno-animism," last modified September 9, 2019, 18:21, https://en.wikipedia.org/wiki/Techno-animism.

6   This is Jennifer Robertson's succinct summary of Kyburz's explanation of

the Japanese view of nature (Robertson 2018, 15; cf. Kyburz 1997, 257–79).

7   Iida's statement during a post-show talk, genre:Gray Project: Humanoid manipulator x Object manipulator, Hyakki Yumehina's "Original Kagura 'Breeze,'" at Kirari ☆ Fujimi Civic Culture Center, May 26, 2018.

8   http://www.zenninkyo.jp/org.html.

Chapter 2

The Rise of Object Theatre

This chapter explicates the introduction and dissemination of Western object theatre to Japan and how it inspired artists to explore creating artistic material performance for adults that could be socially relevant as well as insightful in navigating a posthuman world. Also included is a major analysis of *Avidya—The Dark Inn* (Jigokudani onsen Mumyo no yado, 2015), a play by Kuro Tanino,[1] which indicates how performing-objects for mature audiences can have a profound impact as social critique of gender, the quest for values, the necessity of living within time and history, and the power of the uncanny.

2-1 Paradigm shift

Material performance discourse has evolved since the twentieth century. To clarify the nature of the 1990s paradigm shift, Akiko Kato's revision of some basic terms is provided; this new terminology has become the norm in the discipline, though the average theatregoer may not be aware of the shifts in discourse.

First, the basic term *ningyo* literally means "doll," but in the field refers to the nonhuman as well as human figures, all of which, through manipulation achieve the signification of life. Increasingly, *geki ningyo* (performing-objects for the stage) is used to distinguish objects/figures made deliberately or selected for stage performance from dolls for ornamental use.

The new Japanese term *ningyo engeki* (material performance) now includes both the modern term *ningyo geki* (puppet play) and *ningyo shibai* (premodern puppet plays). It encompasses children's puppetry and TV puppet programs, although mediated, as well as the innovative trends from the 1980s–1990s to the present time including object theatre in the narrower Western sense of a deliberate emphasis on nonhumanoid performing-objects and their equal relations with manipulators and actors (Kato 2007, 235–36).

Although the new Japanese term *ningyo engeki* in English translation does not sound particularly cutting-edge, Kato explains that it was selected to herald a paradigm shift for those in the field—to make them consider the new concept of "performing-objects and humans, liberated of conventional notions of genres, sharing the stage equally in contemporary theatrical performance" (ibid.).

Historically, *engeki* is a term that entered the discourse in the Meiji period when live-theatre artists were deeply engaged in importing modern Western theatre and dramaturgy to transform Japanese performing arts into a modern cultural form of new drama (*shingeki*) that enabled a dramatic forum of ideas about social and other issues rather than a display of emotion, bravado, or spectacle.

Material performance, in particular, has been undergoing a similar kind of paradigm shift from the 1990s, this time under the inspiration and aegis of Western object theatre theory. The general trend has been to transfer focus from human-shaped puppets and "magical" puppeteering skills to an open theatricality with different kinds of "objects" made of a variety of materials like light, sound, or transforming geometric shapes. The visible onstage presence of the manipulator and actor has also raised a more philosophical issue concerning the relations between humans and nonhuman objects.

Alternative & Material Theatre Project 2000

In 1991, material performance historian and semiotician Henryk Jurkowski (1927–2016) was invited by UNIMA-Japan as guest speaker at symposia on material and object theatre in Tokyo, Nagoya, and Sapporo. His seminal text, *Aspects of Puppet Theatre* (1988), had been translated into Japanese by Akiko Kato and published the year before so that some of his audience had prior exposure to his views on sign systems in theatre, transformative opalization in performance, atomization of both performing-objects and the totality of what is called theatre, as well as the need to foster nonhierarchical relations between performing-objects, manipulators, and actors. Jurkowski has continued to inspire Japanese material performers through his writings. His articles "Puppetry and Its Performing Value" (Ningyo geki to sono jikkokachi) and "Ontological Puppet Secrets" (Sonzaiteki geki ningyo no himitsu) were commissioned by UNIMA-Japan and published posthumously in its *Yearbook of Japanese Puppetry* in 2015.

Towards the end of the twentieth century, a number of events and projects became platforms for the reconsideration of the discourse and activation of a paradigm shift. The major groups were the Alternative & Material Theatre Project 2000 (hereafter Project 2000; Ningyo engeki purojekuto 2000), which was supported by UNIMA-Japan, the I.T.O. Project formed in Nagoya in 2001, and the Object Performance Theater (OPT), also active in Nagoya from 1999, and others.

Project 2000 was open to all artists and creators in any field interested in the relations between objects and people. The specific aim was to explore the relations between manipulators, actors, and figures/objects through finding the language of "alternative material performance." Scenographer Petr Matásek (1944–2017), then at DRAK Theatre in the Czech Republic, and Prague-based Japanese object artist Noriyuki Sawa (b. 1961),[2] known professionally as Nori Sawa, were invited to be the lecturer-trainers.

The conceptual base for what is now known as object theatre had been formulated since the 1970s by the famous DRAK trio—director Josef Krofta (1943–2015), Matásek, and actor/composer Jiří Vyšohlíd (b. 1943). Both Sawa and Kurotani had studied and trained under Krofta and Matásek in the 1990s at the Academy of Performing Arts in Prague (DAMU). There is general critical agreement that in the long view, the DRAK vision of modern object theatre "brought puppet art closer to the mainstream of contemporary world theatre" (Dubuska 2006, 42; Francis 2012, 112–13).

Furthermore, according to Russian and Czech theatre specialist Joseph Brandesky, finding a new expressive language included material performance that had acquired Western humanism "to take in animism once again" (2007, 5). Premodern Czech puppetry had been greatly influenced by the country's natural landscape and was rich in superstition, the supernatural, and folk tales of golems and the grotesque. However, over time the society had acquired a secular and humanistic perspective on life. Theatre artists felt that the time had come to loosen ties with humanism and draw strength from other perspectives including the animistic. This approach must have appealed a great deal to the Japanese involved in Project 2000, as the culture already accepts variant religious and spiritual views on life. I will return to this point later in the discussion on Kurotani.

According to Sawa, who now also teaches material arts at DAMU, Krofta's aesthetics of object theatre has at its core the questioning of the dramaturgical validity of performing-objects. Is a nonhuman object necessary for stage performance? Or is it there simply as a decorative attraction for the audience? If the object has intrinsic value, does the manipulator really have to be visible onstage? Each performer must struggle to find his or her own answers to these questions (Sawa 2008b).

For example, when Krofta saw three-person *bunraku* manipulation, he called it "the empire of movement." Sawa explains what he meant:

> [T]he three puppeteers behind the *bunraku* puppet have status and a clear hierarchy, as if an empire were moving the puppets. He went on to say that he found boundless appeal in this tradition, like new land that has never been put to the plow. To them, I think Japanese traditional puppet theater represents a treasure chest of new themes and ideas. (Ibid.)

Scenographer Matásek's reaction was similar but more strategic. He told Sawa that in their intercultural object collaboration, *A Plague O' Both Your Houses!!!—based on Shakespeare's Romeo and Juliet!!!* (2001), he would prefer to have the Romeo figure's manipulators dressed in Montague livery and Juliet's in Capulet attire, rather than in standard black *bunraku* outfits, as the feudal livery would bring home how the two young lovers were always being controlled by their respective families. Thus, while each performer is required to find their own answers to philosophical and practical questions in object theatre, both mentors insisted that unlike in *bunraku*, the presence of manipulators onstage could not be simply treated as a convention, but had to be justified as an integral part of the mise en scène.

Perennial today, Krofta's approach must have been a startling eye-opener in its time. With a tiny seed of an idea, one may choose to start from the light scheme and spend two weeks in discussion on the lights and color design, before there is any script, performing-object, or actor. Or one can start with a chair and an iron and devise an intricate symbolic connection. In fact, these artists tried to avoid settling into a particular modus operandi for deliberately breaking out of conceptual thinking or standard dramaturgy is in itself the creative stimulus.

Memorable also is Krofta's application of atomization as it had a magnetic effect on the audience, drawing them into reimagining the mise en scène to reach coherence. Jurkowski cites an example from Krofta's 1976 adaptation of Don Quixote's punishment scene from the eponymous work.

> The audience saw an actor beating an empty bench, another in the costume of Don Quixote reacting as if he were receiving the beating, a manipulator holding the puppet of Quixote and actually breaking its limbs, another actor who cried as if suffering great pain. (Quoted in Francis, 113)

Matásek also worked with figure and alternative theatre techniques, which connected with the Czech design style called "action design." Brandesky identifies three dominant tenets to action design:

> Designs should be functional and malleable with focus given to the performers and their interaction with the set; authentic properties (items from the surroundings, including trash) should be used and misused to provoke metaphorical associations; and open communication with the audience, using verbal and nonverbal means, should be maintained. (2007, 8)

Sawa's own artistic work displays the fruits of his scrutiny of the "objectness" of everyday things and his respect for nonliving objects as he develops egalitarian, often humorous, and always versatile working relations with them. He does not aggressively pursue creating a sense of the supernatural but does work on the metaphoric level and also enjoys using technology like "overhead projectors to create a shadow play effect" (2008, 1). He received the European Cultural Award Franz Kafka Medal in 1999. His solo *Macbeth*, premiered in 1992, will be discussed in the global Shakespeare segment in the third section of Chapter 4.

In the 2010s, Sawa worked with ART Prometheus, o.s., a Prague-based collective of theatre artists/producers and cultural managers. Their aim is clearly an agreeable one for him:

ART provides an alternative space in the sphere of art, and [...] social spheres. We conceptualize art as a large flow of active access to life. We create projects so its differentness would become a positive device in confrontation with commonly used forms of artistic expressions. (ART Prometheus, o.s., n.d.)

The driving force of Project 2000 was, nonetheless, object artist Miyako Kurotani.[3]

Under her guiding presence and the steering committee's management, seminars, workshops using fiction mainly by writer-of-children-stories-for-adults Kenji Miyazawa (1896–1933)[4] and study sessions were held in 1999. Fifteen participants were selected by audition and the project culminated in a public performance called *Heavenly Forest* at the Ryogoku Theatre X (Kai) in mid-November of the same year. Kurotani received the 2001 Japan Puppet Theatre Achievement Award for her contribution to innovation in contemporary material performance.

In 2002, Kurotani started her "beyond-genres" company, genre:Gray, and highlighted her difference from conventional puppetry arts by replacing standard puppet terms with eye-catching ones: puppeteers are *kugutsume*, an archaic and sibyl-like figure; her performing-figures are *hitogata* (humanoid figures; a different way of reading the same Japanese characters for *ningyo* 人形) or *monogata* (object モノ形); and the stories she weaves are *mono-gatari* (in Japanese script モノ語り , which can also mean object narrative rather than a standard story 物語).

Her best-known work to date is *Half-Moon, Kurosolo Series No. 1* (Kurosolo ichiban hangetsu, 1995). She reworked it after Project 2000, when she felt free of earlier inhibitions. The piece seems to serve as a power-generator whenever she finds herself ascending to a new level in her art. (See fig. 2.2 in the color plates.)

Half Moon presents a "dark" adaptation of three fairy tales, "Little Red Riding Hood," "Peach Boy," and "Blue Bird," with an old figure played by the manipulator, who gives life, protection, and cultural initiation to a child. Due to the constraints of space, I will discuss Kurotani's favorite "Little Red Riding Hood," through which she expresses the motif of interspecies love between the little girl and the wolf. The scene proceeds as a ritual of dressing and undressing with immense contrasts between the two procedures in speed and violence.

Kurotani's style of "peripherality" expresses the girl's acquisition of breath and life through the delicate movement of fabric and selvage that increasingly enwraps the girl's simple body. A sensuous haptic ambience is subtly drawn out by slow handling and lighting. The white-face of the old woman was a choice inspired by Kurotani's 1982–84 experience in a *buto* group called Dance, Love, Machine, an offshoot of the company Dairakudakan. She notes that applying *buto*-like makeup and movement enables her to inhabit an otherworldly place.

In her working relations with performing-objects, Kurotani also values the horizontal and egalitarian relations between objects and manipulators. One interviewer noted that many spectators comment that she and her performing-objects become indistinguishable onstage. Kurotani feels a subtle give-and-take between the object and herself, which is neither unconscious nor fully controlled—just somewhere in-between. Paradoxically, she also feels she is the object's slave and harbors resentment over always having to strive to deepen her relations with the nonhuman; nonetheless, Kurotani continues to place this pursuit of doppelgänger-like identification at the center of her endeavors (2004, 28).

Her artistic purpose is stated in her company name's subheading, "the grotesque performed by a self-centered object and a charitable body." As a contemporary *kugutsume* whose connection to Japanese animism is strong, she desires to visualize the flowing life force that seamlessly circulates between manipulator and performing-object in a gentle bewitching way. Her efforts are rooted in the "exploration for the traces of life in the nonliving and a quest for enabling both the living and the nonliving to 'speak' without muddying that expression with her own egotistic intentionality" (ibid., 32). Incidentally, the term *mono*, which usually means object, harbors, in her case, the connotation of *mamono*, which means evil spirit, *yokai*, or monster.

In general, this otherworldly relational aspect that Kurotani and some of the other object theatre artists in this country actively pursue connects well with the Czech premodern animism and has a stronger spirit-seeking orientation than the new materialisms that have arisen in the West, such

Fig. 2.1. Miyako Kurotani, *Half-Moon, Kurosolo Series No. 1*, 2013, Sengawa Theatre, Tokyo. Photo © kino asa. Courtesy of genre:Gray.

as Jane Bennett's concept of vibrant matter, which are secular in their approach to objects.

The second significant project in the object theatre platform is the I. T.O. Project (f. 2001), a collective of some small string-object companies in the Nagoya-Kyoto-Osaka region led by material artists koichic Iimuro (b. 1948) and Toshihiko Yamada. Having inherited the traditional string-object technology of the famous Kinosuke Takeda (1923–1979), Iimuro[5] builds and manipulates string-objects and is also the head of Marionette MINOMUSHI (Ito-ayatsuri ningyo gekidan minomushi, f. 1975) and Atelier MINOMUSHI (Atorie minomushi, f. 2010). Yamada[6] is an extraordinary inventor/designer of trick string-objects and geometrical objects. His local mentor is Iimuro and his international one, the German puppeteer Albrecht Roser (1922–2011); from both, he learned to value the laws of kinetics, to play from the center of gravity, and engage in creating animated life attractive to adults as well as children. Yamada heads the Puppet Theatre Cocon (Ningyo gekidan kokon, f. 2001).

The I.T.O. Project's mission is to enlighten audiences, disseminate string-object art, and develop successors.[7] With a scientific eye and the mechanical ability to transform images into workable objects that will

Fig. 2.2. Traditional control board. Courtesy of I.T.O. Project.

Fig. 2.3. Yamada-style controller. Courtesy of I.T.O. Project.

surprise and delight, this group basically shares the same perspective of object theatre as Matásek with his action design that, as noted earlier, emphasizes functionality and malleability, authentic properties that provoke metaphoric associations, and verbal/nonverbal communication with the audience. Material performance is not a one-way street of entertainment but a series of insights shared by all involved.

The following achievements attest to their ability to disseminate string-object art, which hopefully is contributing to the development of successors. Yamada himself has twice won the Japan Puppet Theatre Association Grand Prix Gold Prize in 2001 and 2006. He is well known for his adaptation of a Western string-object controller, which enables the manipulator to operate a string-object with only one hand. Iimuro has contributed greatly to keeping performing-objects in the public eye by building more than 600 puppets himself and holding regular workshops in both puppet-making and script-writing. He has also appeared in puppetry programs for the NHK educational TV and other commercial TV channels and served as director of JPTC (2007) and of the Toramaru Material Theatre Institute in Kagawa Prefecture. Their concerted efforts have dazzled audiences with their SFX.

Two productions are outstanding in their collective work. The first is their award-winning *Heitaro's Yokai Diary*, premiered in Osaka, Nagoya, and Hiroshima in 2004. They invited playwright-director Tengai Amano,[8] the head of the Shonen-Ojakan theatre company, as the "innocent and in-experienced" external collaborator. The play is inspired by the *Inoo Yokai Report* (Inoo bukkairoku, 1749). The original documentation tells of a sixteen-year-old samurai youth called Heitaro Ineo and a friend, who climb a mountain to test their courage. At the top, they tamper with an old burial mound. From the following night, Heitaro's home is invaded by *yokai* for a whole month. He manages to persevere, remain calm, and survive the horrors. A high-ranking devil finally appears and gives him a mallet for his courage before flying off forever into the cosmos. (See fig. 2.3 in the color plates.)

The Inari Shrine[9] built in Hiroshima in the early seventeenth century honors Takedayu Ineo, the adult name for Heitaro, as one of their Shinto *kami* (gods). A mallet was also preserved there. This shrine was completely destroyed by the atomic bombing in August 1945 near the end of World War II and later rebuilt twice. These incidents have received much attention from artists, including *yokai* researchers like Hiroshi Aramata, Natsuhiko Kyogoku, and Shigeru Mizuki, known also as a *manga* artist. According to Mizuki, *yokai* come in four types—monsters, the supernatural, shapeshifters, and ghosts/spirits of the dead. The I.T.O. Project not only illustrates this variety, but it also identifies the insidious intent of the *yokai*.

> [A] *yokai* woman's tongue walks alone, caterpillar girls turn into butterflies in an instant, scissors do a death dance. […] The *yokai* keep shapeshifting and threatening Heitaro. However, he is not fazed. (Amano 2007)

The creepy-cute[10] quality of many of the *yokai* can be disarming, but caution is needed.

> They sneak into the void of the human heart, trying to get at Heitaro. A child's wistful thoughts—bewilderment over having forgotten something, trust, and treachery among friends. *Yokai* reside in the blink of the human eye, manipulate the darkness of the human heart, and invite Heitaro to the pit of hell. (Ibid.)

While the play text is largely a pretense for the display of trick *yokai* objects, there is a surprising and worthy social message delivered at the end. See Chapter 7 for an English translation of *Heitaro's Yokai Diary*.

Yamada says that working with director Amano is always highly stimulating because he demands from material performance what performing-object manipulators themselves would not dare ask for themselves. He comments that:

> Amano has broadened my understanding of the potential of object theatre. His scripts are brimming with ideas, images, figures, graffiti/scribbles so that balancing the required movement with the appropriate materials without sacrificing the design becomes very challenging. (Ibid.)

Amano received the 9th Matsubara & Wakao Memorial Theatre Award (hereafter Matsubara & Wakao Award) for *Heitaro's Yokai Diary* in 2004. This is a local prize dedicated to promoting theatre activities in the three prefectures of Aichi, Gifu, and Mie in the Tokai district.

A great inspiration for Amano has been the concept of cosmic nostalgia advocated by boy-love writer Taruho Inagaki (1900–1977). The concept is broader than Marilyn Ivy's nostalgia, which refers to an attachment to a memory of something lost or irretrievable.[11] If Ivy shows that the past is not an entirely knowable body of experience, Inagaki and Amano think that neither is the present nor the future. In Amano's own words, cosmic nostalgia is like a memory "that points to neither the past, future, nor present" (Amano 2018a), but expresses the amorphous predicament of being human, not only in society, but in the universe with no certainty for being or belonging.[12]

Amano contextualized the *yokai* invasion of Heitaro's home with imagery inspired by Inagaki's writings, such as *Stories of 1001 Seconds* (1923), making the mise en scène reverberate with a multidimensional aura, suggesting that Heitaro's particular battle represented the continual activity and evolution of the universe.

On the performance level, the most surprising aspect for this viewer was the standard box set with three to five manipulators standing on a 2 m tall (6.6 ft.) bridge upstage to operate the objects for almost the whole performance. Once the action began, the audience's attention was consumed by the lively display of trick performing-objects and total theatre effects; the "old style" of presentation was clearly no impediment to the performance. Just before the end of the performance, three puppeteers came onstage to showcase the tiger manipulation. Nonetheless, it is worth noting that the two I.T.O. plays discussed here are the only object performances in this book that use a "conventional" modernist puppet stage with hidden manipulators. The "old" can still be fresh and useful again in a different combination.

The specific visual methods employed are first and foremost atomization, mainly of the humanoid form—repetition and multiplication of images, doppelgänger doubling and tripling, dissolution of conventional categories, and transformation. For example, Amano's signature approach in directing is to play with time flow onstage. He states that:

> As time is only an abstract concept, we "cannot tell if time really exists or not." In such a case, we can play with this concept through addition, subtraction, reversion, acceleration, and deceleration. We can re-experience time in a virtual world of fabrication. (Amano 2018a)

Amano also notes that as theatrical performance itself is necessarily locked into time with a beginning and an end, he wants to undermine that linearity.

> Although one intervention would seem to be enough, I repetitively disassemble that inevitable structure in as many ways as possible. I am always questioning where "I" come from. [...] The process of nothing becoming something and then returning to nothing fascinates me. (Ibid.)

The highlights of the moving objects (for this viewer) were the ever-changing rotating face of an extremely creepy-cute *yokai* and the construction in midair of the Japanese character for "dream" (*yume*, 夢) from the disassembled strokes of three characters indicating "eye/eye/I" in different syllabaries.[13] These strokes were made from thin veneer slices and manipulated by string. The wordplay that suggests three kinds of subjectivity (me/me/I) combining into dream connect with the underlying cosmic imagery as this dream-making seems to reference the concept of multiverse or parallel dimensions that Amano and Inagaki share. In-agaki posits a dimension made of strips of veneer (*usuita*), which are visible to the human eye only when peripheral vision is used. These thin strips are said to be made of crystalized dreams that, in the old days, floated in the air. When humans capable of applying peripheral vision enter a sheet, that dimension responds accordingly, spinning out further varieties of thin sheet dimensions. Yoichi Imai (n.d.), in his article, "The Philosophy of Thin Sheets: Taruho Inagaki," notes that the humans who successfully enter this new dimension tend to shed their social, human characteristics and become androgynous. Imai suggests that this thin sheet dimension is Inagaki's metaphor for a utopia permeated by the spirit of innocent boyhood (*shonen*). Amano embeds such moments as alternative ways of relating to the universe.

In the program for Amano's recent play, *1001* (2019), theatre critic Momiichi Unita suggests that the title is a direct reference to how algorithms work according to the 01 principle (2010, 6–7), which seems to suggest that Amano's dreamy visions could be translated into a very contemporary digitalized view of the universe.

Amano contextualizes Heitaro's travails in a universe replete with destructive *yokai* imagery that ultimately suggests a compassionate "cosmopolitan" order that humanity could possibly participate in. The play ends with the demon not simply praising samurai courage and perseverance, but saying: "Depending only on your own strength without acknowledging fear, the Maoo demon's work will continue" (Chapter 7, p. 197).

Knowing, experiencing, and contributing to the "positive and negative" of the universe is important. Knowing so-called negative aspects like fear, using peripheral vision or scientific methodology, relating to and cooperating with other entities, and also accepting that benevolence is needed as well as a samurai's fighting spirit are requisites for a cosmopolitan. In that connection, it is possible to conjecture that the creepy-cute quality of the lesser *yokai* could transform into the cute kind if the balance of the universe were rectified and a compassionate order became viable.

The I.T.O. collective has capitalized on the renewed popular interest, if not belief, in *yokai* in the twenty-first century; their ability to tickle the imagination by combining a mechanical approach in object theatre with the animistic spirit pervasive in Japanese culture is captivating.

The trio came back together in April 2018 for a new I.T.O. production of Tatsuhiko Shibusawa's phantasmagoric tale *The Voyage of Imperial Prince Takaoka* (Takaoka shinno kokaiki, 1987)[14] at The Suzunari in Tokyo and the AI Hall in Itami City, Hyogo Prefecture.

This tale was ideal for displaying their unique brand of object theatre as again a multitude of freakish-looking objects appear. Yamada points out that there are:

[l]iving creatures that look like animals but are much more than that. Some of the humans look like monsters. This all matches nicely with puppet theatre, which transforms objects into humans and living creatures. (Amano and Yamada 2018a)

A prince, whose only shortcoming seems to be insatiable curiosity, proceeds on a grand tour through Southeast Asian countries towards heavenly India (Tenjiku) with his three followers. He encounters exotic creatures like dugongs, anteaters, tigers, birdlike women, honey women with multiple breasts, and carnivorous flowers, which metaphorically carry the motifs of doppelgänger, anachronism, hybridity, mummification as a symbol of eternal life, and much more. In the end, the aged prince is devoured by a ferocious tiger, a splendid mechanical specimen devised and manipulated by Yamada that reveals the prince sitting quietly and Buddha-like inside the raging beast.

This premiere was technically superb, highly surrealistic, but somewhat uneven. The target audience was to be adults but in fact turned out to be more for families as the short-skirted exotic female figures were strangely unerotic; a disappointment as the author, Shibusawa, is known as Japan's translator of the Marquis de Sade. The nonhuman exotic creatures, like the baby-faced anteater, had interesting mechanical abilities but were nonetheless geared for the young.

The revival in November 2019 at the Aichi Prefectural Arts Theatre in Nagoya was a revised and improved performance in that it was clearly framed for family viewing. With projection mapping applied generously, the effect was decidedly brighter and cuter than before, giving the performance an "Asian wonderland" touch with a pink teapot-like creature and more. At the end, the prince became a golden skeleton lying prostrate inside the tiger. The final message seemed to be that death was not something to fear.

The third early bird in the "object theatre" platform was the Object

Performance College (OPC, f. 1998) headed by director Shigeru Kimura[15] and art director Asako Fukunaga[16] and sponsored by the Aichi Puppetry Center (NPO), located in the Sonpo Japan Himawari Hall in Nagoya. In the following year, they opened the Object Performance Theater, under the same sponsorship, for their graduates to perform in. (See fig. 2.4 in the color plates.) New OPT performs abstract puppet plays for adults by inducing motion in powerful objects. Objects that actors, not manipulators, handle lend a variant sense of life and individuality to the animated objects. Their three mottos are:

Objects do not belong to people!
Objects are equal to people!
Set imagination on fire with the fusion of objects and people![17]

More than the other performance groups discussed in this chapter, OPT tries to bring together miscellaneous material culture or found objects as suggested by Matásek and attempts alchemical processes upon them.

If you put your ear to an object, you can hear something like a heartbeat. If you gaze at an object, shapes, and movement you have never seen before become apparent. We start with such experiences and strive to sublimate them into stage-worthy expression. [...] Explosions have often attended experiments. When an image explodes in your mind, it can look like a full-blown chrysanthemum firework or a sparkler. What kind of chemical reaction will happen? (OPT, n.d.)

Major OPT works include *Lakai* (2004), in which performers fight with a huge sheet of paper, and *Sonar Sound* (Soraoto, 2006), made with plastic boxes. The company also uses light and shade as well as geometrical shapes in motion. OPT won a Jury's Special Prize at the 2008 Nagoya City Arts Festival for *The King of July* (Shichigatsuoo), which was made with a scrim. For *Allerleirauh* (Senbikigawa), director Shigeru Kimura won the Matsubara & Wakao Award in 2009. It has been invited to perform at many festivals including Toga Festival, BeSeTo International Theatre Festival in Tokyo, Iida Puppet Festa, and others. OPT's most recent production was a series of adaptations of *Twilight Dream*

Fig. 2.4. Shigeru Kimura (dir.), Asako Fukunaga (art dir.), *Allerleirauh*, 2009, Aichi Puppet Theatre Center (Himawari Hall), Nagoya. Photo © Takashi Horikawa. Courtesy of Object Performance Theatre.

(Hakubomu) by Edogawa Ranpo in Nagoya in 2016. It is presently inactive.

A network of object theatre artists has grown from these three projects and contributed to the development of other experimental groups. Their exploration of the theatrical possibilities of everyday objects tests the boundaries of subjectivity and objectivity and sometimes draws out extraordinarily poetic results. Puppetry arts critic Kathy Foley points out, "because of the abstraction already implicit in the choice of an object as living/talking/performing, the genre invites the audience into non-literal thinking. Metaphor, metonymy, humor, and poetic thinking are evoked by the genre."[18]

2-2 Framing adult and artistic material performance

Trajectory of the *kawaii* aesthetic—from targeting youth to all ages

In the 1980s, unrelated to material performance, postmodern trends made doll-like figures, virtual and otherwise, a common sight in larger society. First came the rise of the *kawaii* aesthetic (cf. Dale 2016); and then, that of the *otaku*, which refers to obsessive fans of *anime, manga,* and so on. Subcultural adult *anime* and *manga* were accompanied by a proliferation of character toys, toy robot transformers, inflatable sex dolls, and sacrificial doll accessories. Doll-like media personalities called idols (*aidoru*) decked in *kawaii* fashion, amateur *cosplay*[19] and fancy dress among young adults have also become part of the urban landscape.

To give a few examples of this phenomenon: some Japan Railways stations hire guides to *cosplay* at work. From a distance, it is difficult to tell if the attractive guide, decked out in a pink and white frilly outfit, and made up in *anime*-style wide-eyed features, is a person or a robot. *Yuru-chara* mascots have also become an integral part of local government and business public relations; *yuru* (loose) refers, in this context, to the disregard for historical or any other kind of authenticity. Many prefectures/cities/companies devise their own specific full-body suited mascots like Kumamon[20] and Hikonyan[21] to advertise their commodities and services; some famous castles now have their cleaning staff dressed in samurai *cosplay* gear. This kind of activity has broadened the range of acceptable adult entertainment and audience/customers to include all ages.

In the 1990s, while new subcultural icons and activities continued to emerge, digital technology development raced ahead. The World Wide Web (f. 1991) enabled the developed world to be connected by the Internet. Programmed robots—like Sony's zoomorphic AIBO (1999), Honda's Asimo (Advanced Step in Innovative Mobility, 2000–2018), Mitsubishi Heavy Industries' Wakamaru (2005–2018), Softbank's Pepper (2014), Vstone's Robovie (2001), ATR's Geminoid (2006), and Daiwa House's Paro, a harp seal-shaped therapeutic robot (2001)—have been designed with *kawaii* looks included.[22] Some continue to work in hospitals, banks, and department stores; such operable robotic performing-objects have become ubiquitous in urban areas. At this point, clarification of the meaning of the *kawaii* is called for as it has become distorted over time. Hiroshi Nittono,[23] a Japanese experimental psychologist, takes the position that *kawaii* refers to the emotional response of the viewer to a particular object, not the attributes of the object itself (2019, 26). However, the term has been used in both ways and thus can cause puzzlement as something can be seen to be *kawaii* but not felt to be so.

The following is Nittono's translation of the *kawaii* entry from the second edition of the *Great Japanese Language Dictionary* (Nihon kokugo daijiten, 2001):

kawai-i (adjective) (1) looks miserable and raises sympathy. pitiable. pathetic. piteous. (2) attractive. Cannot be neglected. cherished. beloved. (3) has a sweet nature. lovely. (a) (of faces and figures of young women and children) adorable. attractive. (b) (like children) innocent. obedient. touching. (4) (of things and shapes) attractively small. small and beautiful. (5) trivial, pitiful (used with slight disdain). (Quoted in Macpherson and Bryant 2018, 39–55.)

The first and last definitions of *kawaii* concern something vulnerable and to be pitied (*kawaiso*) and even disdainfully so, while the middle three definitions are more in line with the cute, adorable (*kawairashii*) (Nittono et al. 2019, 21) quality of contemporary usage. From the beginning, this term covers a wide spectrum of feeling.

Nittono adds the caveat that the word "cute," the present English translation for *kawaii*, is an abbreviation of "acute," which meant "crafty" in the eighteenth century. Cute in that sense became popular in the US in the nineteenth century and has only recently gained a more positive meaning (ibid., 25–26).[24]

Moreover, in psychological studies, "cuteness" is considered an attribute of the targeted object such as in the "infant physical attractiveness" of Konrad Lorenz' baby schema (1943),[25] while in Japanese, *kawaii*, as noted earlier, refers more to the viewer's positive feelings toward the target. Yet both the Japanese term and its English translation harbor somewhat negative and infantile connotations.

Nittono identifies the characteristics of the emotional response of *kawaii* as positive, unthreatened, on an appropriate level of arousal, an approach motivation for caregiving, and desire for social interaction (thus it is not only about babies) buttressed by attention to other visual aspects like smiles, roundness, and colors, which are not necessarily related to baby schema (2019; cf. Chapter 5). If *kawaii* is an emotional response, two points can be made: first, it arises from cognitive appraisal, which requires some level of consciousness and evaluation and thus is not in-stinct- or reflex-based, however fast the response may seem to be; sec-ondly, it is expressed through subjective, behavioral, and physiological changes (ibid.).

Opposite pairings or other complex associations with *kawaii*, which create a sense of the anti-cute, are also plentiful. Nittono claims that the compounds *kimo-kawaii* (creepy cute; abbr. *kimokawa*) and *busa-kawaii* (adorably ugly: abbr. *busakawa*) have been in use for 2000 years (ibid.,12). Other popular combinations are *guro-kawaii* (grotesquely cute; abbr. *gurokawa*) and *ero-kawaii* (erotically *kawaii*; abbr. *erokawa*). Further offshoots of *kawaii* have led to characters whose names indicate anti-cute qualities, without the addition of the telltale *kawaii*. The visuals usually indicate the level of *kawaii* evocation, such as Sanrio's anima-tions of Gudetama[26] and Aggretsuko.[27]

Marilyn Ivy provides a plausible explanation for a quality like cute-ness to be easily reversed into its opposite. Its inherent vulnerability can lead easily to its deformation when the attraction to interact with it turns aggressive. She points out that, "the cute, in its very vulnerability, inevi-tably entails the uncanny (*bukimi*)."[28]

Let us now take a closer look at *kimo-kawaii*, as it is a key aesthetic in understanding *Heitaro's Yokai Diary* and other performances targeting adults. *Kimoi* means "disgusting" and indicates a desire to move away or terminate relations with the source. The compound indicates a mixture of opposite feelings so that while there are strongly repulsive qualities, the desire to approach and become involved remains active. The *kawaii* at the end of the compound implies continuing interest and alleviates the sickening quality of *kimoi* (Nittono 2019, 113).

To facilitate understanding, the best-known popular examples of *kimo-kawaii* are in Hollywood movies—the eponymous creature in the American science fiction film *E.T. the Extra-Terrestrial* (1982) and the *mogwai* monsters in the American comedy horror film *Gremlins* (1984). In material performance, Brazilian dancer-object manipulator Duda Pai-va, who uses foam rubber objects to delicately stir pain and joy in his dance-puppetry, excels in the *kimo-kawaii*, as can be seen in *Blind* (2015), his recent work on disabilities. In Japan, creepy cute "dancing baby" characters drew attention in the late 1990s. A real life example would be the gangly, asexual male comedy duo the Ungirls (abbr. Anga), who were called *kimo-kawaii* when they first appeared in the early 2000s.

Returning to *Heitaro's Yokai Diary*, we can see that many of the *kimo-kawaii yokai* are pliant shapeshifters skilled at transmuting between a whiny, forlorn post-pretty state to revolting deformity suggestive of moral decrepitude. They appear harmless enough at the beginning of their undertaking to harass Heitaro, when his entourage is with him. But once Heitaro is on his own, they close in for the "kill." Their basic tactic is to trick Heitaro into self-destruction, physically or mentally. Knowing that the *yokai* are mere illusions, he is able to ride out the psychic storm.

Yet Heitaro is pulled both ways, as he is inquisitive about the *yokai* and their leader, the Maoo, or Demon Lord of the Sixth Heaven. Dressed in traditional formal samurai attire and retaining a curious civility, it is concerned for the evolution of the universe, not just petty vengeance. Despite the horrendous ordeal Heitaro has been through, he hankers to meet the Maoo again one day as he has felt something beyond the *kimoi* or *kawaii* in this *yokai*. In Buddhism, it is said that the Maoo interferes with the devotion of Buddhist practitioners when they make progress in their practice. But if the practitioners truly persevere in their devotion, the Maoo's interference can become an opportunity for spiritual growth.[29]

Today, the term *kawaii* on its own seems to have lost any pejorative quality it may have had. *Kimo-kawaii* is one of the preferred negative forms for subverting the straightforward adulation of the *kawaii* and, through its nauseating and abhorrent qualities, seems to be a suitably complex aesthetic for adult object theatre.

Framing object-centered adult material performance

Despite the social acceptance of mobile "figures" off- and onstage, material performance is still largely expected to be conventionally illusionistic and regarded as children's fare. Careful framing or contextualizing or, in more pragmatic terms, marketing, is necessary to transcend assumptions and mitigate bias. At the least, most companies provide guidelines in small print in flyers and online; in fact, the title, venue, and show times are often ample indication of the targeted audience. Nonetheless, concern for box office returns can compel many companies to cater predominantly to family audiences. Individual artists and companies rarely focus exclusively on growing an adult clientele, but more are offering a limited number of adult-specific productions as part of their repertory.

Jo Taira (b. 1981)[30] is one such artist. Knowing the importance of framing a production, Taira tried to make an age-appropriate guide system for potential audiences. At first, he restricted the age ranges for adult viewing to R15 and to over twenty.[31] He has now settled for an overall more orthodox age division with four overlapping groups—family/primary school pupils/preschoolers; 5–6th graders to adults; adults only; and he was the first in Japan to make a zero-to-terrible-twos age bracket.

Furthermore, besides age, other contextualizing signs can be added to capture adult interest in an attractive manner so that adults will have the choice, if they so wish, of exposure to more serious, risqué, or taboo-breaking productions, some of which employ the *kimo/ero/guro* versions of the *kawaii*. Jo Taira's strictly adults-only 2004 adaptation of Shuji Terayama's *La Marie-Vison* is an excellent example. For this work, he won the 2007 Japan Puppet Theatre Grand Prix Silver Award at the age of sixteen and continues to be the youngest recipient of that award to date. (See fig. 2.5 in the color plates.)

Taira's version faithfully follows Terayama's live theatre script on the sadomasochistic relationship of the transvestite Marie with his/her purported son, Kinya, conducted in vengeance against the boy's biological mother, who had sexually humiliated Marie in front of their female coworkers. As *buto* critic Tatsuro Ishii points out:

> Beneath this "mother-son relationship," there are layers of other elements such as confinement, captivity, pederasty, homosexuality, incest. [...] These and other taboo images pile up in various combinations. (2004, 25)

This play, replete with eroticism, cruelty, the grotesque, the relentless desire for total domination and destruction of others, all presented in a *kimo-kawaii* style is even now a challenge for adults to watch.

Approximately ninety minutes long, Taira's solo performance unfolds on an open stage that suggests a large residence with multiple reception rooms offstage. The set itself is Marie's private parlor with a bathtub center stage. Interestingly, in object theatre fashion, a single teacup set conspicuously on a stand, centerstage left, represents the bathtub plus Lake Chad, and is also used as a teacup.

Taira enacts Kinya, the "beautiful boy," and also manipulates the rest of the thirteen characters and delivers their lines by skillfully modulating his voice. His costume is a white top with a longish white tutu skirt that is neutral enough to "match" all the characters he manipulates as well as the narrator's role. He sings songs without musical accompaniment, calls out the stage cues, which do not necessarily produce any effect, and also takes regular breaks onstage in full view of the audience to drink water and wipe off his perspiration. As such, the audience sees the creative process, the results or lack thereof, together with what is usually kept backstage. They are not allowed any respite from Taira/Marie's domination of the stage.

The major co-performing objects are different types manipulated in different ways. Marie-Vison is a metal-rod object with droopy "come-hither" eyelids. The servant, "Oh, the longed-for Mr. Stroheim," is represented by a primitive-looking mask. Monshiro, the "beautiful girl" upstairs, is a colorful hand-object with eyelids similar to Marie-Vison's but bristling with eyelashes. Kinya, frightened by her sexual aggressiveness, strangles her and then forgets her body onstage. The "ghosts of six beautiful girls" are six circular foam rubber finger objects that get squeezed into oblivion, foreshadowing Monshiro's destiny. At the very end of the play, Kinya returns "home" after a brief escapade, to totally acquiesce in being Marie's slave for life. Marie is triumphant.

Besides *La Marie-Vison*, Taira has other exclusively-for-adults productions, including his 2005 version of *The Castle Tower* (Tenshu monogatari, 1917) by Kyoka Izumi, and his 2014 version of Euridipes's *Medea,* both tour-de-force solo performances.

Fig. 2.5. Jo Taira, *La Marie-Vison*, New National Theatre, Tokyo, 2012. Photo © Daisuke Omori. Courtesy of Jo's Group.

Actor-centered adult material performance

Mainstream theatre does not generally venture forth to use performing-objects as a promotional tool for their productions. However, even without framing devices, if their presence is sufficiently innovative or significant in the play, it is possible to call such productions material performance.

Live theatre has been enriched by the entry of performing-objects as they add a different kind of flavor to their mise en scène. The cynically humorous *Favonia's Fruitless Fable* (Kemiko no fumowa, 2016) by playwright-director Satoko Ichihara[32] does not publicize the deployment of performing-objects onstage but has a ventriloquist accompanied by a dummy's head that is used for miming outrageous encounters with outsized, fake reproductive organs.

Theatre Company ARICA (hereafter ARICA, f. 2001),[33] a collective of artists from various fields—acting, artistic direction, poetry, music composition, digital art, art installation, architecture, textile design, etc.—has a reputation for entangling actors with performing-objects, with a particular penchant for "hanging" both. Independent artist Kubikukuri (Hangman) Takuzo (1948–2018), whose specialty was self-hanging, was a guest performer in their *Butterfly Dream* (2009). Director Yasuki Fujita believes that stage elements—objects, properties, sound/music, lighting, etc.—"are not merely for stage effects, but through their relationality with the performers' bodies, activate the whole stage to move persistently like a life form" (*KIOSK* pamphlet, 2020).

ARICA's recent work *On the Island* (Koto, 2019), written by Shino Kuraishi and directed by Fujita, is about a woman (played by Tomoko Ando) who has lost her human companions and is left alone on her own mobile piece of land.[34] Manipulating the island from underneath, Ando manages to launch it on the imaginary sea of the stage and in this tiny personal space compensates for the lack of human contact by interacting with food, two-thirds of a chair, a slice of a concrete slab, buoys and a loudspeaker that echoes back her pronouncements. The play could almost be a latter-day, aquatic version of Samuel Beckett's *Happy Days*. (See fig. 2.6 in the color plates.)

The performance piece resembles object theatre, but is not publicized as such. The framing is subtle—the venue is a theatre-cafe called BUoY,[35] a former bowling-center-cum-public-bath by a canal in Tokyo.

Fig. 2.6. ARICA, *On the Island*, 2019, BUoY, Tokyo. Photo © Katsu Miyauchi.

Housed in a building erected in 1964, the same year as the first Tokyo Olympics, the venue exudes an atmosphere of resistance despite the ongoing renovation—rather like an arthropod struggling to molt.

The stage is in the basement, which used to be the bathing area. The large baths are still in place and are filled with water. Light is made to bounce off the bath water and onto the rough beige stone walls, creating an eerie sight that makes the viewer think visually not of expanses of water spotted with islands, but rather of a limestone cavern, which may point to the state of the woman's mind, where thoughts and memories trickle incessantly. Through using a liminal space, the production suggests that the viewing experience will be at variance with conventional expectations of theatre.

2-3 Case study of Tanino's *Avidya—The Dark Inn*[36]

Introduction

Kuro Tanino's most famous play to date is *Avidya—The Dark Inn*, premiered at the Morishita Studio, Tokyo, in 2015. He won the prestigious 60th Kishida Drama Prize and his company won the ACA National Arts

Festival Excellence Award for it. (See fig. 2.7 in the color plates.)

As with Taira and ARICA's plays, Tanino's is also an example of theatre that highlights performing-objects as a fundamental aspect of its production. In *Avidya—The Dark Inn*, the homunculus figure and the revolving stage set are crucial to the meaning of the work.

First, to frame the cultural significance of this play, I will apply anthropologist Marilyn Ivy's concepts of "the vanishing" and "phantasm," and then situate the homunculus' contemporary relevance as that which signals the modern uncanny.

In this narrative, as autumn gives way to winter, two puppeteers, a dwarfish man called Momofuku, and his reticent son, Ichiro, head to a mountain inn in the hinterlands of Japan with a single puppet tucked away in a suitcase. Invited to put on a show, they find on arrival that the proprietor is deceased and the locals and others, like Sansuke, a former *yakuza*, have appropriated the hot spring lodge as a refuge from the world. The pair mingle with these hot spring junkies, who are in denial of the imminent changes about to erase their already tenuous grip on life, and add their own miasmic indulgences to the bubbling memories, regrets, desires, hopes, and fears at the spa.

Marilyn Ivy's notion of "the vanishing" is particularly appropriate for analyzing Tanino's *Avidya—The Dark Inn*. It refers to the consciousness of how a way of life is "going, going—but never entirely gone" as traces of the past still stimulate nostalgia for their regeneration. In Ivy's view, the fascination and engagement in the manipulation of culturally marginal sites enabled the Japanese to negotiate loss of tradition and foster continuity of national-cultural identity during their venture into modernity in the Meiji period and on, through promoting as "Authentic Tradition" peripheral rural practices, folklore, domestic tourism, and *itako* mediums to resolve personal and collective trauma, and more (1995, 10). Such operations continue to be conducted by Hato Bus sightseeing tours and other cultural industries as a standard part of Japanese capitalist modernity.

Tanino's play is set in the Hokuriku region, which comprises the four northwestern prefectures of Niigata, Toyama, Ishikawa, and Fukui. It has long had an unfortunate reputation as an isolated, rural, snow-bound mountainous area left behind by Japan's national economic development and modernization. The ongoing construction of the high-speed Hokuriku Shinkansen railway, in accordance with government policy, started from Takasaki City, Gunma Prefecture, in 1997. To be completed in the

2020s, this line will eventually serve to link Tokyo and Shin-Osaka via the cities of Nagano, Karuizawa, Toyama, Kanazawa, and Tsuruga. The most recent extension between Nagano and Kanazawa cities was finished on March 14, 2015, five months before this play was premiered. Tanino's dedication at the beginning of the play alludes to the various troubles that have occurred during its protracted and yet-to-be-completed construction.

At the same time, the focus of the play is on how the so-called vanishing people, practices, vocations, and sites enact their cultural marginalities rather than on strategies for actual revival of so-called tradition and stabilization of the national-cultural imaginary or the framing of a new era of technology by the imminent arrival of the Shinkansen bullet train. For what is important is often not so much the revival of the past but the affect. In his article "The Taste of Nostalgia: Vanishing Flavors from the Ancestral Japanese Village," Ryan Anderson is in agreement with Ivy that nostalgia is "epitomized by a desire to reconnect with something lost. The issue at hand is not resistance to change but instead keeping alive a deeply emotional and intimate pleasure" (Anderson 2019). Ivy notes ironically that "restoring what is lost is not only impossible but more unwelcome than the original loss itself" (Ivy 1995, 10). We do not actually want the past to return if we have moved on already, but wish to retain the frisson of the old attachment. In Kan Kikuchi's play *Father Returns* (1917), for example, the father, who ran off with a lover, returns alone twenty years later to the consternation of the grown-up family members, who have now exchanged a manageable bittersweet memory for a problematic presence.

Avidya Inn as a phantasm

Closely related to vanishing is the notion of "phantasm." Epistemologically, phantasm is understood as something "which apparently exists but is not real; a hallucination or vision,"[37] not simply a self-deceiving fabrication, but a suspension between presence and absence (Ivy 1995, 22). As Ivy points out, this concept can be applied to the Avidya Inn: "Japanese investment in the continuity of tradition discloses a phantasmatic structure" (ibid.).

Since the demise of the owner, the inn is and is not an inn. It no longer exists as a hot spring business, but seasonal regulars stay and Sansuke, the self-appointed bath attendant and all-round house staffer, keeps the spa clean and running. He is the only one who gets tipped for his considerable hard work, while the others cooperate to keep each other fed and taken care of in a low-key, barter economy.

The hot spring junkies are like an endangered species gathered in this strange shelter away from their real home, whether near or far. They are the locally marginalized among the regionally marginalized and most threatened by the arrival of the bullet train and the enormous changes it is expected to bring to their district. The self-established freeloaders have every reason to fear losing their present, leisurely lifestyle. Eighty-year-old Otaki takes perverse satisfaction in reminding the others that their boarding arrangement will soon end, as she assumes that the creaky building will be one of the first to be demolished. She also tells the two geisha, Iku and Fumie, that due to the new convenience of easy travel to and from Tokyo, they will lose their *shamisen* gigs to a younger generation of attractive women who will enter the job market and displace them. Her dogmatic "prophecies" on the imminent demise of their phantasmatic lifestyle are proven wrong as the inn escapes demolition, i.e., total vanishing, and Iku and her baby become the links to the next stage of nostalgia and continual vanishing.

Momofuku's performance as a phantasm

Is it possible to say that master puppeteer Momofuku's performance also has a phantasmatic structure? How is the border between presence and absence suspended or obscured? The "absent" repressed returns into "presence" and causes a simultaneously awkward familiarity and alienating frightfulness of the uncanny. One is assailed by a sense of confusion-when the border between presence and absence has shifted without reason. How then does Momofuku conjure up a sense of the uncanny from his art? It triggers the repressed.

On one level, Momofuku has devised an affective concoction reminiscent of the fare offered by pre-modern puppeteers, to set up his clientèle into expecting something "traditional," nostalgic, as well as vaguely numinous. On another, he exploits the promise of nostalgic familiarity only to reveal what is, in fact, much more relevant to his audience's psychological state, the modern uncanny, hence his ultimate popularity.

In places like Tottori Prefecture, stick puppets called *dokunbo* were used in the short rituals of the *kadozuke* ("at the gate") New Year celebrations by traveling performers, who could possibly be divine visitors (*marebito*), to call in happiness and prosperity to the musical accompaniment of *shamisen* and *kokyu*.[38]

In terms of facial features, Momofuku's performing figure seems close to the *yozo-deko*, a stick puppet with a misshapen head made from a gnarled knob of a pine tree. It also resembles a creepy-cute human face like a *hyottoko*[39] or worse. Yet his performing-object is not a stick puppet, as it has hands and legs that can be manipulated and its head has internal mechanisms for facial expression.

Momofuku and Ichiro's visit both resembles and differs from that of *kadozuke* traveling performers. Consistent with them, the pair arrive at the change of seasons if not exactly at New Year's. Unlike *dokunbo*[40] puppeteers, who are expected but do not have to be invited in, and can be turned away, the pair have been invited to perform but once on the premises, though they are ironically treated as if totally unexpected. They wait for a considerable time for the owner at the inn entrance, the metaphoric boundary between the inner and outer worlds. Unlike the *kadozuke* performers who are recipients of monetary offerings, Ichiro tips the bath attendant excessively, and later on, the father and son conduct a secular bathing ceremony for their homunculus. Ichiro does play the *kokyu* and the women performers play the *shamisen* in the same room but more in reciprocity than in ritual.

Small foreshadowing touches are also embedded in the master puppeteer's name: Momofuku shares the same initial Japanese character for *momo* (百) of Momodayu, the ancient *kami* of puppetry: the *yozo-deko* was said to pray for *fuku*, which means happiness.

In this way, some of the elements and aspects overlap with the trajectory of *kadozuke* performance; however, the purpose is clearly not to replicate an older ritual but to provide just enough of an aura of the alien and numinous to suggest a kind of performance that had vanished in the early Showa period (1925–1940), even though they had no direct experience of it.

In the pair's informal entertainment piece, what powerfully conjures up a sense of alterity is the performing-object's disproportionate features paired with Momofuku's dwarfishness. In terms of the puppet's contemporary relevance, Tanino identifies Momofuku's puppet as a Penfield type of sensory homunculus in the stage directions, if not through the dialogue. Such a figure, when in 3D form, displays the size of each body part in ratio to the density of sensory receptors in the human cortex, hence the huge hands, eyes, mouth, and tongue all bulge grotesquely in scientifically accurate sensory innervation.[41]

If the homunculus represents the healthy inner sensory networking of the human physiology, the characters themselves are specimens of the dysfunction or vanishing of sensory and other physiological functions in such forms as blindness (Matsuo), speech impediment (Sansuke), aging (Otaki, Fumie, Ichiro), and loss of virility (Ichiro, Matsuo, Momofuku). They reflect some ordinary breakdown in the inner mechanisms and wiring of human bodies, which is socially unproblematic. Momofuku's microsomia, according to the medical definition, refers to an adult of less than 147 cm (4.8 ft.) in height, is more unusual and in the eyes of the occupants places him close to the uncertain borderline between the freakish and the normal. For most of the play, Momofuku is regarded prejudicially as a freak but harmless and his puppetry is, by association, anticipated to be strange.

When the onstage audience sees the performing-object, most are shocked by its grotesqueness rather than enchanted or amused by its infantile sensuality. The naked form of the childlike figure, which is about a meter (3.2 ft.) tall, is familiar yet disproportionate, giving rise to a sense of the uncanny, exacerbated by the doubling of the two short figures. The occupants of the inn, unfamiliar with homunculi, are appalled by this gross caricature. Unable to quite pin down the reason for their repugnance, they are unwilling to talk about the strange figure even among themselves. The effect of the homunculus is thus to bring the occupants face-to-face with the uncanny (darkness).

The modern uncanny

The modern uncanny is a complex concept related to the "strangely familiar" and with various interpretations about its nature, ranging from Ernest Jentsch's intellectual uncertainty in "On the Psychology of the Uncanny" (1906), Sigmund Freud's castration repression in "*Das Unheimliche*" (1919), to Jacque Lacan's mirror stage of ego development, roboticist Masahiro Mori's fear of death ("The Uncanny Valley," 1970/2012), Sadeq Rahimi's Lacan-based, specular-oriented approach in "The Ego, the Ocular, and The Uncanny: Why Are Metaphors of Vision Central in Accounts of the Uncanny?" (2013), and John Bell's discussion in "Playing with the Eternal Uncanny" (2014).

This section will apply Ivy's perspective, which is an extension of Lacan's approach and also refers to recent and related views by Sadeq Rahimi. A slightly abbreviated excerpt of Ivy's discussion of the "modern uncanny" follows.

> Freud's uncanny refers to initially familiar objects or experiences that return out of time and place to trouble the stable boundaries between subject and object, such as ghosts, automata, doubles, etc. [...] For Lacan, the anxiety of the uncanny occurs when the part of oneself repressed in order for one to become a subject ([...] one's "self-being" before the necessary split introduced by the mirror stage) returns in the guise of a double, a ghost, or repetition. To become a subject requires an initial lack, as the very possibility of recognizing oneself in a mirror implies that one has already lost some unmediated self-being. The uncanny lies in the uncertainty about what is real or imaginary, self or other. But Lacan says that the uncanny effect does not arise from a simple lack of knowledge; it instead erupts from an excess of what was supposed to be kept repressed. Lacan would call this the Real. [...] Thus an insufficiency of lack can be said to be an excess of the Real. The repressed part of being has somehow reappeared in an alienated form. (1995, 84–87. Emphasis added.)

To clarify, Lacan's Real refers here to the Primordial Real, or what was called primary narcissism before the Mirror stage, or what Ivy calls the unmediated self-being. The homunculus could be seen as a symbol of any of these formulations. Repressed material cannot be consciously recovered. Such emergence happens by chance like a memory triggered by an association like Proust's madeleine in *À la recherche du temps perdu* or through therapy. The horror and anxiety felt by the onstage audience derive from the unexpected outburst of repressed narcissism. The specific content may vary with the human subject but in Lacanian terms is likely to be the "dark knowledge" of the facility of self-disintegration, lack/loss of meaning and coherence (cf. Rahimi 2013).

Matsuo's predicament

Matsuo became blind in an accident, lost his job, and stays at the inn during the milder seasons, leading an ascetic lifestyle committed to "third eye" development and physiological purgation in the hope of curing his blindness. Although he cannot actually see the homunculus and is not even in the room during the performance, his revulsion is the strongest. The encounter with the homunculus triggers the abandonment of his already impossible belief in a cure when his tactile exploration of it leads him into an experience of the uncanny side of human nature. Tanino makes it clear in the stage directions that a blind person cannot be expected to fathom the significance of the homunculus without external knowledge: "a homunculus drawn in the imagination from the sense of touch alone is a horrendous monster" (Chapter 9, p. 309). Overwhelmed by anxiety, Matsuo gives up and leaves the spa for good.[42]

Is there more to why Matsuo feels the horror and anxiety the most and is driven to break out of the Avidya Inn? In this regard, Rahimi points out the significance of the ocular/specular in ego development: that it is a process of identification with the ideal specular self. First:

The very appearance of the ego is formulated in specular terms (i.e., the "mirror stage") and the "ego" itself is the seat of the uncanny, always doubled, always self-alienated, and always narcissistically self-aggressive. (2013, 453–76)

The ego is the seat of the uncanny in the sense that ego development requires the mirror effect of doubling images to maintain and extend self-preservation. As noted earlier by Ivy, the nascent ego grows from the split with unmediated self-being (primary narcissism) towards identification with its ideal specular image, but it can never truly discard what has seemingly vanished and continues to harbor unawares the repressed in self-alienation and passive aggressiveness until an occasion appears for its emergence.

Matsuo is the youngest, most knowledgeable, and most concerned about self-development. But the imagery Tanino employs indicates that he is metaphorically in the worst condition as his sight is damaged beyond hope. His actions show he has not developed a third eye or even an acute sense of other people's physical presence or absence, and his extreme dietary program suggests that he is doing more harm to his health than good. Paradoxically, he has set himself up for extreme anxiety in the uncanny moment.

In psychoanalyst Mladen Dolar's terms, Matsuo has gained too much and is now flooded by the Primordial Real as he has lost the specular ideal image that ensured coherent reality for him. Dolar's explication of the modern uncanny indicates:

> Anxiety is not produced by a lack or loss. [...] It is not the anxiety of losing something. It is, on the contrary, the anxiety of gaining something too much, of the too-close presence of the object. What one loses with anxiety is precisely the loss—the loss that made it possible to deal with a coherent reality [...] the lack lacks and this brings about the uncanny. (1991, 13)

At the end of the play, the amazingly reliable, omniscient Old Woman says that Momofuku's puppetry is becoming popular due to the wild times.

> As the whole country has gone insane and is craving blood, Momofuku's dwarfish figure and puppetry were in much demand. People want to see misery, overwhelming misery. (Chapter 9, p. 314)

Momofuku doesn't feel miserable himself; he represents misery for ordinary people through his iconic short stature. It seems that the vanishing art of traveling puppeteers does not die out completely, due to the social needs of the times for such qualities as grotesqueness, horror, misery, and the uncanny, actual or projected.

A comment is due on the Buddhist context Tanino provides prominently in the name of the Avidya Inn in the title. Within the play, Matsuo gives a listing of the twelve *nidanas* in Scene 5, and Tanino himself adds a long note of explanation after the play. Briefly, the twelve Buddhist *nidanas* or causes, which are interlinked, refer to Avidya (ignorance), constructing activities, consciousness, name-and-form, six senses, contact, feeling, love, clinging, becoming, birth, and aging-death. Love is subdivided into the craving for becoming, death, and stimuli, which refer to sensations and self-generated stimuli like ideas, images, and so on. These *nidanas* all arise in relation to each other. In this teaching, transient suffering, which arises from attachment, is the nature of human existence (cf. Chapter 9, p. 316).

Before proceeding to the performance aspects of *Avidya—The Dark*

Inn, I would like to reiterate that I have applied Marilyn Ivy's concepts of the vanishing and phantasm to explicate the dynamics of shoring up "tradition" against the necessity of proceeding on into the future. In addition, Matsuo is most affected by the homunculus, as he is the only one to touch, feel, and know it directly. He senses that its representation of pure primordial narcissism is totally alien to his ascetic self-delusion. The homunculus triggers chaos in Matsuo, who has striven relentlessly yet ignorantly against meaninglessness. The other characters do not struggle so hard and ironically seem able to sustain a fragile balance in their existence.

The performance aspects of Avidya Inn

Tanino acknowledges the significance of the following factors in his creative process: the patients he had when he was a psychiatrist; surrealism, which gave him insight into how to warp time; Juro Kara's theory of the privileged body of the actor, which he found exciting in its use of theatrical space; and Tadeusz Kantor's stage art, especially as regards effects of color and light (Tanino 2011). Inspired by Marcel Duchamp, Tanino considers his sets and plays to be like fully formed pictures, in which he can arrange performers like parts of an installation or tableaux (ibid.). Of the major performing-objects in this play, the revolving Avidya Inn will now be discussed.

Tanino comments that, "[s]tage sets are functional and vibrant objects that contain diverse wisdom. There is a lot to learn just by looking at them" (2014). Creaking and groaning like an aging life form, the inn reveals four areas—the entrance hall, the men's guestroom with the women's guestroom directly above it, the changing room, and the open-air bathing area, which are connected by an inner courtyard visible through the windows facing inwards to the yard. In a filmic moment, Momofuku's son, Ichiro, walks through room after room of the entire downstairs, revealing splendidly the all-too-human goings-on of this microcosm.

In addition to serving the needs of its sojourners, the inn separates yet connects the human world with the surrounding wilderness. While sheltering people from the cold weather, it enables the sharp cries of wild birds and the sound of gushing hot spring water to penetrate the building and lets smells and scents from *sake*, tea, spa water, pickles, overripe persimmons, urine, and vomit collect in nooks and crannies, thus conjuring up a pungent ambience of pleasure and decay.

At significant moments in the play, the setting sun captures the hue of the ripe fruit of the persimmon tree in the courtyard, spreading a sheen of orangey-red across the upstairs and also sends shafts of light into the changing room of the spa downstairs. The inn is like a permeable living entity that interacts with both human and natural activities.

Chapter summary

In the twenty-first century, while continuing to have a substantial role in enriching children's early education, material performance is making a significant contribution to the performing arts, due to the leveling of the field by which performing-objects, their manipulators, and actors are now considered equal players. Taira's rendering of *La Marie-Vison* indicates that performing-objects can hold their own as a sophisticated art form, while works like Tanino's *Avidya—The Dark Inn*, framed for the live theatre, can feature performing-figures in thematically significant ways as well as providing tantalizing spectacle.

1   Born in Toyama Prefecture in 1976, Tanino is resident playwright, director, and head of Niwa Gekidan Penino. He founded his company in 2000 and has written and directed all the plays produced by it to date. His company has been invited to many theatre festivals both domestic and foreign. His plays that have numerous performing-objects are: *The Frustrating Picture Book for Adults* (Irairasuru otona no ehon), which went to Belgium and Germany in 2011; *Your Room That Nobody Knows* (Daremo shiranai anata no heya), which toured the US in 2014, and *The Box in the Big Trunk* (Okina toranku no naka no hako), which toured Germany, Austria, and Switzerland the same year. For *Avidya—The Dark Inn* (2015), Tanino received the 60th Kishida Drama Prize, the North Japan Newspaper Fine Arts Award, and the 71st ACA National Arts Festival Excellence Award, all in 2016. Starting the M Project with German fine arts designer Caspar Pichner in 2017, Tanino is exhibiting both in Japan and overseas (Tanino 2019b, 155). http://niwagekidan.org/.
2   Nori Sawa is an object theatre artist, director, and educator. He creates his own fusion of Japanese and Czech approaches to material performance. His works are nonverbal and devised from objects, masks, movement, and music. In 1992, Sawa went to the Czech Republic and trained with Krofta and Matásek at DAMU. He has performed in twenty-five countries and

taught courses and workshops at many institutions including DAMU, Stanford University, and London School of Puppetry. He received the prestigious Franz Kafka Medal in 1999. His two-and-a-half-hour solo *Macbeth* (1992) is well known. A prolific creator, he has several full-length performances to his name and countless shorter works.

3   Miyako Kurotani, object artist, trained under Matásek and Krofta at DAMU in Prague in 1994, after which she started solo performances that pursued the relationality between objects and the human body. She considers women to have the sensuous ability to feel the "life force in all the world and be the conduit for memory." She has performed widely in Europe and Asia and participated in a 2001 Japan-Malaysia modern theatre collaboration. She started her own company, genre:Gray, in 2002. She received the Japan Puppet Theatre Gold Prize (officially, Excellence in the Puppet Award Recognition System / National Specialized Puppet Theater Association) in 2007 and the Grand Prix at the 2014 Kurgan International Festival of Puppet Theatres, and others.

4   Kenji Miyazawa was a poet and writer of children's stories. Also known as an agricultural science teacher, vegetarian, cellist, Buddhist, and utopian social activist, he brought together his religious devotion, love of nature, and scientific perception in artistic forms. Extremely popular among performing-object artists, his best-known story is *Night on the Galactic Railroad* (Ginga tetsudo no yoru, published 1934).

5   Born in Kyoto, Iimuro joined the traditional string puppet company Takedaza in 1966 and receive training in marionette construction and manipulation from master Kinosuke Takeda (1923–1979) and Sennosuke Takeda (b. 1930). He founded the Marionette Theatre MINOMUSHI in the Kyoto-Osaka district in 1975. He gained an adult following with his *Laugh Out Loud! Comedic Storytellers Hall of Fame* (Wahaha kamigatatei dendo yose) shows by recreating *rakugo* masterpieces with his marionette doubles of the master entertainers. https://www.puppet-house.co.jp/phg/japan/iimuro/iimutop.htm.

6   In his amateur period between 1991 and 2000, Toshihiko Yamada founded puppet theatre Gig in 1991, won awards at the Suita Puppet Theater Competition, and received instruction in string puppetry manipulation and production from master puppeteers koichic Iimuro and Albrecht Roser. In 1993, he formed the Moretsu Tohoho Unitto (Furiously Miserable Unit) with Sayoko Nishimiya (d. 2012) of the Negibozu SAYO (Onion-head SAYO). Beginning professional activities in 2001, he established the Pup-

pet Theatre Cocon, and won the prestigious Japan Puppet Theatre Grand Prix Gold Award for *Marionette Collection* and won the same award again for *Chahaha Maru and Hehehe Maru* in 2006. His company received the Yanase Takashi Cultural Award in 2019. Yamada is a founding member of the I.T.O. Project.

7   Cf. http://itoayatsuri.com/Profile.html.

8   Cf. the introduction to Tengai Amano in Chapter 7.

9   Inari refers to the Shinto fox god.

10 The local term for creepy-cute is *kimo-kawaii*; both *kawaii* and *kimo-kawaii* are discussed in the second section of Chapter 2.

11 Ivy's nostalgia is discussed in the third section of Chapter 2.

12 Seigo Matsuoka, an intellectual who has written much on Inagaki, prefers to use the paradoxical expression "memory of the unknown" (*michi no kioku*).

13 One character signified an eye in *hiragana* (め); the second represented eye again in Japanese character (目), and the third, I (*watashi*, myself) in *katakana* (ワタシ).

14 *The Voyage of Imperial Prince Takaoka* takes the standard format of a high-status personage with loyal companions going on an adventurous pilgrimage in search of enlightenment, which they find through virtuous conduct.

15 Shigeru Kimura is a director, artist, and scriptwriter. After working at puppet theater Musubiza, he turned independent and delved into expressing the inner depths of the human heart/mind with moving-objects and figures. His "modern art in motion" method became the basis of his Object Performance Theater (f. 1999). Masks, *bunraku*, dance, open-air performance, narrative, and narration are also important aspects of his work. In addition to receiving many awards, he has served as General Director of Japan Directors Association and Director of Nonprofit Organization Aichi Puppet Theater Center since 2016.

16 Asako Fukunaga graduated from Kyoto City University of Arts, where she studied Japanese painting (*nihonga*). After working at Kyogei Puppet Company (Ningyo gekidan kyogei) and Musubiza, she became an independent artist, engaging in object performance, script-writing, directing, and commissioned art work for dance and opera. As art director of OPT, she was in charge of the artworks for the open-air performance at the first Aichi Triennale in 2010.

17 Available on the OPT profile page on CoRich Butai Geijutsu. https://stage.

corich.jp/troupe/5271.

18 Cf. *World Encyclopedia of Puppetry Arts*, s.v. "Object theatre." https:// wcpa.unima.org/en/object-theatre/.

19 *Cosplay*, a portmanteau of the words "costume" and "play," is a performance art in which participants called *cosplayers* wear costumes and fashion accessories to represent a specific character (Stuever 2000).

20 Kumamon, the mascot of Kumamoto Prefecture, is a black bear with red cheeks, created in 2011. https://kumamon-official.jp/kiji0031657/index. html.

21 Hikonyan, the mascot of Hikone City in Shiga Prefecture, is a white cat wearing a samurai helmet, created in 2006. https://hikone-hikonyan.jp/.

22 The Geminoids are generally not very *kawaii* as they are made to represent humans naturalistically.

23 Hiroshi Nittono (b. 1971) is a professor of experimental psychology and cognitive psychophysiology at Osaka University Graduate School of Human Sciences. His objective is to clarify the mechanism of human psychological activities in daily life using brain waves and event-related potential (ERP), as well as autonomic nervous system indices and behavioral indices. Currently, he is investigating "cute" psychology and behavioral science.

24 Cf. Dale 2016; May 2019.

25 In baby schema, cute things are thought to have the following juvenile attributes: a large head, a round, soft body; short and thick limbs; large eyes and chubby cheeks; small nose and mouth, and an unsteady gait. Cf. Dale, 2016.

26 Gudetama literally means "lazy egg." Created in 2013.

27 Also known as Agurreshibu Retsuko, Aggretsuko combines the Japanese word for "aggression" and the female name Retsuko; *retsu* in this context means "ferocious." She is a cute red panda office staffer who works off her aggressions singing karaoke. Created in 2015.

28 For her discussion on the uncanny, see Ivy 2010, 13–16; also see page 51 of this chapter.

29 Maoo/Tenma. Wikipedia, s.v. "天魔," last modified September 25, 2018, 11:47, https://ja.wikipedia.org/wiki/天魔.

30 Jo Taira is a puppet manipulator and actor. His method lies in the fusion of solo acting and versatile puppetry manipulation. In 2001, Taira founded Jo's Group in Tokyo and received the Japan Puppet Theatre Grand Prix Silver Award for *La Marie-Vison* in 2004. His other Taira-style adult pro-

ductions are *Cinderella* (2004), *The Castle Tower* (2005), *Ballad of Orin* (Hanare goze Orin; 2011), *Medea* (2014), *The Little Prince* (2007); *Eric, the Phantom of the Opera* (2013), *Hamlet* (2016), and *Salome* (2019), as well as original works like *Candlelight* (Tomoshibi, 2018). He has performed in Germany and the US. https://tairajo.com/.

31 The Japanese Film Classification and Rating Committee (Eirin) restricts film viewing by age: the rating R15+ indicates that persons aged fifteen and above will be admitted to view a film and R18+ indicates admission for those aged eighteen and above.

32 Satoko Ichihara is a playwright, director, novelist, and head of Q. She studied theatre at J. F. Oberlin University in Tokyo. Her plays are about human behavior, the physiology of the body, and people's unease over these subjects. Life is portrayed through the viewpoint of women, the audience is showered with physically stimulating verbal rampages, and the actors deliver their lines using their entire body. Ichihara won the 2011 Aichi Arts Foundation Drama Award for *Insects* (Ichihara 2019b, 154). She won the prestigious Kishida Drama Prize for *The Bacchae—Female Holsteins* (Bakkosu no shinnyo—mesu no horusutain, 2019) in 2020.

33 Theatre Company ARICA was founded in 2001 by five artists sharing a fascination with Shogo Ota's theatre of quietude for its plenitude of expression that precluded words or narrative. ARICA's central topic is labor and its many forms, with the members developing expressive performances through the application of Beckettian minimalism, poetry and visual arts, and new ways to relate to the performance space. Yasuki Fujita, the director and art designer, has directed all their productions to date, including *Love is Blind* (Ai wa yami, 2012), *Listen, Dear* (Ne anta, 2015), *Happy Days* (2014), *Butterfly Dream: Inspired by Samuel Beckett* (2016), and *On the Island* (Koto, 2019). Poet Shino Kuraishi formulates the concept and writes the text; Tomoko Ando, a former actor with Ota's Theatre of Transformation, conducts the physical training and performs in the piece. Producer Keizo Maeda, composer-musician Osamu Saruyama, and others complete the list of members. The company toured *Kiosk* (2006) to Cyprus, New Delhi, and New York. Ando received the Jury's Best Solo Performance Award for *Parachute Woman* at the 17th Cairo International Avant-Garde Theatre Festival in 2005.

34 The island is designed by synthetic media artist Nao Nishihara.

35 http://buoy.or.jp/.

36 This English title is Tanino's choice, which puts sharper focus on the Bud-

dhist concept of *avidya* (ignorance) as one of the twelve *nidana* (causes) that link relations, than the Japanese title, which refers equally to the environment. A literal translation of the original title would be *Hell Valley Spa—Avidya Inn.*

37 Cf. Oxford English Dictionary, s.v. "phantasm."

38 A *kokyu* is a traditional Japanese three-stringed instrument played with a bow.

39 See. Chapter 4-2, p. 77 for more detail on *hyottoko*.

40 *Dokunbo* also referred to persons, manipulators or puppets who could appease and entertain the *kami* (Law 1997, 158–59).

41 Cf. Wikipedia, s.v. "Homunculus," last modified December 15, 2019, 06:56, https://en.wikipedia.org/wiki/Homunculus.

42 The impossibility of a cure is indicated when Matsuo removes his dark glasses to reveal only black holes where his eyes would be.

Chapter 3

Rupture and the "Real"

3-1 What is the "Real" ?

What do adults want from material performance? Presumably, they want thematic content that is socially and artistically engaging as well as entertaining. The overarching concerns from the twentieth century form the background against which a specific topic or issue can be treated on the local level by artists, practitioners, critics, and others. The most significant concern would be the shift in human awareness from a modernist/ anthropocentric mindset to a postmodern subjectivity and an emergent posthuman ontology that includes the nonhuman in its vision. The fragmentation or multiplication of subjectivity and the dissolution of artificial/humanistic categories in general enable transcending boundaries and globalization to continue as positive trends. Thus, we could posit that adults desire a sense of the Real from material performance that includes life perspectives beyond the limits of present society as well as challenging present sociocultural values, ethics, and issues.

What the Real is depends on the individual. It can refer to objective reality based on sense perception and the material order as well as to the totally opposite—the infinite and absolute.[1] What follows is a somewhat dogmatic selection of approaches on the nature of the Real that is useful in comprehending the Japanese sociocultural context and performances discussed in this book.

Today, the Real most commonly refers to that which is "authentic" for the individual. For robot theatre playwright Oriza Hirata, the Real is what cannot easily be perceived, like the oscillation of the mind/emotions or the uncanny. For J. D. Bolter and R. Gruisin, the authors of *Remediation*, the Real is the "subjective authentic"—that is, whatever enhances experience or knowledge.

As already noted in Chapter 1, the Real in animism includes spirits that inhabit nonhuman life and objects as well as the new animism, which does not offer a formal philosophy, but can be effective on a local, pragmatic level. Its Real involves meta-communicability between both human and nonhuman entities. Also already noted is that the new materialism takes seriously the vital agential power of seemingly inert nonhuman matter, what political theorist Jane Bennett calls "thing-power." Posthumanist Rosi Braidotti does not use the term "the Real" but considers "nomadic becoming" the crucial point of the posthuman future. This indeterminate/fluid existence would reject humanism and individualism and embrace a Zoe-centric worldview. Zoe refers to:

the mindless vitality of Life carrying on independently, regardless of rational control. This vital energy is the [...] privilege attributed to nonhumans and to all the "others" of Man [sic]. (2011, 99)

It is the "dynamic, self-organizing structure of life itself" (ibid., 60).

Jacque Lacan's "real," in lower case, emerges in the post-mirror stage, when the subject has repressed what s/he no longer identifies with and is opposed to the imaginary as something outside the symbolic order of language. The "real" may only be experienced as ruptures in that symbolic order.

In philosopher Alain Badiou's view, "reality is grounded on a 'void' of 'inconsistent multiplicity,' which is his Real. An Event happens that ruptures the fabric of society to expose the chaos underneath, an insight that could open the way to change, if not necessarily progress" (Robinson 2014).

The Real that Maurice Merleau-Ponty's phenomenology offers is the concept of "decentered subjectivity"—i.e., an embodied subject is both subject and object to itself—and is characterized by an oscillation of perceptual modes. This embodied subject evinces an ambiguity of presence and absence that can be related to material aesthetics. For instance, the audience can perceive the specifics of performing-objects but can simultaneously imagine a more aesthetic, surreal, or simply different image/vision from the material performance as a whole.

Merleau-Ponty's reference to the physiological structure of the human eye and its optic disc is also useful to remember when viewing and interpreting genre-breaking or intra-/intercultural theatre in the context of globalization. All tend towards more complex or "fragmented" stage [re] presentation. The human eye is not made to gain a holistic view immediately, but has the ability to complete what it sees by drawing on previous experiences. Those with cataracts or glaucoma may have their vision partially blocked by attending symptoms but their mind/imagination will automatically complement the view with appropriate imagery, meaning that the visually impaired are tricked into thinking their sight is still intact. This compensatory mechanism does not apply only to illness; looking at a Picasso could provide just as much stimulus for the mind to activate this mechanism as a naturalistic painting.

3-2　The process of rupture

"Creating illusion through rupture" is a well-known quote from Steve Tillis, indicating that creating art afresh requires breaking out of accepted, conventional artistic thinking that has stultified. Genre-breaking and collaboration with diverse practitioners, who possess very different notions of what art is and how it may reflect the present and galvanize innovation, seem to be the two major ways of attaining such rupture. This section will focus on genre-breaking, while Chapter 4 will address ventures into intra-/intercultural diversity.

In the case of modern material performance in both Europe and Japan, the convention has been the magical invisible aesthetics of puppets seemingly moving autonomously without a manipulator in sight.

Brecht's alienation principle was applied to European material performance in the postwar period to prevent the audience's emotional identification with characters and the logic of inevitability by exposing the mechanics of staging. His use of a predominantly bare stage, reminiscent of Shakespeare's open stage, was also useful for experimental staging (cf. Penny Francis).

As Penny Francis points out, with the addition from the 1950s of *bunraku* multi-person manipulation to "rupture" further standard conventions, the Western principles of homogeneity and formal specificity were largely abandoned. In Japan, Brechtian methodology certainly drew much attention among live-theatre practitioners in the 1950s when the theatre company Actors Theatre (Haiyuza) introduced it, and again in the 1960s, when the experimental company Black Tent (Gekidan kuro tento) based their style on epic theatre. Among material artists, familiarity with Brechtian concepts was fostered through the educational policy of UNIMA -Japan. By the late 1970s, Taiji Kawajiri had taken PUK to perform at the post-Brechtian Berliner Ensemble in East Berlin and had dialogues on the modern and traditional characteristics of puppetry with a Brechtian theatre expert at Humboldt University and others (Kawajiri 1986, 296). Furthermore, the traditional marionette theatre Youkiza preferred to collaborate with directors and playwrights of this mobile Black Tent.

Today, the modern Westernized Japanese manipulator steps onto the stage to manipulate his performing-object openly. Whether he follows object theatre's emphasis on the rationalization of the mise en scène is also up to him. He can also borrow from traditional Japanese puppetry and calibrate the degree of visibility by wearing color-coded attire with or without a hood. The Western-derived, genre-based barriers have collapsed and the contemporary Japanese stage now welcomes both traditional staging and alternative devising, and various fusions thereof. Artistic direction enables the crossing of boundaries, whereby the movers' dramaturgical effectiveness is greatly enhanced. They can handle and speak for multiple performing-objects, just as Jo Taira does in *La Marie-Vison*; furthermore, they can separate from them and become actors to play different characters, as Taira also does. Actors can also enter the mise en scène to hybridize the theatrics.

The new freedom for the manipulators has also increased demands on their professionalism. Many contemporary Japanese manipulators still see material performance as a specialized vocation often dedicated to one style of puppet manipulation, while regarding acting a separate and optional discipline. Others take the new opportunities in their stride and pick up the necessary skills willingly to work in an expanding theatre environment that welcomes performing-objects.

In this writer's view, it is important that Japanese manipulators gain the flexibility to temporarily cast aside their single-minded dedication to what is at present still called puppetry and embrace the vast possibilities of their contribution in diverse, high-tech, global performance environments.

As for the content of the new artistic "illusion," i.e., the vision that is the Real, recent Japanese material performances share with other art forms an awareness of accelerated technological advance overtaking human abilities and the need to find methods to cope with the resultant sociocultural changes. Favorite subjects at present are antiwar activities, denuclearization, alternative energy sources, ecological concerns like global warming, aging and the family, gender and sociocultural identity, a "numb with peace" attitude,[2] which more recently has been superseded by alarm over the fragile position of Japan in Asian politics and economics; finally, the development of AI and its social repercussions, including a concern over the diminishing value of the performing arts.

3-3 Genre-breaking in Youkiza's *Choan and the Ripped Umbrella: Heisei Trick Peep Show*

Youkiza's *Choan and the Ripped Umbrella: Heisei Trick Peep Show* (2008; hereafter *Choan and the Ripped Umbrella*) provides an excellent example of genre-breaking. It is also an intracultural collaboration, a point that will be discussed briefly in a note at the end of this chapter.

Application of the phenomenology of perception to aesthetic attitude

As further clarification of the phenomenological notion of the oscillation of perceptual modes discussed in the first section of this chapter will increase comprehension of *Choan and the Ripped Umbrella*, a summary is given on Steve Odin's analysis of aesthetic attitude in his *Artistic Detachment in Japan and the West*. Taking beauty as an example, he explains how in ancient/medieval theories, beauty was seen as an attribute of harmony located in the object. In contrast, Kant's perception of beauty/sublime depends on the disinterested attitude of the subject.

Objects of perception in the phenomenological sense according to Kant are not simply fixed or given but are constituted by "acts" of consciousness. So beauty is not a fixed property of an object, but is now something posited by mental acts of a constitutive subject. The objective content (*noema*) is constituted by the subjective act (*noesis*) of consciousness. *Epoche* is a suspension of judgment, which comes in two parts: (1) neutralization of habit and/or disinterestedness; and (2) fantasy variation—i.e., creativity. The aesthetic attitude comes in two parts: detached sympathy and then, as the unfamiliar aspects fall into place, reconstitution of perceptual field.

The phenomenological method requires a shift from the "naturalized attitude" of already sedimented interpretations in the noetic context of the "phenomenological attitude," which either requires *epoche*—i.e., suspension of judgment—to neutralize habitual constructs, or involves spontaneous reorganization of the perceptual through the (Husserlian) technique of "fantasy variation" in creative imagination. We will now see how an audience's perception can be encouraged to oscillate through a genre-breaking process that leads to a novel interpretation of the play.

Youkiza's *Choan and the Ripped Umbrella*

Youkiza is the oldest active string puppet company in Japan, boasting a history of 385 years. Moreover, they have innovatively broken away from their standard performance style over those long years. Starting as a traditional string puppet company that did sideshows for *yose* entertainment, they had developed a *kabuki* performance style by 1903 with puppeteers appearing onstage and delivering their characters' lines. From 1957, they introduced guest actors to perform with their marionettes and manipulators. In 2008, after their principal *shamisen* performer and narrator Sokyo Takemoto passed away, they gradually eliminated those traditional qualities, and now invite guest musicians, often with very different musical instruments, and actors to join their collaborative performances. What has not changed is the structure of their marionettes and their manipulation method. (See fig. 3.1 in the color plates.)

Youkiza's *Choan and the Ripped Umbrella* is an adaptation of a premodern *kabuki* play, written and directed by Kiyokazu Yamamoto (1939–2019) and performed at Theatre Tram in Tokyo.

The tale unfolds rapidly as follows. The eponymous Dr. Choan Murai helps his brother-in-law, Jubei, pay off debts by selling his niece, Oume, to the licensed pleasure quarters. He then kills Jubei, steals the money, and foists the crime onto samurai Dojuro Fujikake, who forgets his umbrella at the doctor's house. Accused of the murder, Dojuro dies in a holding cell during the investigation. The case is closed. When Choan's sister Osoyo visits to see her daughter, who she thinks is working for a wealthy family, Choan has his buddy Sanji kill Osoyo. The plot thickens when Oume's client, young Sentaro of the Iseya Pawnbroker's, wants to buy her out. Pretending to assist him, Choan takes the money Sentaro has prepared for her release by selling a dagger pawned by Sanji. Then Choan instructs Sanji to extort money from the pawnshop owner for disposing of an item without permission. In order to protect Sentaro from exposure and humiliation, the head clerk Kyuhachi takes the blame and is promptly fired. Three years later, Kyuhachi, now a rubbish dealer, and another man happen to meet Dojuro's impoverished widow. The man tells her that he spotted Choan near the scene of Jubei's murder on that fateful night, and belatedly they report this to the authorities. Meanwhile, Sanji has confessed to having killed Osoyo on Choan's instigation. Choan is arrested.

As with many contemporary adaptations of premodern plays, Yamamoto has broken out of the traditional genre and the theme of upholding the social order. First, on the script level, he has simplified the plot and reduced the number of acts, characters, and relationships, while modernizing the language. There are also some significant changes in the title, characterization, and ending worthy of further attention.

Choan and the Ripped Umbrella: Heisei[3] *Trick Peep Show* is based on the 1862 *kabuki* play by Kawatake Mokuami, which has two titles: *Kanzen choaku nozoki karakuri* (Poetic Justice Trick Peep Show) and *Murai Choan takumi no yaregasa* (Choan Murai, The Master's Ripped Umbrella). Furthermore, the play was also popularly known as simply *Murai Choan.*

Yamamoto has clearly combined the two original titles to inform the potential audience that the adaptation is of a familiar work that has passed the test of time. In addition, he removed the promise of "poetic justice" from the title as well as the final act with its court trial and certainty of deserved punishment, thus intensifying the play's disturbing and threatening milieu. The adaptation ends with Choan captured, but magnificently defiant—a delicious ambiguity. Furthermore, Choan's character is adjusted to fit this bravura ending. Obsessed with money and out of control, he murders Jubei with little planning. In the original, Choan carefully plots to awaken Jubei earlier than promised so that it will still be dark when he kills his victim; he also thinks ahead of using the umbrella to incriminate Dojuro. The new Choan is clever but not careful.

Another difference is that, in this reimagining, the young Sentaro and older Kyuhachi are not biological brothers. The Confucian concept of loyalty in master-employee relations is operative; however, the equally

Confucian notion of a younger brother's duty to honor and obey his older brother has been abandoned, thus partially disassembling the Confucian pillar of morality that sustains the original play (cf. Boyd 2010, 30–31).

In performance style, breaking out of marionette manipulation conventions is evident. Magosaburo XII is the driving force behind the performance with his deft manipulation of nine characters, together with their voices so that their personalities and movements are lively and easy to distinguish. In *kabuki*, the wild Choan and the steadfast Kyuhachi are traditionally performed by the same actor. Youkiza breaks this tradition by having actor Kushida (b. 1942) play Choan and his buddy Sanji, and further breaks with genre specificity when Kushida shares the Sanji role with a stringless doll, which he brought in himself.

As Youkiza has an informal policy of collaborating with only non-performing-object groups, allowing Kushida to use his figure onstage was a considerable concession in style. Although it had moveable limbs, it was mainly an icon that Kushida carried around, sat next to, and ventriloquized for. Nonetheless, a magical moment occurs at the beginning when Kushida-as-Choan unwraps a checkered green cloth to reveal the Sanji figure dressed in the same green material. From this point, Kushida as actor then continues to play Choan and simultaneously Sanji. Kushida occasionally enacts Sanji so energetically that the doll tends to get left behind. Using a performing-object as a prop rather than an object to animate has conventionally been considered taboo. Yet as a postmodern technique of genre rupture, it cleverly suggests an internal split in Sanji that would support his final "betrayal" of Choan to the authorities despite his heavy complicity in Choan's machinations. Admittedly, Kushida does not always use the green cloth as a Sanji marker, making it difficult for the audience to keep the two characters separate. The challenge and risk in directing audience perception and relying on their imagination to make connections in genre-disassembling is revealed in such moments.

Many of the genre-breaking aspects were achieved improvisationally. Kushida is well known as a stage actor and director, but this production was his first time to work closely with marionettes. At first, he had difficulty adjusting to his 70 cm (28 in.) co-players, and looked at or interacted with the manipulators instead. Magosaburo XII found this taboo-breaking attractive and worked some of Kushida's freewheeling actions into the Youkiza performance style. For instance, when Choan kills his brother-in-law, Kushida grabs Magosaburo XII by the neck instead of the marionette. In the pawnbroker's extortion scene when Kushida-as-Sanji roughs up the pawnbroker puppet, he pulls out its head and estimates its weight to shock and convince the pawnbroker that his life is worth more than he's willing to pay. In the performance this writer attended, after an *epoche* hesitation, the audience laughed at being suddenly cornered into acknowledging that a marionette is after all an object cobbled together from pieces of wood rather than a character. In the same scene, Kushida-as-Sanji and a manipulator squabble with each other over the marionettes' heads about how much money they could squeeze out of the pawnbroker. This prominently visible shifting and doubling of identity between marionette/object and manipulator was expertly handled.

In the finale, resisting arrest, Choan slashes through the police reinforcements. The *mezashi* policemen[4] are ripped open and bright red blood[5] bursts out. Using an actor for Choan is particularly effective here as the contrast in scale makes his sword play bigger and wilder. It symbolizes both his insurgence and the fragility of civil order. From the umbrella in the first murder to the police in the last act, props and figures are smashed and broken in this extravaganza of violence and bloodletting (cf. Boyd 2010, 30–31).[6]

To sum up: the rupture of standard magical illusionism drawn from modern Westernized puppetry was accomplished largely by moving from an invisible aesthetics to a visible one and then on to a fluctuating state of devising. Of this process, this chapter focused mainly on breaking out of genre specificity. The following chapter will address the hybridization of dramaturgical strategies deployed in domestic and international collaborations that now proliferate in the pursuit of artistic diversity.

1   Carol Martin's "theatre of the real" requires some explanation. In her case, the real does refer to "life" and theatre is the "professional fictional" (2013, 30). Her "theatre of the real" uses reality as a force in theatre—as fact, history, and memory (individual, social, historical), and often through the verbatim use of archival material available through digitization and the Internet. As far as I know, there is not yet any substantial evidence of its deliberate application in Japanese material performance.
2   The postwar US-Japan Security Treaty enabled Japan to devote its ener-

gies to a successful economic recovery. People took peace for granted and became disinterested in assessing their national security in Asia and the rest of the world.

3   Heisei refers to the period of Emperor Akihito's reign, January 1989 to April 2019.

4   Cf. Chapter 1, n. 3, p. 20.

5   Following tradition, the blood is made of strips of red cloth.

6   As for the intracultural aspects of *Choan and the Ripped Umbrella,* the following cultural traditions are brought together not simply to be juxtaposed, but to interact and hybridize—premodern string-figures operated by contemporary manipulators in black-coded outfits; a nineteenth-century *kabuki* play in the hands of 1960s underground theatre artists for its adaptation, direction, and acting, as well as music and effects by avant-garde improvisational pianist Yuji Takahashi (b. 1938). Thematically, the placating cliché of poetic justice proffered by the original *kabuki* play and the 1960s underground theatre's countercultural subversive "pushing and pulling" hybridize into an uneasy yet viable relationality of in-betweenness. Such encounters have enriched the performing arts as a whole.

Chapter 4

Collaborative Productions: Local and Global

This chapter will continue the discussion on how rupturing magical illusion to create the Real was accomplished. The method of genre-breaking was attended to in Chapter 3; here, the application of dramaturgical innovation will be discussed in intracultural and intercultural/globalized contexts.

4-1 Cultural globalization and other key terms

Cultural globalization

This part presents a clarification of the present global cultural environment in which performing-object theatre is devised and produced, starting with the larger term of "globalization" and proceeding to the smaller one of "text."

Globalization is now seen as a long-term process of large-scale human integration, inter-connectivity, and hybridization at various historical phases. It gives rise to what sociologist Jan Nederveen Pierterse calls a "global mélange" (2019, 81). The contemporary phase of globalization, which became apparent around the 1990s, has emphasized economic internationalization and the spread of capitalist market relations. This globalization can be divided into the economic, political, and cultural. The economic principle is at the center and also enables the flourishing of cultural globalization, if not impeded by negative political globalization. From this point, the focus of discussion will be on the cultural kind.

Contemporary cultural globalization refers to the circulation of ideas, information, cultural practices, and social values around the world, by which new social relations are made and extended. This process is characterized by the consumption of commodities and cultural practices diffused by the Internet, popular media networks, and international travel including migration.[1]

Within cultural globalization, three perspectives are identified by Pierterse and others. The first is cultural differentiation, i.e., lasting difference such as "an intense commitment to local difference and ideology." A major advocate of this view is Samuel P. Huntington, American political scientist, who contends that, "[c]ivilizational-consciousness is increasing; conflict between civilizations will supplant ideological and other forms of conflict as the dominant global form of conflict" (Watum 2017). The second is cultural convergence, i.e., increasing homogenization as in the spread of Westernized consumer culture like McDonaldization. The last is hybridization, i.e., ongoing cultural blending of differences that can foster new diversity and plurality. This last view is what Pieterse advocates.

The general effect is a growth in global awareness, a sense of both interconnectedness and diversity. The banner concept is the new cosmopolitanism that concerns what connects humans across difference and inequality—sameness over difference, homogenization over differentiation.

What has theatre, including performing-object theatre, to offer this expanding world? Theatre's social function as an institution can develop cultural/artistic exchange and cosmopolitan identity formation as well as enable marginalized identities a voice in the world. It can reveal that what seems unrelated is actually connected.

One method is the large-scale international performing arts festivals celebrating diversity and commonality that are organized and/or funded by major government agencies like the Japanese ACA and the Japan Arts Council as well as by smaller municipal agencies and cultural institutions to promote their collective agendas. The method is to find a supportive locality with adequate venues to present an intercultural program with notable, established artists or though lesser-known, experimentally daring ones. Speedy communication, easy travel, and access to funding enable them to find professional and amateur collaborators at home and abroad. Among the more recent large-scale annual events are Festival/Tokyo (F/T),[2] Kyoto Experiment: Kyoto International Performing Arts Festival,[3] TPAM—Performing Arts Meeting in Yokohama,[4] and Theater Commons Tokyo.[5]

Last but not least is the Iida Puppet Festa (Iida ningyo geki fuesuta, f. 1999),[6] the largest puppet festival in Japan, located in Iida City, Nagano Prefecture, and organized with the support of Iida City and their Board of Education. Approximately 2000 volunteers assist to make this large-scale event possible. Every summer, about 450 performances are held at 120 venues, drawing an audience of around 50,000.[7]

In terms of content, theatre in general can address global topics such as conflict over resources and migration,[8] minority issues,[9] gender relations[10] and link well with new media performance.[11]

Increasing homogenization of performance style is already evident in the high replicability achieved through franchising and performance kits, such as those for *The Lion King* and *Avenue Q*, both of which champion performing-objects and have been produced in Japan.

Review of other key terms

This section provides a brief review of some of the basic performance concepts closely related to globalization and cosmopolitanism, such as "text," "intertextuality," "hybridity," and "intra/intercultural theatre." Text, since Derrida, has referred widely to any "symbolic system a culture may construct, be it religious ritual, clothing fashions, or the script of *Hamlet*" (McConachie et al. 2016, 498). Intertextuality refers to the intermingling of such texts, and the fusion is frequently complex, diverse, and innovative; this hybridizing trend has grown as the scale of cultural exchange has widened from intracultural to the intercultural and global. Hybridity, originally a biological term that meant the "cross between two separate races, plants or cultures," has already been used in discourses on essentialism, racial theory, postcolonial identity, cultural studies, and globalization.

Pieterse's position is that cultural globalization as hybridization functions on the institutional and cultural levels and leads to the formation of translocal *mélange* (blending) cultures. As a cross-category process,

hybridity functions as a power relationship between center and margin, hegemony and minority, and indicates a blurring, destabilization, or subversion of that hierarchical relationship. (2019, 94–95)

He adds that items or categories can be situated between two polarities: "assimilative hybridity and destabilizing hybridity" (ibid., 96). As examples of cultural globalization's hybridization process, he cites syncretism, migration *mélange*, intercultural crossovers when the adaptability is positive, and community-making. The negative side is alienation and sense of homelessness without fostering a sense of agency for the hybrid (ibid., 95).

In this respect, Pieterse's notion of hybridization seems amply applicable to the intra/intercultural collaboration projects that have increased in theatre. They can function as intercultural brokers, which can be plotted along a continuum of assimilation and destabilization.[12]

4-2 Collaboration: Local and intracultural productions

While material visibility may not by itself be the answer to all the issues in contemporary material performance, the visibility rupture has been crucial in enabling performers to break out of genre expectations and has undeniably opened the floodgates to a richly varied intertextuality—the intermingling of various theatrical vocabularies (scenic, visual, verbal, physical, etc.), technologies, and training methods—inspired by different disciplines and cultures in both local and global performance. While the tendency of such developments to eschew verbal texts and literary language is sometimes seen to be limiting, they can also be emancipating. Furthermore, technology now enables simultaneous surtitling in multiple languages. This discussion will begin with local intracultural collaborations, as they are numerically the more common mode of sharing artistic creativity in Japan in both material and other kinds of stage performance.

Japanese theatre practitioners have traditionally had a powerful drive to develop and perfect a particular aesthetic style and have banded together strongly for that purpose. While this sense of exceptionalism has faded through the changing times that value speed, stylistic variety, and interconnectedness, encouraging them to collaborate with other artists or companies, a wariness still attends their search for stimuli from the diversity of their locale. For instance, even today open auditions are rarely conducted. Thus, much of the local collaborative theatre work takes place on a modest level between Japanese practitioners in various genres and subgenres to galvanize innovation or juxtapose/collage their talents in unusual combinations without necessarily reaching a high level of genre-breaking or hybridity. Specular diversity can sometimes lead to pre-designed harmony rather than a new insight or rupture.

A local collaborative project is often de facto in the hands of one theatre or production company that has its own performers and invites individual guests to write, direct, animate, act, sing, dance, design, and so on. Thus, much of the decision-making at the production and selection levels is managed, and indeed controlled, by one company. This privilege ensures consistency across the board. Also, the median number of members in an object theatre company is two, with only a few companies reaching a double-digit membership, such as Youkiza (between twelve and fifteen), Kyogei (twenty-one), La Clarte (thirty-eight), Hitomiza (forty-two), and PUK (seventy).

Intracultural theatre, according to Rustom Bharucha, denotes "cultural encounters between and across specific communities and regions within the nation state" (quoted in Lo and Gilbert 2000, 38). It should serve a critical function in challenging "organicist notions of culture by highlighting the deeply fragmented and divided society" (ibid.).

Japan is not as monocultural as it likes to present itself. According to the Ministry of Justice (2018), approximately 2.73 million foreigners reside in Japan (i.e., 2.16 percent of the total population). Korean and Chinese residents comprise 44.5 percent of the foreign residents in Japan: about 449,600 are Koreans including about 71,000 permanent residents and 288,700 special permanent residents, while about 764,700 are Chinese including approximately 260,900 permanent residents. Other long-term ethnolinguistic minorities include the 25,000 officially recognized Ainu people and the 1.3 million Ryukyuans in Okinawa alone, though they are not recognized as "foreign." Cultural encounters are possible; for example, a collaborative venture between an urban object theatre group from Tokyo or Kyoto and a cultural minority with a political agenda from Hokkaido or Okinawa would certainly raise the level of challenge. But such events are uncommon.

Wishing Chong's *Doll Town* as diaspora

One example of an intracultural project that does work towards emancipatory identity formation for cultural minorities is the Japanese-Korean joint production of *Doll Town* (premiered 2007, revived 2017) by Youkiza and playwright/screenwriter Wishing Chong (b. 1957). Chong belongs to the second generation of Koreans born and bred in Tokyo, who, due to politico-historical reasons, identify with Korea despite limited experience of the life or people there. The 385-year-old Youkiza marionette family rose out of the premodern caste system (abolished in the Meji era with the proclamation of the equality of all people), which had relegated performers to the outcaste category, to become a high-profile nationally and municipally designated cultural property today. Although this particular production does not address Japanese-Korean relations in any detail, that the collaborators chose to perform about historically deep-rooted discrimination is significant. (See fig. 4.1 in the color plates.)

The play portrays the desperate conditions of various minorities in the Kyoto-Osaka district during World War II. Besides the poverty-stricken

Fig. 4.1. Youkiza and Wishing Chong, *Doll Town*, 2017, The Suzunari, Tokyo. Courtesy of Youkiza.

Japanese locals, there were Koreans, an illegitimate blonde girl of Japanese and American parentage as well as members of two groups excluded from the former caste system—a leather worker of the *burakumin*, who were ostracized due to their taboo occupations connected with death, dying, and defilement, and performers such as puppeteers, as they did not engage in so-called productive work.

Two itinerant puppeteers, Hyottoko (acted by Magosaburo XII) and his sister/partner Okame (acted by Chie Youki, Magosaburo's real-life sister), provide the frame story of the play.[13] Bringing out his boyhood double, puppet Kota, Hyottoko recalls how miserable life had been during World War II and how in a single air raid, he had lost everything—his mother, his chums like the blonde, and the whole tin-roof shanty neighborhood condescendingly known as Doll Town. As he recalls those events, they begin to materialize on stage.

The names of these framing characters are telling. Hyottoko, meaning "fire-maker," is a comedic stock character in the traditional performing arts with a distinctive *kimo-kawaii* mask that shows a lopsided face with one eye squinting and the mouth puckered up as if blowing a bamboo pipe to start a fire. Okame is a plebian version of Ame-no-Uzume-no-mikoto, the Shinto goddess of dawn, mirth, and revelry. Okame masks are always smiling and promise happiness. However, as a comedic stock character, she is sometimes portrayed as an ugly, noisy nuisance, as well as a plump, humorous matron. In performance, Magosaburo XII and Chie Youki do not wear those masks but display many of the characteristics of their namesakes. Incidentally, the leather sandals hanging around Hyottoko's neck are an important memento of the special "friendship" both he and his mother had in their different ways with the leather worker.

In this way, the Youki siblings act traditional types that represent the Japanese comedic folk tradition, just as in real life, the Youki marionette family is now representative of the continuing material performance tradition of Japan. Both they and Chong cast an ironical eye at how the nation finds them useful.

Chong is known for portraying life as a cycle of laughter, tears, and energy through his fictional world. It is the tumultuous vitality of his characters despite their desperate predicament that raises audience consciousness and recognition of the indomitable spirit of the deprived to "keep on going on." He has said (2007) that he despises drama about self-discovery: "The poor don't have existential crises. They have no time to ask 'To be or not to be.'"

The local children in the play constantly taunt and fight each other, reflecting the divisions in the larger society. Mitsuru and Ume, another brother-sister pair, are from a family with the resources to evacuate when living literally gets too hot. Rough and tough, they never miss a chance to beat up on the blonde and the penniless Kota. The blonde girl retaliates with ferocity, howling and screaming as she struggles. Their sudden and wild animation almost reassures the audience that the younger generation has the energy and potential to find a way to survive the horrendous troubles that surround them, but not completely, as Kota stays weakly on the sidelines, trips over, and is not able to hold his own.

The highlight of the performance is the figure of Kota's mother catching fire (in real time onstage) during the Allied Forces air raid that destroys the town. She burns to death on the railway bridge, a dangerous trick for the manipulator Chie to accomplish especially as in the 2017 revival she had already broken her arm in a fall from the same bridge during rehearsal.

Furthermore, in the same scene, Magosaburo also acted the role of Kota for one moment, and swam through a sea of flames (made of cloth) to safety. His acting was superb, conveying the deep emotion of a ten-year-old boy unable to save his mother whom he both loved and hated. When a master manipulator is also an impressive actor, the stage takes on the aura of the Real.

To sum up, the cultural aspects deployed in this play indicate how the past continues in the present: premodern marionettes, premodern comedic characters continue and adapt to the times; stylized characterization and fighting seem new and contemporary but retain traces of traditional martial arts. In thematic terms, social stigma from the premodern caste system, twentieth-century postcolonial animosities, and World War II hostilities and prejudices, meet in this play to make a crucible of discrimination.

Three intracultural productions featuring *bunraku*

So far in this study, little mention has been made of traditional *bunraku* theatre. Some reflection is appropriate here before discussing intracultural projects that take license with the *bunraku* performance style.

Bunraku is the modern popular term for three-person puppetry, traditionally called *ningyo joruri*, and invented by the famous manipulator and *karakuri* automata artist Bunzaburo Yoshida (d. 1760) around 1734 amidst the rivalry between the Toyotake Ningyo Joruri Theatre (Toyotakeza, 1703–1765) and the Takemoto Ningyo Joruri Theatre (Takemotoza, 1684–1767), to which he belonged. Through various innovations, the puppets were almost doubled in height up to a maximum of 140 cm (55 in.) and, while weighing an average of 2–3 kg (4.4–6.6 lb.), could weigh up to 4–5 kg (8.8–11 lb.).

The master puppeteer manipulates the head and right arm; the second puppeteer, the left arm; and the third, the feet. The three stand very close to the puppet and each other so as to share the rhythm-tempo of the master. To conduct the sophisticated puppet head movement, the master inserts his left hand into a hole in the puppet's back to operate a handgrip with small levers attached to strings that move the eyes, mouth, eyebrows, and nose. This handgrip is part of a rod that extends down from the neck of the puppet.[14]

Today in the West, the term *bunraku* is used very differently from that in traditional Japanese theatre, commonly referring to multiple, visible animators who manipulate puppets or objects hands-on. Other aspects of the traditional eighteenth-century performance style—such as the *tayu* vocalist who recites all the voices as well as the stage description and narrative background in the script, the *shamisen* musicians, and the split-level stage floor with rails allowing more space for the leg animator to work—are usually not included in the Western conceptualization.[15]

The puppetry aspect of *bunraku* has been an immense inspiration for Western animators since the 1950s and 1960s in exploring novel devising, unencumbered by history, tradition, types, style, specific techniques, or precision (Bidgood 2015). But it has not had such an effect or presence in its country of origin.

As premodern Japanese puppetry employed a visible aesthetic with black as a code color for invisibility, when visibility again became attractive in the late twentieth century as a "novel" method of material stage representation, it was easy to access traditional methods and apply or modify them to suit the needs of specific performances. In that sense, some aspects of *bunraku* have always been available resources. However, respect for the living tradition as represented by the Bunraku Kyokai (Bunraku Association) in Osaka and the desire for "authenticity" tends to discourage local manipulators from modifying or deconstructing *bunra-*

ku for alternative purposes. Thus, there have been relatively few intracultural *bunraku* adaptations by contemporary local groups or artists. However, when there are, those productions may explore conceptual experimentation in finding alternative approaches, like satirical treatment of the genre or the patriarchal content, or downplaying the hierarchical work relations of premodern theatre. In the performance aspects, innovation is discernable in the addition of audiovisual projection, radically different music, speed, and scenography that does not highlight the visibility of puppet operation.

The memorable productions are almost inevitably those that include professional *bunraku* puppeteers of the Bunraku Kyokai, thus ensuring an impeccable level of text comprehension and technical skill. *Sonezaki Shinju Rock*, Sugimoto *bunraku*, and Mitani *bunraku* are in this category. No modification of the puppet structure was made in any of these productions.

The earliest major experiment was the 1980 *Sonezaki Part II*, Ryudo Uzaki's rock and roll adaptation of Chikamatsu's *Love Suicides at Sonezaki* (1703), in which the Bunraku Kyokai puppeteers performed in front of his Downtown Fighting Boogie Woogie Band on a flat stage at a rock music house in Tokyo (Uzaki, n.d.). While there was limited on-stage interaction between the two types of performers, the music, which was carefully modulated to match the Sonezaki themes and human situations, received high praise in reviews (ibid.). For the thirtieth anniversary of his band in 2002, Uzaki renamed it the New ☆ Ryudo Group and revived his 1980 piece with a new title, *Sonezaki Shinju Rock*, at the Sogetsu Hall in Tokyo with puppeteers Monju Kiritake (d. 2017) and Bungo Yoshida (1934–2008) plus fourteen other *bunraku* performers. Uzaki composed fresh music, and invited popular singer/songwriter Amii Ozaki to compose the lyrics. This version also included the opening prologue on Hatsu's pilgrimage to the Kannon deity of mercy, which is usually omitted from the official *bunraku* theatre program. A three-tiered platform was provided upstage for the three vocalists and musicians. (See fig. 4.2 in the color plates.)

Since the turn of the twenty-first century, artists have been taking up the challenge to hybridize or reassemble *bunraku* puppetry performance more proactively. Modern artist and photographer Hiroshi Sugimoto (b. 1948)[16] premiered his *bunraku* vision of the same Chikamatsu play with a new version, *Sonezaki Love Suicides Kannon Pilgrimage* (*Sonezaki*

Fig. 4.2. Hiroshi Sugimoto, *Sonezaki Love Suicides Kannon Pilgrimage*, 2014, Kanagawa Arts Theatre. Photo © Hajime Watanabe. Courtesy of Odawara Art Foundation.

shinju tsuketari Kannon meguri), with members of the National Bunraku Theatre and performed at Kanagawa Arts Theatre in 2011. (See fig. 4.3 in the color plates.)

The production brought together modern performer/artists and *bunraku* practitioners in the standard three-in-one formation of puppeteers, narrators, and *shamisen* accompaniment. Living National Treasure Seiji Tsuruzawa (b. 1945) newly composed and directed *shamisen* music to accompany Shimatayu Toyotake (b. 1948) and four other narrators. For this premiere production, the National Bunraku Theatre provided the puppets and manipulators, with master Kanjuro Kiritake III (b. 1953) performed the lead role of Hatsu with Living National Treasure Minosuke Yoshida (b. 1933) playing her lover Tokubei.

Director Sugimoto's concept was to restore the Buddhist Amida belief that provided the religious rationale for the expeditious journey from love to double suicide by employing two religious symbols, a large statue of the Kannon deity of mercy and a tall *torii* gate[17] and being faithful to the original script. He notes that:

Doomed to live apart in this life, [Hatsu] and her lover Tokubei come to believe that if they kill themselves for true love then the Kannon will reunite them in the afterlife. (Sugimoto 2014)

In the staging of this ideal love, Sugimoto experimented boldly. Retaining all the lines, he accelerated parts of the chanter's delivery to rap-style speed so as to keep the performance within two hours while instructing the puppeteers to move gracefully like *danseurs*. What is more, he decided to explore visual extension through perspectival depth by using a 40 m long (131 ft.) *hanamachi* passage onstage. This factor alone transformed the mise en scène from its usual horizontal lineup and movement for the *bunraku* puppets to a radically vertical one. To this, he added two huge screens for dark and bright images to conjure up the dark, flickering ambience of premodern Edo. For Sugimoto's 2013 European tour to Madrid, Rome, and Paris, popular contemporary artist Tabaimo designed gorgeous visuals of butterflies, will o' the wisps, and more on an 875 cm (350 in.) screen with 8K super hi-vision.[18]

For professional puppeteers, some of these techniques were disorienting, as they had to accelerate to the fast chant, discard many of their accustomed movements, and move about in the dark with their hoods on (Toyotake 2013).

The celebrated comedic writer/director Koki Mitani[19] (b. 1961) directed *Much Ado About Love Suicides* (Sorenari shinju) at the Parco Theater, Tokyo in 2012. It is a pastiche of various love suicides near the woods of Sonezaki, where a cake shop owner has to solve the combined problems of plummeting cake sales and rising double suicide attempts. (See fig. 4.4 in the color plates.)

Mitani's inventive concept was to change the tragic journey to suicide into a hilarious comedy and also direct the puppeteers to do totally new segments onstage such as having the cake shop owner "haunted" by the original characters, having the playwright Chikamatsu appear in the performance, and an underwater double suicide attempt. Gathered for staging was an impressive cast and crew from the National Bunraku Theatre, with Rosetayu Toyotake for the narrator. According to Rosetayu, the twenty-one professionals, expecting to do *bunraku*, were bewildered by Mitani's approach, as *bunraku* does not have a single comedy in its repertory, though comic scenes (*chariba*) do exist. Neither is there a director, for the traditional repertory is by and large fixed and audiovisual recordings suffice as guidelines; nor do they workshop or rehearse for weeks at a time as do actors in modern theatre (Toyotake 2013). Both sides had to negotiate their way to reach what finally became a laudable performance. Mitani clinched his underwater scene with the puppeteers' goodwill, but Rosetayu's conclusion was that the *bunraku* performers did not learn much. He commented that:

The performance of new works that provide new viewpoints from which to look at *bunraku* is a very good thing. However, if asked whether I learnt anything new from them in terms of performing technique, I would say no. (Ibid.)

In this way, collaborations are not easy explorations to carry out, but can be immensely satisfying. In general, it seems that contemporary directors and artists deploy conceptual variation, and in performance, apply a principle of addition, particularly of contemporary effects that downplay the visibility of the mechanics of *bunraku* puppet operation.

In the following section of this chapter, the discussion will proceed to artistic hybridity on the intercultural level in a world interconnected through globalization.

4-3 Intercultural theatre in a globalized world

Expanding forms of intercultural theatre

According to Bharucha, intercultural theatre is a hybrid:

"derived from an intentional encounter between cultures and performing traditions" and "has more latitude to explore and critique alternative forms of citizenship and identity across and beyond national boundaries; but some state mediation is likely." (Quoted in Lo and Gilbert 2002, 36)

From the 1970s to 1980s, Western intercultural theatre endeavors focused on how to adapt, naturalize, or transpose out of context the original play or performance style, often Asian, for easy consumption by the target and mainly Western audience. In his review of Dan Rebellato's *Theatre and Globalization* (2009), A. Walsh quotes his point that "since the 1990s, intercultural performance has become a contested area in which performance producers and creators make claims for the kinds of cultural borrowing that result in hybrid and syncretic work on world stages" and adds that, since then there has been an increase in voices arguing that interculturalism tends toward appropriation (2012, 111).

Today in the twenty-first century, intercultural performance in the context of globalization has focused on the process or relationality of transformation itself—the in-between devising. Western countries are no longer the central figures in intercultural theatre, and globally, artists, now sensitized to the differences between replication, representation, appropriation, and collaboration are more adept at negotiating their way through the intricacies of such collaboration.

Rather than having any intrinsic differences, intercultural/global theatres may be products of changing eras and expanding global parameters of socio-cultural and economic activities. Extending Bharucha's view, we can say that both are hybrids derived from an intentional encounter between cultures and performing traditions. The differences may lie in the extent of the intentionality and how that is realized through technological advance, motilities, and funding as seen in its international touring and rapid world dissemination by cybernetic means. At present, intercultural theatre can still be a one-way cultural consumption in the target country, while globalized theatre is assumed to be made more widely available to an international audience.

The changing environment opens up new potential and facilitates different innovations. Consideration should be given to whether the production is performed onstage globally and also on whether it is released through other audiovisual media as dissemination is greater in the latter case. The following section will discuss the borderlessness of Shakespeare and other intercultural theatre.

Borderlessness around the Globe

In terms of world cultural iconicity, Shakespeare's *oeuvre* is particularly attractive as the plays are already famous, widely translated, and also dramaturgically complex or problematic enough to demand, capture, and satisfy the attention of a worldwide audience.

Pieterse's concept of a hybridization continuum, already introduced in the first section of this chapter, will be applied to see if or how intercultural material performance can be successfully plotted between the two poles of assimilative hybridity and destabilizing hybridity.

In the postwar period, performing-object productions of Shakespeare *à la japonaise* were not as numerous as in live theatre. Hitomiza and Youkiza have led the way in adapting drama Shakespeare's drama since the 1960s, while Sawa joined in with his object theatre renderings in the 1990s. The early productions started from the assimilative hybridity with replication and imitation, reinforcing the cultural authority and extending the brand capital of the institution that is Shakespeare. Production strategies then fanned out to localizing hybridity, increasing hybridization, or homogenizing the universality of Shakespeare. Some reached a destabilizing hybridity, but most remained within the beneficial glow of Shakespeare's brand. The movement between the two poles is not so much linear and orderly like Pieterse's imagery suggests as multifaceted and explorative.

Puppet Theatre Hitomiza is well known for its periodic engagement with the Shakespeare canon. The company has produced and regularly revived four of Shakespeare's tragedies—*Macbeth* (premiered 1961), directed by Koji Shimizu; *Hamlet* (premiered 1970), directed by Kiyohiko Yamamoto; *Romeo and Juliet* (premiered 1971), directed by Katsundo Morimoto (b. 1942); and *King Lear* (premiered 1988), directed by Shiro Ito (d. 2018)—and, to a lesser extent, *The Tempest* (premiered 1971), directed by Yamamoto. The translations are predominantly from the well-established *Iwanami Bunko Shakespeare Plays* series, guaranteeing literary and poetic quality. (See fig. 4.5 in the color plates.)

Its 1961 production of *Macbeth*, geared for children, won the company three major awards: the Yomiuri Children's Theatre Award, the Minister of MEXT Award, and the Tokyo Children's Puppet Theatre Award. This early *Macbeth* and also their *Lear* had life-size and Western-featured figures, emphasizing the dignity and cynosure of European nobility. Methodologically, they aimed for authenticity through replication. From 1971, their mask and rod performances of *Romeo and Juliet, The Tempest* (1971, 2011), *A Midsummer Night's Dream* (1993), and even revivals of *Macbeth* ventured away from Western production style and translations considered conventional at that time. Localized assimilation to Japanese pop culture became a growing concern and the characters acquired increasingly nonhuman characteristics, variant sizes, and striking colors. An impressive example is the 2009 *Macbeth*, replete with elaborate animal/insect imagery, making the characters look more like postmodern toy robots than humans. Thus, while retaining Shakespeare's text

Fig. 4.3. Hitomiza, *Macbeth*, 2009. Courtesy of Hitomiza.

to develop the themes and action, the company has distanced itself radically from European archetypes.

Increased interweaving in performative hybridity can be noted in Hitomiza's introduction of co-performers from the 1972 *Romeo and Juliet* and in the shift to a modified visible aesthetics with one or two visible manipulators in black per figure, using the *marionnette portée* style with the head controlled with a short stick at the back of the head. As their figures are human-size and wear robes that spread wide when the arms are stretched out in large theatrical acting, the figures continue to be grand and regal while the manipulator's presence is muted. A veil covers the manipulator's face but leaves the ears somewhat exposed.

Radical and experimental hybridization that challenges or subverts the original works can also include exploiting the original as a springboard to generate a different kind of work. Such trends are not yet evident in Hitomiza's Shakespearean adaptations. The Hitomiza directors of Shakespeare plays are advancing in age and Shiro Ito has passed on. Though the Hitomiza website declares that it does not unilaterally equate puppetry with education and entertainment for children and youth, their present developmental focus seems to be solidly in those directions.

In the Japanese postmodern theatre of the 1980s, the Youkiza versions of Shakespeare's works started with their well-known *Macbeth* (premiered 1982). It evinced radical experimental hybridization, in which the constitutive parts of the play were atomized rendering the adaptation into a reinvention or subversion of the original. This was achieved under the direction of Brechtian Makoto Satoh with the translation by Yushi Odashima, whose penchant is strongly for the vernacular. Youkiza took its *Macbeth* on a 1986 European tour that included Serbia, where it won a Belgrade International Theater Festival Award, as well as Finland, Yugoslavia, and Belgium. The second international tour of *Macbeth* in 1990 went to Sweden, Norway, Denmark, and the former Soviet Union. With *Hamlet* (1986), Youkiza chose a different approach by using Yoshiyuki Fukuda's poetic translation under his direction at the Musashino Geino Theatre, Tokyo.[20]

Other notable examples of the experimental hybridization of Shakespeare as material for new work can be found in Sawa's collaborative object theatre adaptations. Of the three Shakespeare fusions[21] he has done to date, the focus here is on his wordless, solo *Macbeth* (1993), using masks and performing-objects. For the concept, Sawa acknowledges that his mentor Matàsek provided some words of wisdom: "Aren't there men who think they are dominating their wives but in fact the wives are manipulating them?" (Sawa 2008b).

Sawa realized that he could create a relationship in which he, the manipulator wearing a mask, acts the character of Macbeth, but is unknowingly controlled by his own puppet, Lady Macbeth. Furthermore, in the creative process, he discovered that drawing "pictures to check the balance of the symbolic elements of what appeared onstage" was a more

Fig. 4.4. Nori Sawa, *Macbeth*, 1993, Prague. Photo © Masahiko Takeda.

Fig. 4.5. Marionette Company Isshiza, *Artaud 24 Heures++Encore*, 2014, Tokyo Metropolitan Theatre (Theatre East). Photo © Yasushi Yaginuma. Courtesy of Isshiza.

flexible approach than continually rewriting the script and stage directions (ibid.).

Concerning other intercultural theatre, a rising star is Marionette Company Isshiza (f. 2015). To be accurate, it is not really "new," as the leader Isshi Youki[22] has reorganized his company a few times: in the past, it has been called Office Acephale (2003–2005) and Edo Marionette Company (Ito-ayatsuri ningyoza, 2005–2015). An offshoot of Youkiza, its manipulators use the same kind of traditional Edo string-puppetry control panel and puppets. It is deeply conceptual and often produces adaptations of historical Western avant-garde theatre. Its *Artaud 24 Heures* (Aruto 24 jikan, 2011) was based on Soshi Suzuki's novel *Antonin Artaud's Return* (Antonin Aruto no kikan), directed by *buto* dancer Masahiko Akuta, and premiered at the Akasaka Red Theater in Tokyo. (See fig. 4.6 in the color plates.) It was a passionate attempt at staging Artaud's restless spirit, attended with cameo appearances by other Western philosophers such as Derrida and Lacan, holding forth on their theories in a "con-fusion" of *buto* dance, acting, and performing-objects. This company's target audience is Japanese, though its material is mainly Western. It

Fig. 4.6. Setagaya Public Theatre and Complicité, *Shun-kin*, 2013, Setagaya Public Theatre, Tokyo. Photo © Tsukasa Aoki. Courtesy of Setagaya Public Theatre.

also has international connections and has performed *Artaud 24 Heures++Encore* (2014) in Pilsen, the Czech Republic, and hosted a Japan-Czech international collaborative production of *Golem* (2016) in Tokyo.

The emerging characteristics of globalized theatre

Globalized theatre refers to theatre production that intentionally involves eclectic participants from multiple countries and cultures; it often depends on substantial funding from public and/or corporate sources and includes touring of some international cities. Content-wise, it is theatre that reflects on or problematizes globalization, disassembles cultural, national, and ethnic stereotypes and taboos, and holds cosmopolitanism as one global aim. In comparison to intercultural theatre, globalized theatre is often larger in scale, wider in range, and easier to replicate and share among global performers and audiences. The performing-object productions cited in this section—*Shun-kin* and Kuo Pao Kun's *Descendants of the Eunuch Admiral*—will exemplify these points.

There is no set style, and the visibility aesthetic is assumed to be common knowledge for the audience of material performance. A recurring cluster of aspects can be noted. The portrayal of humanity is more general and abstract than in conventional living theatre, as are the figures' identity. Time and space are transformative and elusive so that figures from different historical periods may share the same space, suddenly teleport to a parallel world, and so on. Unifying principles are usually not based on language or logic. They experiment with cutting-edge technology like projection mapping and other digital techniques. The practitioners' ingenuity is spent on devising various dramaturgical strategies, which often result in highly complex structures.

One globally directed work from its inception is *Shun-kin*, a Setagaya Public Theatre (SEPT) and Complicité co-production of the blind protagonist Shun-kin's sadomasochistic relationship with her male attendant, Sasuke. According to SEPT artistic director Mansai Nomura's statement in the performance program (SEPT 2008), this collaboration is the fruit of a tripartite encounter of the modernist literature by Junichiro Tanizaki,[23] Complicité's artistic director Simon McBurney (b. 1957),[24] and contemporary Japanese actors. While performing-figures were used to portray Shun-kin's childhood, they were not given equal status in the promotional materials.

Besides being a self-consciously global endeavor on the part of the project team, the reinvention is at the destabilizing hybridization pole of cultural globalization through the way the original story is fragmented and distributed among many voices as well as times and spaces, yet connects the past with the present and reveals to the viewer both the extreme and mundane ways in which passion may be expressed.

The play's Tokyo premiere was held at SEPT in 2008, and its international premiere at Barbican Theatre in London the following year. Over the years, this production also toured to many international cities such as New York, Paris, Singapore, and Los Angeles, and concluded its final run in 2013. *Shun-kin* received the 2008/9 Yomiuri Theater Awards Grand Prix in three categories: Best Play, Best Director (McBurney), and Best Actress (Eri Fukatsu for her performance as the adult Shun-kin). Fukatsu also won the Kinokuniya Theatre Award for Outstanding Achievement the same year. Internationally, the play won the 2011 French Drama Critics' Award Grand Prix for Best Foreign Play.

This hauntingly atmospheric play is based on novelist Tanizaki's erotic story *Shunkin-sho* (1933) and his monochromatic essay *In Praise of*

Shadows (1933). Indeed, the stage is kept so dark that it is difficult to register fully the subtle maturation of Shun-kin, a blind female *shamisen* player who develops a codependent relationship with her disciple, Sasuke.

The inspiration the project team received from *bunraku* is notable, but it is important to bear in mind that unlike the traditional puppets in the intracultural *bunraku* projects discussed in the second section of this chapter, the performing-figure's structure is radically simplified from the traditional one and thus cannot be called a *bunraku* puppet. In addition, professional *bunraku* puppeteers are not employed. (See fig. 4.7 in the color plates.)

The Shun-kin figures were designed and constructed by the London-based Blind Summit Theatre to portray the childhood and adolescence of this strong-headed and passionate woman. In the succinct words of Blind Summit's co-founder Mark Down:

We made a *bunraku* [sic] eight-year-old girl and taught the cast to bring her to life. She then grows into a young woman made from the head of the eight-year-old and a kimono on a coat hanger, then into a human puppet. (Blind Summit Theatre, n.d.)

As a maximum of five manipulators operate the delicate body of the maturing girl, the visibility aesthetic is quite prominent. Shun-kin's sophisticated puppet head movement is achieved through *bunraku*-like devices and manipulation as described earlier in the second section of Chapter 4. What is innovative is that an extra handle was added to the back of the puppet's head to facilitate the switching of manipulators, and an identical handle added to the back of the Shun-kin actor's head to extend the illusion of objectness. An eye-catching dramaturgical moment occurs when, in a fit of jealousy over Sasuke's kindness to a female disciple, the Shun-kin manipulator casts aside her object form and as actor strides into the role to rule and possess him. Character continuity is maintained by having Fukatsu always speak Shun-kin's lines.

The female manipulators, who, incidentally, wear black business suits, also function as actors in character-appropriate costumes and play multiple roles. A professional *shamisen* player, Hidetaro Honjo, is featured in the performance and sits downstage left much of the time. He is the only performer to actually play live *shamisen*; the other masters and pupils hold a white rod and mime *shamisen* strumming to piped-in melodies. However, as if to compensate for such simplicity, the spoken environment is enriched by having four narratorial figures haunt the stage: the *shamisen* musician/chanter narrates to his music; the author Tanizaki appears as a character who observes, narrates, and even intervenes in the action; well-known senior actor Yoshi Oida, who plays the aged Sasuke, shares autobiographical information with the audience to contextualize the story on a personal and local level; and finally, the periodic appearance of a woman voice-actor narrating and recording the original *Shunkin-sho* for a radio drama functions as a contemporary frame story, in which she is also struggling with a difficult love affair. By the last production in 2013, her personal entanglement seems to be resolved.

How does this play reflect a globalized world? The discrete mix of contemporary clothing worn by the manipulators in a dark, minimalist, multi-shifting staging of life, work, and passion in the 1930s, which ebbs and flows in a bleak modern recording studio reflects the almost effortlessly liquid passage of different times and spaces. A multidimensional and multi-perspectival structure of meaning is offered for our delectation.

The next case study is a 2010 international collaboration led by Youkiza of Singaporean Kuo Pao Kun's major work *Descendants of the Eunuch Admiral* (1995, hereafter *Descendants*). (See fig. 4.8 in the color plates.)

The original *Descendants*, already a hybrid script/story with floating voices, features Zheng He (1371–1434), a court eunuch who served under Emperor Yongle (1354–1424). Born in poverty, Zheng He rose to the heights of the imperial hierarchy: as admiral, he made international tributary voyages of unprecedented pomp and circumstance, and held the title of Defender of Nanjing for life. Through his portrayal, Kuo reveals how unfree even Zheng He was in maneuvering the "real" voyages as a citizen of the world.

This production is also an example of destabilizing hybridization in intercultural theatre. Though the production is faithful to Kuo's message and his striking alienation methods, it recontextualizes on the global business level, and employs Japanese visionary techniques of revisiting spirits.

This collaboration was produced by a diverse team of artists—Magosaburo XII and his company, French artists, and well-known Japanese actors—at Theatre Tram, Tokyo, and the Spoleto 53 Festival of the Two

Worlds in Italy in 2010. For this tour de force performance of sixteen scenes *sans* interval, Youkiza provided twenty-seven marionettes and nine manipulators, who also acted roles. Frédéric Fisbach (b. 1966)[25] was the director and the script adapter. Concerning his approach to experimental directing, his work at Festival d'Avignon 2007, where he served as associate director, indicates that he values research as much as production, involves his audience before/during the performance, adapts different perspectives to frame stage texts, and strives to apply methods and styles that challenge Western approaches.[26]

Laurent P. Berger,[27] an accomplished stage designer, was in charge of the scenography, costumes, lighting design, and performing-object art. Guest actor Yukikazu Kano (b. 1960)[28] played the lead role of a disaffected businessman, while guest actor Taka Okubo (b. 1943)[29] was an off-stage narrator.

Concerning the play, drama critic Lin Ke Huan states that Kuo examines the "vagaries of history to protest and resist the spiritual and cultural castration of the individual by harsh political repression" (Lin 2003, 130–31).

Director Fisbach's statement in the 2010 program indicates that he is in agreement with Lin's interpretation:

Descendants of the Eunuch Admiral is a shocking, angry and fierce piece on what our life in contemporary liberal democracies too often is. It talks about the desire for freedom and the assertion of truth, which is a prerequisite. Through a dive into history, and identifying with the great Chinese explorer Zheng He, the protagonist of the play realizes that "true life is elsewhere." (Youkiza 2010)

Fisbach goes on to identify Kuo's historification strategy of telling Zheng He's tale as a way to circumvent "the censorship in force in his country and to make us understand what could not have been said, being a citizen of Singapore" (ibid.). To negotiate the divide between Zheng He's medieval world and the modern global business one, Fisbach's own strategy in reimagining Kuo's play is to deploy the traditional Japanese theatre that

allows a visionary theatrical approach, where the invisible worlds come true, making ghosts appear onstage and enable the audience to look at the world across the portrayal given by the Asian world, according to which Europe is relegated in the upper left-hand corner on the world map, where we usually place Alaska. (Ibid.)

Furthermore, at the beginning and the end of the performance, the audience is reflected on a world map embedded in the office wall upstage, incorporating them undeniably into the global situation.

Similarly to McBurney, Fisbach uses a frame story and narrators to juxtapose two worlds that are historically apart. To this end, the stage set is a slick impersonal office of an upscale global trading company, where employees sit at identical desks in neat rows, working on identical computers, and taking identical photocopies on a copy machine. The ceiling lights give what Fisbach likes to call a convenience store glow—an extremely artificial glare that eliminates shadow. In addition, on the aforementioned map, the world's major cities light up and indicate the course of Zheng He's nautical travels. (See fig. 4.8 in the color plates.)

One businessman lingers behind after the other workers leave, starts daydreaming about Zheng He's adventures as explorer, diplomat, admi-

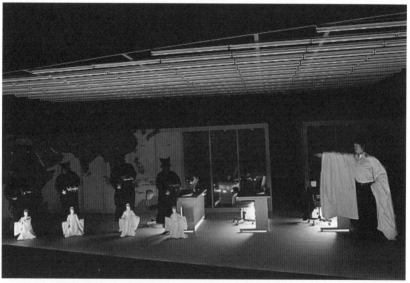

Fig. 4.7. Youkiza's international collaboration with French artists, *Descendants of the Eunuch Admiral*, 2010, Theatre Tram, Tokyo. Photo © Jun Ishikawa & So Kuramochi. Courtesy of Youkiza.

ral, and eunuch, and ends up staying there overnight. He fears the empti-
ness of his life and wonders if Zheng He also felt such foreboding as he
traversed the oceans. "By facing up to his own fears and anxieties, he
feels closer to Zheng He, who also experienced humiliation, solitude,
and fear. So much so that he feels he must be his descendant" (ibid.) A
digital clock is placed prominently on the wall and provides vivid contrast in time flow with the businessman's imaginative meanderings.

Similarly to *Shun-kin*, the insertion of narratorial figures complicates
the play, first by adding a new prologue and having some scenes actually
in the original played by the lead puppeteers who both performed themselves while manipulating their doppelgänger figures. The Otaka narrator
also participated in some of the onstage scenes but mainly stayed offstage as the businessman's alter ego.

During the prologue, the lead manipulators, Fisbach, and an interpreter officiated with their string-figure counterparts, which helped to famil-
iarize the audience of the performance style of the production. The rationale for the prologue was to clarify Kuo's objective. Fisbach came out
quite baldly to speak about the censorship issue in Singapore—that Kuo
is illustrating that people in the country are free economically but unfree
politically. Singaporeans know that Kuo is displacing the story to fif-
teenth-century China and that Zheng He represents the average Singaporean. They enjoy how Kuo with his craft and intelligence gets around the
censorship rules. Fisbach emphasized that this prologue was designed to
enable the Japanese viewer to join and enjoy the playwright in his
scheme. In addition to this delivery, which was in French with Japanese
interpretation, the team advised the audience to read the explanation in
the program, had members of staff walk the aisles to sell copies, and
even provided time and house lights for the audience to comply.

This tactic seemed forced, yet the largely Japanese audience complied
good-humoredly. Is such directive needed to communicate a performance
adequately to a global audience? The censorship issue may have benefit-
ed from pre-show clarification, but the sense of alienation and emascula-
tion in the business world was not difficult to understand, as it seems a
common aspect of office business, global or otherwise, and did not require explication.

What may have been puzzling were some of the alienation effects.
The periodic reappearance of the lead manipulators as themselves, and
the Otaka narrator's interventions, such as to fix the ceiling lights, were

part of the original work as informative alienation effects. The manipulators' work break in the middle of the play is actually in the original, though it was arranged to look like a spontaneous grumbling session. To summarize this global project, the *Descendants* production employed an extravaganza of dramaturgical strategies to enhance the multi-perspectival quality of the play: aggressive education of the audience to enable their understanding of the play according to Kuo's own objectives; theatrical alienation tactics modeled on those in the original, making historical memory feed contemporary life; a contemporary business re-framing; and traditional Japanese methods of using ghosts, memory, and animism for layered surreal effect.

In this chapter, the importation of the aesthetics of object theatre and material performance from the West in the 1990s was shown to accomplish a paradigm shift by which purity of style formerly highly valued by the Japanese gave way to diversity and hybridity without loss of artistic incentive or rejection of animism or even traditional performance concepts and skills when they served a contemporary purpose.

Intra- and intercultural collaborative performances both utilize hybridization as a major method in their respective contexts. Breaking out of genres, hybridity, and collaboration on the domestic level in performance can be seen in diasporic minority theatre and between traditional *bunraku* and contemporary performance artists or groups. On the intercultural/global level, dramaturgically intricate works like Shakespeare's and high-quality collaborative global projects that seek a worldwide audience are prominently showcased, though are still not large in number.

1   The digital revolution has led to the rise of Society 5.0, whose innovative characteristics are advanced broadband that raises data transfer speed to a hundred times those of Society 4.0, expanding big data, and multi-connectivity with minimal delay. The Japanese government announced that Japan entered Society 5.0 in April 2020.

2   F/T is organized by Toshima City, Toshima Mirai Cultural Foundation, and NPO Arts Network Japan.

3   Kyoto Experiment is organized by Kyoto City, ROHM Theatre Kyoto, Kyoto Art Center, and Kyoto Performing Arts Center at Kyoto University of Art and Design.

4   Previously known as Tokyo Performing Arts Market, TPAM is organized

by the Japan Foundation Asia Center, Kanagawa Arts Foundation / Yokohama Arts Foundation, PARC – Japan Center, and Pacific Basin Arts Communication.

5 Theater Commons Tokyo is co-organized by Minato Cooperation Project for Cultural Program, Tokyo.

6 The predecessor of Iida Puppet Festa was the Iida City sponsored Puppet Carnival Iida (Ningyo geki ka-nibaru Iida, 1979–1998).

7 The Iida Puppet Festa aspires, in spirit, civil cooperation, and diversity, to be like the mammoth Festival Mondial des Théâtres de Marionnettes that biennially transforms the French city of Charleville-Mézières, where the UNIMA headquarters are located.

8 Cf. Yudai Kamisato's *The Story of Descending the Long Slopes of Valparaíso* (Baruparaiso no nagai saka wo kudaru hanashi, 2017) and *Isla! Isla! Isla!* (Isura! Isura! Isura!, 2015).

9 Cf. Chong Wishing's *Doll Town* (2007) in Chapter 4-2.

10 Cf. Taira's version of *La Marie-Vison* (2007) and Ichihara's *Favonia's Fruitless Fable* (2016) in Chapter 2-2.

11 Cf. Chapters 5 and 6.

12 By comparison, the term "hybrid arts" refers to the new areas in which artists work with scientists and engineers in emergent scientific fields such as robotics, information visualization, interface engineering, media studies, and AI. Hybridity in this sense will be addressed in Chapters 5 and 6 on technological innovation and performing-objects.

13 All the other characters are string-puppets handled openly by manipulators.

14 Cf. World Encyclopedia of Puppetry Arts. s.v. "Bunraku," https://wepa. unima.org/en/bunraku/.

15 Cf. Adachi (1985) for staging details.

16 Hiroshi Sugimoto has lived and worked in New York since 1974. His fascination with objects has led him to activities ranging from photography, sculpture, installation, drama, architecture, landscaping, and writing to cooking. His art reflects on the transience of history and nature, while his specific objective is to bridge Asia and the West through empiricism and metaphysics. He also explores themes on human perception and the origin of consciousness. He established the architectural design office New Materials Research Institute in 2008 and the Odawara Cultural Foundation in 2009. His recent awards include the 2013 French Order of Arts and Cultures. He was designated a Person of Cultural Merit in 2017. https://www.

sugimotohiroshi.com/.

17 A *torii* gate symbolizes the transition from the secular to sacred space. The one used in the performance was modeled on the Ise Grand Shrine *torii*.

18 It was revived in Tokyo and Osaka in 2014 and at the Lincoln Center, New York in 2019 as part of the Japan 2019 project.

19 Koki Mitani, a Japanese playwright, director, actor, screenwriter, and film director, excels in comedic work celebrating humaneness. He has written two sophisticated puppet series for TV family viewing. His adaptation of *The Three Musketeers* was broadcast by NHK (2009–2010) and his scripted "puppet entertainment" *Sherlock Holmes*, again by NHK (2014–2015). For televising, the rods of the musketeer puppets were erased from view creating a new kind of attractive magical illusion. *The Three Musketeers* series won five awards; the *Sherlock Holmes* series won the Japan Sherlock Holmes Award in 2015. Video recordings are available at the NHK Archives website: for *The Three Musketeers*, https://www2.nhk.or.jp/archives/search/special/detail/?d=backstage008; for *Sherlock Holmes*, https://www2.nhk.or.jp/archives/tv60bin/detail/index.cgi?das_id=D0009040449_00000.

20 Youkiza continues to produce Shakespearear productions such as *Hal and Falstaff* (1989), *Richard III* (1993), and *The Tempest* (1994), all directed by Yoshiyuki Fukuda, a 1960s counterculture playwright/director. Its most recent, *A Midsummer Night's Dream* (2012), directed by Tadashi Kato at the theatre iwato, Tokyo, was a more straightforward production.

21 Sawa's work with DRAK on the Japan Foundation + DRAK: *A Plague O' Both Your Houses!!!—based on Shakespeare's Romeo and Juliet!!!* has already been discussed in Chapter 2. His own adaptation of *King Lear* (2004) employed shadow theatre techniques.

22 Born in 1948 as the third son of Magosaburo Youki X and brother to Magosaburo XII, he assumed the name Isshi Youki III in 1972. He left Youkiza in 2003.

23 Junichiro Tanizaki (1886–1965) is a major writer of modern Japanese literature. His novels and short stories are characterized by eroticism and ironic wit. He was shortlisted for the Nobel Prize in Literature in 1964.

24 Simon McBurney is artistic director, co-founder, and head of the famous performance company Complicité. He says himself, "Most of my influences come from outside the UK" (McBurney 2011). Included is Japan, as he seems to have an easy receptivity to this country's theatre arts. He has good working relations with SEPT, which has staged three adaptations directed by him: Bruno Schulz's *The Street of Crocodiles* in 1998, Haruki

Murakami's *The Elephant Vanishes* in 2003, and, of course, *Shun-kin*. With each production, the collaboration has intensified, drawing out more complex interweaving dramaturgy and performativity. Incidentally, Mc-Burney's wife is of Japanese descent. http://www.complicite.org/ourhistory.php.

25 Frédéric Fisbach is an experimental French director and recipient of the 1999 Villa Medicis Prize Japan, a French award for research in Japan. He has since continued to contribute to exchange between artists and productions in the two countries. He introduced Oriza Hirata's work to Europe when he directed *Tokyo Notes* (1994) in 2000 and *Citizens of Seoul* (1989) in 2005. He also directed Youkiza's 2002 performing-object version of Jean Genet's *Screens* (Les paravents) in France (revived 2004 in Tokyo) as well as Kuo's *The Descendant* in 2010 (Japan Foundation 2007).

26 Cf. the Festival d'Avignon 2007 website: https://www.festival-avignon.com/en/shows/2007/les-paravents (accessed August 25, 2019).

27 Laurent P. Berger is an interdisciplinary artist in the visual and performing arts and architecture and design. He received the Villa Médicis Prize Japan in 1999. He has maintained and developed his Japanese ties through various residencies including the Shizuoka Performing Arts program in 2010. In the same year, his company, Berger&Berger, was one of the international teams for director Kazuyo Sejima's 2010 Architectural Venice Biennale (Berger 2011; n.d.)

28 A versatile *neo-kabuki onnagata* (female impersonator) and head of Hanagumi Shibai Theatre Company.

29 A principal actor in Juro Kara's Situation Theatre (Jokyo gekijo), and Karagumi company.

Chapter 5

Robot and Android Theatre

This is the first of two chapters that address the dynamic relations between technology and performing-objects. In particular, the rapid development of digitalization and robotics has transformed the performing arts, where hands-on work has always been considered a precious talent. The impact goes far beyond what has been called mixed media in Japan, a simple addition of attractive video/digital backdrops to enhance the mise en scène.

In this chapter, the area of innovation and growth to be addressed is Japan's new robot theatre led by a playwright and a roboticist in an interdisciplinary project that features robots and androids performing characters and interacting with human actors in a series of productions. The second area, to be treated in Chapter 6, is New Media Theatre, the hybridization of actor-object performance with different media. A case study will analyze the live video transfiguration of a Chinese-Japanese collaborative string-figure performance.

5-1 Context of national branding for robot development and theatre

So far, material performance in the postwar era has been discussed as emerging from children's education to evolve into art for adults. While these categories continue to coexist in the twenty-first century, robots, which at this point in time are still limited in terms of AI and stay largely within the definition of conventional performing-objects, have been taken up at the national level as a significant way to brand Japan as a next-generation robot-human collaborative society.

The Japanese government and industries' vision for the future is the daily coexistence of robots with humans as a solution to the nation's aging and declining population and work force. This new direction will create new markets outside the manufacturing sector and will be valuable for the growth of the robot industry. Specifically, its realization requires a major shift from industrial robots to service robots that can mingle easily with people at work and home. A number of government initiatives have been implemented over the past twenty years or so to this effect. I will discuss the various governmental projects and how the initiatives have provided a conducive environment for the humanoid experiment that is called the robot theatre.

The first major government initiative was the Humanoid Robotics Project (HRP, 1998–2003). Headed by Kawada Industries, this project was sponsored by the Ministry of Economy, Trade and Industry (METI) and the New Energy and Industrial Technology Development Organization (NEDO, f. 1980), and supported by the National Institute of Advanced Industrial Science and Technology (NAIST) and Kawasaki Heavy Industries.[1] The Kawada HRP series was designed as social robots that resembled the human figure and could blend into the average household, both on the service and social levels without disturbance or threat to the inhabitants. In addition, NEDO's robot technology section also aimed to drive the development of next generation robots as part of everyday life.

While the early humanoid bipedal robots were large, cumbersome, and rather intimidating, by 2010, the HRP4 robot, the most technically developed of the series, had evolved into a "slim athletic" type, 151 cm (4.9 ft.) tall and only 39 kg (86 lb.) in weight. It has thirty-four degrees of freedom[2] and can track faces and objects, as well as respond to voice commands. It is capable of working safely side by side with humans and costs about ¥26 million (approx. $240,000).

The next platform is Innovation 25 (2007–2025). This is a long-term strategy initiative to be completed by the year 2025 so that "each field, such as medicine, engineering and information technology, [can be] new energy for Japanese society for the creation of innovation contributing to economic growth" (Prime Minister of Japan and His Cabinet, 2007a). The five aims identified in the Long-term Strategic Guidelines of Innovation 25 are given below:

1. Setting the goals high and anticipating challenges for the future
2. Timely and effective response to globalization and advancement of informatization
3. Significance of the perspective of ordinary citizens
4. Change with diversity and reform of a society filled with possibilities
5. Primary importance on human resources development—encourage people who think creatively

(Prime Minister of Japan and His Cabinet, 2007b)

Putting the rhetoric aside, the basic key concepts especially for robot engagement are convenience, security, and comfort. The objective is to develop an environment with full-scale social infrastructure for networking and robots for individual/family as well as corporate/industrial use. An important part of the expected results is a society with diverse work styles and communication robots that provide smooth and intuitional conversation and exchange.

To assist people in imagining the future Society 5.0 that would succeed the information age of Society 4.0, a *manga* booklet, *One Day in the Life of the Inobe Family* (Inobe-ke no ichinichi, 2007), was published. The three-generation, six human-member Inobe[3] family has an enviable number of labor-saving gadgets, security wearables, enhanced communication and health-monitoring devices, flexible work hours, and a young male robot called Inobe, who is the "brains" of the household. Convenience, safety, and comfort are ensured in their home as never before.

However, the human roles and relations remain much the same as in the 2000s or even earlier. Granted, the father is cast as a risk-taker, who failed with his first venture company but succeeded in his second start-up. He works in a virtual office but, on the day in the story, has to go to the real company office for a meeting with his business associates. As he is not at home, we cannot tell if he is an *ikumen* type, that is, a man who proactively participates in the daily management of home activities.

This futuristic ethnography states that 30 percent of the workforce in

2025 will already telework from home.[4] Presumably both men and women are included in that percentage. However, the mother, who is an exemplar teleworker, emerges from her home office at five o'clock to confer immediately with the Inobe robot about the progress of the housework. This particular narrative seems to suggest that she has two jobs, teleworking and supervising the robot so that when the other members return home, *they* can relax. This sounds suspiciously familiar.

Others have also caught a whiff of the reactionary quality lurking in the proposal. Anthropologist Jennifer Robertson, in her *Robo-Sapiens Japanicus* (2018), gives a polemic against the traditionalist drive that underlines the seemingly futuristic vision. She argues that far from innovatively "generating new values to provoke major social changes" (ibid., 35), the reality will be "the renewal of old values—especially those represented by the patriarchal extended family and wartime ideologies" (ibid., 82). For Robertson, the robot agenda, Innovation 25, and the Japanese robot industry in general exemplify "retro-tech," or "advanced technology in the service of traditionalism." She warns that we "should not assume the technology per se is liberating" (ibid.).

Another major government initiative that started in 2014 was the Robot Revolution Realization Council (RRRC), which advocated that 2015 be the Robot Revolution year with a fresh proposal called New Strategy for Robots, but was a de facto reformulation of Innovation 25. The rhetoric has increased the social value of robots from a sign of technological success to a sense of Japanese uniqueness.

[T]o make Japan the world's most advanced robot showcase and achieve a society in which robots are utilized more than anywhere else in the world, from nursing care and agriculture to small- and medium-sized enterprises. To that end, we are engaged in achieving a "robot barrier free" society through regulatory reform and establishing the highest level of artificial intelligence technologies in the world. (Prime Minister of Japan and His Cabinet 2015)

Robots in this context refer mainly to next-generation robots (mentioned in the NEDO section of research), which are intelligent, mobile, and service-oriented, such as the "new industrial robots" that work with humans and various humanoid or zoomorphic service robots for cleaning, security, welfare, care, or amusement.[5] Examples include Honda's

Asimo; Toyota's third-generation humanoid robot T-HR3; the University of Tokyo JSK Lab's Kengoro, the exercising robot, and the Ishiguro/ATR's Erica.

The New Strategy for Robots also includes a new event popularly known as the Robot Olympics (Robertson 2018, 197–98), the objective of which is to "promote and showcase cutting-edge Japanese technologies, including robot taxis and wearable robots" (ibid., 28). Robots will compete for best product in five fields: manufacturing and service; nursing and medical care; disaster response and construction work; and the agriculture, forestry, fishing, and food industries (ibid.).

It is clear that "robot development is inextricably intertwined with and mediated by Japanese corporate and government aims concerning national identity, consumer acceptance, technology, and futurism" (Sone 2017, 82) as well as global competition. It serves as a national branding of Japan as a Society 5.0.

On the second point of consumer acceptance, Sone applies the concept of framing (ibid., 82) already touched on in this study's Introduction; in other words, Sone uses framing in the sense of creating an imaginary space where a robot or a social issue can be experimented with.

The government has already framed robotics as the key factor in transforming the basic social unit, the family in all its varieties, into a high-powered human-robot collaboration, which would guarantee its economic stability and viability. As far as the three initiatives are concerned, it is not difficult to imagine such a community becoming the norm in urban areas.

Unlike regular factory-based industrial robots with limited functions, the next-generation robots need to be increasingly humanoid and user-friendly. It is this urgency in enhancing humanoid qualities that has led to the involvement of theatre-makers in robotic theatre, the topic of the following section of this chapter.

The high interest and deep affection Japanese people have for robots have been identified by Sone as arising from the following four cultural aspects: the respect for craftsmanship (*monozukuri*) as seen in *karakuri* (trick) automata and the eighteenth-century Gakutensoku automaton[6] that was capable of facial expressions and writing; the tradition of anthropomorphism and animism, which enables people to link humans and robots on a natural continuum; the *manga*/*anime* robot characters like Astro Boy (Tetsuwan atomu), a symbol of the peaceful use of nuclear energy, and Doraemon, an advanced and feeling feline robot from another dimension; and Buddhist thought, which encourages mindfulness in all things (Sone 2017, 7–10). The Japanese approach to robots is very different from the Western fear of powerful robots overtaking the world.

5-2　Automata/robots/androids in Japanese theatre

The *karakuri* beginning

In addition to the present government policy to support robot research, the twenty-first century development in Japanese robot theatre has its roots in *karakuri* automata popular far back in the seventeenth and eighteenth centuries. A brief introduction to this early automaton will be presented, followed by discussion of the new robot theatre.

The word *karakuri* means a mechanical device to tease or trick and implies magic and deception. *Karakuri* puppets are dolls or objects with clockwork-like mechanisms that perform tasks when activated. They were shown in private homes as collector items, onstage, and at festivals. This new mechanical technology was not applied to industrial or military purposes as the Tokugawa government forbade the development of machinery (Yamaguchi 2002, 72).

The fortunate family connection between the (Izumo) Takeda Karakuri theatre (1662–1768) and the Takemoto Ningyo Joruri Theatre facilitated the application of *karakuri* techniques in developing *joruri*/*bunraku* from small stick puppets to the present large three-person puppets. Furthermore, the rivalry between the Takemoto Joruri Theatre and the Toyotake Ningyo Joruri Theatre added fuel to the fire of puppet development. The Takemoto Ningyo Joruri Theatre won out by inventing three-person puppets and doubling the puppet's height to 140 cm (55 in.).[7]

Modern robot theatre

A robot, which means "forced labor," is a mechanism made to work for humans; a humanoid is a robot with some generic human characteristics and abilities; an android is a robotic copy of an actual person or persons. Early robot/android theatre was written for and performed by human actors; the best-known example is Karel Čapek's *Rossum's Universal Robots* (1921), which was performed in 1924 at the famous Tsukiji Little

Theatre in Tokyo and triggered a robot literature boom.

With today's robot theatre, award-winning playwright-director Oriza Hirata[8] has taken the lead. His android *Sayonara* (2010; second version in 2012) is a widely known venture into globalized theatre born of a unique collaboration with roboticist Hiroshi Ishiguro[9] of Osaka University and ATR Institute International. The objective of their collaboration, Seinendan (Youth Group) + Osaka University Robot Theatre Project (2008–2018),[10] was to explore firstly "what it means to be human" and, second, "what human sociality is" by developing better communication between robots and humans through building androids with humanlike expressive abilities rather than highly developed mobility as in industrial robots. In fact, in 2008, Ishiguro made a paradigm shift to the second point of human sociality in his research. This would address the relations between humans and robots through multi-party interaction and equip robots to handle complex, multitasking situations as well as standard one-on-one communication. (See fig. 5.1 in the color plates.)

The original twenty-two-minute play is about a terminally ill woman (performed by Bryerly Long) and her female android companion, who recites Japanese, French, and German poems to her young owner. The woman, however, wants happier poems. The android speculates that maybe Germans look for happiness while Japanese want to escape loneliness. The woman asks the android which she would prefer, but she cannot answer. Technically, her silence is probably due to the limited AI that disallows value judgments but it alerts the viewer of the crucial difference between the human ability to think and the robot's ability to retrieve. With further development in AI, androids may no longer be considered performing-objects but super actors.

The coda added to *Sayonara* after the triple disaster of the 2011 Great East Japan Earthquake has a technician collect the now dysfunctional android, fix it, and send it to an off-limits contaminated beach in Miyagi Prefecture to recite poetry in requiem for the disaster victims. The audience is left with the open-ended question "What do life and death mean to humans and robots?" This ending "adds a new layer to the human-robot relationship [...] the shift from the human/nonhuman towards a posthuman landscape" (Rosner 2019).

There is also a 112-minute-long film version of *Sayonara* (2015), adapted and directed by film director Koji Fukada, a member of Hirata's Seinendan. Referring to the well-known statement that awareness of

Fig. 5.1. Seinendan + Osaka University Robot Theatre Project, *Sayonara Ver. 2*. Japan Society, New York, 2013. Courtesy of Seinendan.

Fig. 5.2. Seinendan + Osaka University Robot Theatre Project, *La Métamorphose, version androïde*, 2014, Kanagawa Arts Theatre, Yokohama. Photo © Madoka Nishiyama. Courtesy of Seinendan.

death separates humans from other animals, he says that he was fascinated by the situation of an android observing a terminal ill woman slowly die. He felt that the contrast between the android that is not concerned with death and the dying woman reflected the tragedy of modern humans. Aware of the ultimate approach of death, how do we deal with the fear and confusion churned up by the thought of dying? He says that he does not subscribe to any religion, but feels that his involvement in filmmaking is a preparation for death (Fukada 2015). It is interesting to note that his film ends with the android committing suicide after Tanya dies.

A chronology of the plays produced by this Robot Theatre Project indicates, among other things, the rapid development of robot/android performance.[11]

Human expressivity engineering

In general, three overlapping considerations can be identified in the application of new technology to human expressivity: the illusion of living presence, the cultural construction of *kokoro* (heart/mind/soul), and design methodology.

Since 2012, the illusion of living presence is created mainly by teleoperation. It autonomously controls an android by transferring the operator's movement measured by a motion-capturing system (Advanced Telecommunications Research Institute International 2006). The autonomous control of eye-gaze and small business is also available. Large motion has never been of great concern for Ishiguro's androids; they are fixed to their seat or stand in one spot, because the pneumatic cables have to be connected to the compressor offstage. By combining this programming with on-site remote control and use of sensors, a semblance of human agency is achieved.

Other specific considerations are timing, skin, and breath. In speech and response, timing is culturally constructed. The programming and onsite remote control can manage this relatively easily. For the face, the soft skin is made of silicone elastomer; the eyes blink to the human average of twenty times per minute. Breathing is simulated by mouth movement, together with chest and shoulder heaving. In the early days, lip-synching was de facto ventriloquism as a backstage actor/operator was delivering the android's lines; from 2012, recordings of actors' voices have been used.

An external contributing factor to the illusion of presence is lighting.

Subtle adjustment of stage lights can greatly enhance the mystery or scientific impact of androids. For example, in *Sayonara*, the stage was kept dark and very atmospheric with a special yellow light trained on the android at the beginning to mask her physicality and make her indistinguishable from the human actor sharing the stage.

Construction of *kokoro*

In psychology, *kokoro* no longer means heart or soul, but action. In fact, the term *kokoro*, together with *seishin* (spirit), has disappeared from Japanese psychology dictionaries. For example, the buzzword for the 2020 Tokyo Olympics was "hospitality" (*omotenashi*), which can be viewed as an action that signals *kokoro*. Ishiguro considers it a cultural construct that can be replicated in the android through programming and design methodology. One day, androids will have the AI acumen to tell white lies. Now, they are still learning. In Hirata's *I, Worker,* the two house robots discuss the human concept of beauty and concur that, for humans, sunsets are "beautiful" (Hirata 2019a, 363–64).

Design methodology

I have mentioned a few design factors already and will now summarize the major points of design methodology to facilitate understanding of the rest of the discussion .

There are three purposes to design modification: to enhance expression of positive humanlike qualities in robots; to evoke expression of positive humanlike qualities in the interaction between robots and humans; and to preempt the uncanny valley effect.

For the first purpose of enhancing expression of positive humanlike qualities in robots, face tracking, involuntary movement, and gaze management are important. Face tracking is used for smooth shifts in facial expression. Good-quality skin needs to be made from malleable, silky silicone to achieve such smoothness. Furthermore, humans often engage unconsciously in involuntary "idling" like twiddling fingers, rocking, or head tilting. These actions are called microslips or ideomotor actions (*yuragi*) and are meaningful in indicating the state of mind of the mover. Such actions can be added to the robot's repertory so that it, too, can oscillate "movingly" as the human body does.

Regarding gaze management, incorporation of the following scientific viewpoints can improve the interactional quality of the robot. Arousal reduction theory indicates how periodically looking away when talking to someone can keep external stimulus low. Differential cortical activation hypothesis suggests that brain activity can induce shifts in eye movement. According to social signal theory, such gaze shifting can also signal to the other party that one is thinking.

The second purpose of evoking expression of positive humanlike qualities in the interaction between robots and humans can be accomplished through *kokoro* construction and language adjustment. *Kokoro* construction refers to what humans learn through "socialization," which can be programmed into robots.

Hirata has a nine-category taxonomy of language: address, speech, debate, teaching, dialogue, greetings, conversation, reflection, and monologue. For him, theatre amplifies dialogue and conversation. Dialogue is an exchange of ideas, information, opinions, and values. Theatrical language is dialogue-based. Conversation tends to be more private and abounds with assumptions of shared knowledge. One can get caught between a dialogue-based culture that emphasizes explanation and a conversation-based one that stresses rapport. The subtle calibration of three factors can make a robot's speech approach the human: timing, redundancy, and mirroring.

Timing in speech refers to pausing in speech or response, silence, or adding speech fillers. "Redundancy" (*jochoritsu*) refers to the percentage of unnecessary sounds or words in a unit of speech. It tends to be high in dialogue and low in conversation. We all need to adjust redundancy according to the situation or topic (Hirata 1998, 124–25). "Mirroring" here refers to replicating or echoing someone's phrasing, actions, and postures to enhance empathy.

The last purpose is to preempt the uncanny valley effect. First, what is the uncanny valley? This phenomenon is sometimes brought about intentionally or unintentionally through the failure or manipulation of the illusion of living presence. The bourgeoning interpretations of this key term that is creating some controversy among roboticists can be traced. First, the word, uncanny (in German, *unheimlich*; in Japanese, *bukimi*), in this context has a predominantly negative meaning. As noted earlier in Chapter 2, Ernest Jentsch claimed that the uncanny is a product of "intellectual uncertainty." Sigmund Freud's position was that it unconsciously reminds us of our own id, so that our super-ego perceives our repressions as threatening (Freud [1919] 1988).

The full term, the "uncanny valley" (*bukimi no tani*) derives from Masahiro Mori's yet-to-be-proven 1970 hypothesis on how "a person's response to a humanlike robot would abruptly shift from empathy to revulsion as it approached, but failed to attain, a lifelike appearance" (editor's note in Mori 2012). Three hundred years ago, the most famous *joruri* and *kabuki* playwright, Monzaemon Chikamatsu, also referred to something similar. His story is of a noblewoman who had a doll made in the likeness of her lover. It was so realistic that:

> the only difference between the man and this doll was the presence in one, and the absence in the other, of a soul. However, when the lady drew the doll close to her and looked at it, the exactness of the reproduction chilled her, and she felt […] rather frightened. Court lady that she was, her love was also chilled, and as she found it distressing to have the doll by her side, she soon threw the doll away. (Hozumi [1738] 1955, 389–90)

Robertson states that Mori's translator, McDorman, took liberties with the original graph. He combined two of Mori's charts—one for still items and the other for moving items—and added new figures—the industrial robot and healthy person, while omitting the disabled person. Whether he had permission to do so in not clear (Robertson 2018, 158).

According to Mori:

> As healthy persons, we are represented at the second peak […] (moving). Then when we die, we are unable to move; the body goes cold, and the face becomes pale. Therefore, our death can be regarded as a movement from the second peak (moving) to the bottom of the uncanny valley (still), as indicated by the arrow's path. […] We might be glad that this arrow leads down into the still valley of the corpse and not the valley animated by the living dead. (2012)

Fear of death is, then, a major factor in the apprehension of the uncanny: Evidently live humans are never still: unconscious movement, breathing, blinking, physiological processes, involuntary movement are ongoing. We do not consciously look for microslips, but notice quickly if someone is totally immobile.

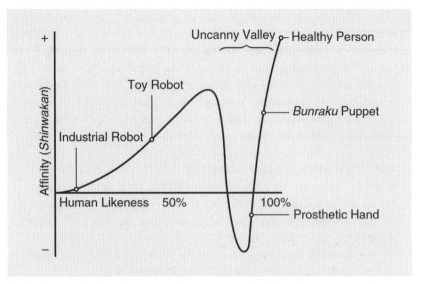

Fig. 5.3. The graph depicts the uncanny valley, the proposed relation between the human likeness of an entity, and the perceiver's affinity for it (Mori 2012).

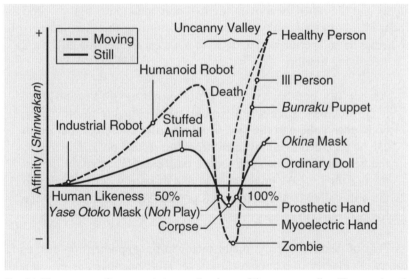

Fig. 5.4. The presence of movement steepens the slopes of the uncanny valley. The arrow's path represents the sudden death of a healthy person (Mori 2012).

A cognitive experiment conducted by Ishiguro and Shoji Itakura of Kyoto University supports this point. To summarize, the participants were asked to identify the color of the clothes of the person they would be shown for two seconds. The person was actually an android. The follow-up question was whether the participants had noticed anything strange about the person. Regarding the still android, 70 percent said that it was not a human being. In contrast, regarding an android in movement, 70 percent said that there was nothing strange about the person (Ishiguro 2007, 238–39).

As already noted, the uncanny valley is not a proven theory. Many roboticists continue to experiment with the valley idea to see if it can be modified. Ishiguro's first android, Ripliee R1, was modeled on his four-year-old daughter, who must have felt that it plunged deep into the uncanny valley, as she never wanted to see it again, although the android on seeing the girl is alleged to have said, "There I am" (*watashi ga iru*) .

When the child android is still, it does not look so strange. It has ten motors controlled by USB, can simulate sleepiness, and nod, but is prone to excessive shaking. The skin is soft yet deteriorates within a year as this model generates much body heat. Furthermore, subsequent research has revealed that two-to-four-year-olds are particularly susceptible to the uncanny valley as they are learning how to distinguish between humans and other beings.

Since that first attempt, he has devised an extended uncanny valley chart with an extra dimension for movement so that the synergetic effect of appearance and movement can be better clarified. He notes that the congruence between appearance and movement is crucial. Indeed, Ishiguro defines the objective of android science as:

To tackle the problem of appearance and behavior, two approaches are necessary: one from robotics and the other from cognitive science. The approach from robotics tries to build very humanlike robots based on knowledge from cognitive science. The approach from cognitive science uses the robot for verifying hypotheses for understanding humans. We call this cross-interdisciplinary framework android science. (2005, 1)

Returning to the starting point on how to preempt the uncanny valley effect, there are two main ways: match movement, voice, and appearance; and provide continual low oscillation (breathing, blinking, rocking) that replicates autonomous nervous system-centered vibration.

The discussion will now proceed to Hirata's second android play, *Three Sisters, Android Version.*

Case study: *Three Sisters, Android Version*

Three Sisters, Android Version, a futuristic adaptation of Anton Chekhov's *The Three Sisters* (1900), features three robots: Robovie 3 plays the butler; Geminoid F plays the youngest sister, Ikumi; and an elfoid, a smartphone pocket robot, is itself. The play exploits the idea of the uncanny. I will provide a synopsis of the play and also clarify Hirata's dramaturgy and how it applies to this play with a focus on the construction of the uncanny. (See fig. 5.2 in the color plates.)

The Fukazawa family resides in a declining provincial town with a dwindling robotics industry and low-ranking regional colleges ninety minutes away by train from Tokyo, their original home. The father, a famous roboticist, is deceased and the siblings, as with the Prozorovs of Chekhov's play, frequently allude to the lively life they might have had in the big city.

The patriarch still seems to remotely control his family through his idiosyncratic and somewhat morbid will. It contains such directives as the transfer of the family grave with his ashes from Tokyo to their present town three years after his demise, and after two more years, notification to his former science student, Nakano, that his youngest daughter, Ikumi, who had suddenly disappeared and been (publicly) pronounced deceased, was still alive. In fact, she had become a shut-in and her father had built an android version of Ikumi, a Geminoid F, as a companion for her.

The eldest sister, Risako, draws a decent income as a teacher (like Olga); the second sister, Marie, is unhappily married (like Masha) and contemplating divorce. The last sibling, Akira, who (like Andreyev) showed some academic ability as a young man, nonetheless grew up in his father's shadow and cannot escape that debilitating influence even now. The play begins on the day of Risako and Marie's viewing of the new family grave in a cemetery nearby, and a modest farewell party for Nakano, the former student, who is about to move to Singapore.

Hirata takes his concept of "contemporary colloquial theatre" (popularly known as quiet theatre) that was originally for his actors and applies it wholesale to robot-actor theatre. Hirata's theoretical objective is to forgo ideology, *drame à thèse*, or sensationalism, and reconsider drama and dialogue from the perspective of the quotidian in a hyper-pictorial or naturalistic way. The resultant "quiet" style is dialogue-based yet emphasizes nonverbal communication and has an affinity with Chekhov's use of non-sensational dramaturgy and silence to draw out subtext or what Hirata calls "oscillations of the mind/consciousness" (Boyd 2006, 60). However, despite these similarities between the look of Chekhov and Hirata's mise en scène, Hirata is not interested in deep psychology, but in the construction of subjectivity through identifying sameness and difference with the (human) environment, especially otherness-in-sameness.

The major characteristics of Hirata's methodology can be summed up as follows: focus on the quotidian rather than the sensational; the discourse of the said, unsaid, unsayable; alterity in intimacy; insider, outsider, intermediary functions; and semi-public setting (ibid., 48–57). All these aspects can be observed in *Three Sisters, Android Version*, but the focus will be mainly on the first three.

The quotidian

The father's glorious achievements as a robot inventor are downplayed, and the desultory family conversations contain frequent allusions to how the family cannot carry on or keep up with the innovative drive of their deceased father's followers or rivals' scientific discoveries. The outdated Robovie 3 model is an indication of Risako's attachment to her father and the past. It has fitted into family life with humans to the extent that it is largely taken for granted. The same applies to Android-Ikumi, who has been Ikumi's avatar for five years. Hirata makes sure that the audience does not mistake either robot for a glamorous sign of the future.

The only son, Akira, cannot build on the family reputation in scientific research due to lack of the ability and/or desire. What he wants is not clear probably even to himself. He has stopped chasing dreams of studying abroad and resigned himself to sinking into what he realizes is mediocrity.

The discourse of the said, unsaid, and unsayable

The "said" is what is articulated openly. The "unsaid" refers to what is assumed and need not be articulated, or is simply irrelevant to the current conversation. The closer the family members are, the less they need to explain or repeat themselves, and the more the audience is left to figure out what the allusions are about. For example, the play begins with Risako returning home and immediately starting to chat with Akira about the new cemetery. But the audience is left out of the conversation as the characters do not actually name the place. The audience catches up three pages into the play. While each instance of such discursive exchange is small, the cumulative delay in transmission to the audience can be disturbing.

The "unsayable," refers to taboos, negativity, and prohibited content at various levels, such as Ikumi's secret existence, Akira's lack of academic acumen, or Akira's withholding from his sisters the abandonment of his plan to study abroad.

Alterity in intimacy

In Hirata's drama, alterity within the inner circle is manifested by the widening gap in perceptions caused by misinterpretation of what is left unsaid. Small misunderstandings accumulate through unspoken assumptions in the members' exchanges. For example, the sisters assume that Akira will study abroad. Marie's husband brings red wine as a contribution to the dinner, because he assumes that the *entrée* will be some fancy beef dish, and is mortified when it turns out to be homely mackerel.

Android-Ikumi, confined to a wheelchair, is Ikumi's avatar and is updated regularly to be in sync with both the live Ikumi (played by an actor) and the changing environment. Neither she nor Ikumi herself are ever allowed outside, and nothing untoward has happened thus far. The family members, accustomed to their dual presence at the Fukazawa residence, are very relaxed.

Interpretations may vary as to what happens in the scenes from 4.1.1, when Android-Ikumi joins the party when all the guests—i.e., Dr. Maruyama and his young wife, Mineko, Nakano, and Akira's uninvited girlfriend—are assembled with the family in the living room, to 4.1.3, when Ikumi herself abruptly enters and wheels Android-Ikumi offstage.

As a nonhuman, Android-Ikumi is after all not the same as the family. Factual and logic-oriented, she purportedly cannot "read the situation" and articulates blunt questions to Mineko about her age and her connection with Nakano, and then recalls how Maruyama kissed Ikumi lewdly when she was a sixth grader working on a jigsaw puzzle. Thus Android-Ikumi dredges up the unsayable to the surface without intention.

Or Ikumi may be intentionally steering Android-Ikumi to expose the older man's predatory behavior as a warning to Mineko. Or Android-Ikumi's artificial intelligence may have developed to the extent that she has figured out what had happened to her original model and intentionally taken the opportunity to warn Mineko.

When Dr. Maruyama readies to pull the plug on the android, Ikumi enters in identical dress and hairstyle as the android to the immense astonishment of Nakano, the Maruyamas, and even the family, who of course know that Ikumi is alive.

The uncanny quality of the twin-like Ikumis together arises from confusion over who is alive and who is dead. But the two seem to resemble each other only in appearance. The single conversation they have onstage is not only full of disagreement but also suggests that this android has learned to think independently. Ikumi claims not to remember the jigsaw puzzle incident. A brief exchange exemplifies their differences:

Ikumi: Humans are capable of forgetting. […] We can forget.
Android-Ikumi: But my brain is synched with yours/
Ikumi: *Shut up.
Android-Ikumi: I'm sorry.
Ikumi: I secretly burned that jigsaw puzzle of the Gauguin painting.
[…]
Android-Ikumi: But I wonder, was it really the cause/
Ikumi: Quiet.
Android-Ikumi: Did that make her unable to leave the/
Ikumi: Shut up.
Android-Ikumi: …
Ikumi switches off Android-Ikumi.

(Hirata 2012b)

Insider, outsider, intermediary functions

As much of the dialogue/conversation is among relatives or colleagues, the exchange is difficult for the external audience to comprehend unless a stranger onstage can comment or ask questions naturally to clarify the relations and issues among the characters. While some of Hirata's live theatre plays have extremely complicated relationships, *Three Sisters, Android Version* is not so difficult to unravel. Hirata inserts Akira's partner, Sakamoto (Natasha), as a noisy intervention that draws familial attention to the fact that their brother has his own life plans. Furthermore, Nakano alerts them to the possibility of fraud by Dr. Maruyama over the license renewal of the robots. Such matters which tend to lead to conventional plots with conflict will however be kept offstage, for with Hirata (as with Chekhov), nothing climactic is allowed to happen onstage.

Ishiguro's view regarding communications is that people construct their own image/illusion of whom they interact with. Yet they cannot afford to become unmoored from social reality. So, they must balance these two tendencies of relying on their own imagination and being socially realistic. Ishiguro believes that robots enable us to become aware of this balancing act. Thus, he thinks they can serve as a mirror of what human nature is like.

For example, to the end of the play, the echoes of the original three sisters reverberate. In Chekhov's play, the three sisters come together and declare their intention to work, something they have never had to do as female members of the Russian gentry. Irene is the most serious in her aspirations to change her life. In Hirata's play, Marie and Risako are left in the living room and declare that they must eat dinner as it is being served in the adjacent room. Eating happens to be an activity androids cannot take part in. Humans must eat but do not necessarily want to work. Robots must work but do not need to eat. The two sisters may have found a modest way of winning their right to existence by reminding themselves of their difference from robots—a small homely rectification of the balance between the two entities.

Minimal design robots

Apart from naturalistic androids, other considerations such as expense, portability, and availability have led Ishiguro to introduce a branch of minimal design robots. These smaller products are very abstract so that the user is invited to project images of family and friends onto the hugvie, telenoid, or elfoid (see fig. 5.1 in the color plates), with some encouragement from the device that has a touchy-feely texture, heartbeat vibration and sound quality that reflects the tone and volume of the other party's voice. The phone that Dr. Maruyama whips out of his jacket is an elfoid.

Success or failure?

The scientific standpoint is that the robot theatre project is a success—

Ishiguro has supported the hypothesis that robots/androids can function in human social situations that are purposeful and sufficiently framed.

From a theatrical viewpoint, Hirata also considers the project a success as his contemporary colloquial theatre principles have worked in directing robots/androids just as in living theatre. He considers human communication as a code system that can be acquired. Moreover, for indicating biological and social existence, digitizable aspects like timing, pause/breath, and spatial relations can be more important than language. The insistence on micromovement is not just superficial manipulation. As Sone notes, "Hirata directs his robots at the limit of human cognition" (2017, 93). A delay of half a second is enough to make a person look for meaning in the time lag, such as hesitation, uncertainty, secrecy, and deception. Hirata's stage directions require pauses that are 0.3 of a second long; furthermore, his *Three Sisters* script has a legend of icons (☆ */○...▲ △) indicating various kinds of pauses, overlaps, and moments of speech.

The high expectations of viewers and critics regarding robot theatre were not quite met. Even though they were aware that they were having a novel experience, they expressed disappointment at the limitations of the robots/androids in expressiveness, movement, gender attribution, character variety, setting, and themes, as they seemed technically underdeveloped compared to, for instance, the full-bodied Asimo, who can run and kick soccer balls. The Ishiguro androids are deliberately limited to mainly upper body acting, rather like when filming TV drama, which tends to disregard the lower body in indoor, seated situations. As Hirata's theatre resembles standard modified realism that is rather slow-paced and unclimactic, the audience and critics cannot see why it is considered "Japanese"; in other words, they cannot see the value of the "quiet" method, which makes one reassess what is usually considered marginal in life.

Another view is that as the android characters are paraplegic or incapacitated in some way, they can be read as metaphors for technological failure. Android-Ikumi is confined to a wheelchair; Gregor Samsa in Hirata's *La Métamorphose version androïde*, unlike the one in Kafka's original *Métamorphose,* has transformed into a metallic shell of a robot with a *no*-like mask and is confined to a bed throughout the play; the companion android in *Sayonara* never stands up, and in the coda, a technician literally picks her up to be repaired, for she has become dysfunctional and spews out fragments of poetry like a demented actor. In this connection, Hirata has not indicated any particular interest in disability theatre, so his motivation is likely in line with the project objectives.

Since 2015, Ishiguro has been building more advanced models of his androids in the ISHIGURO Symbiotic Human-Robot Interaction Project, to which research teams from Osaka University, Kyoto University, and ATR contribute.

The Project aim is:

> to develop autonomous robots that naturally interact with multiple humans of all ages in a range of social contexts. It involves developing skin-like materials for safe interaction with humans, speech recognition technology, and autonomous communicative functions that are context-and task-sensitive. The project's long-term goals are for robots to occupy supportive roles in elderly care, public facilities, public transportation, and education. (Ishiguro, n.d.)

Ishiguro hopes these androids will eventually pass the Total Turing Test, which adds visual acuity and physical interaction to the textual interrogation a computer must pass. The increase in spontaneous conversational ability bodes well for robot theatre.

ERICA (Erato[12] Intelligent Conversational Android, 2015) is a twenty-three-year-old woman android, designed for conducting interviews and counseling. Her features are a CG composite of what is considered "beautiful" in women across the Internet. Although there are still traces of jerkiness and slow response that require the human to adjust to the robot, the improvement in speech content, voice quality, mood, and sense of humor is welcome.

Another example is ibuki (2018), a ten-year-old autonomous android with naturalistic upper body features and two large and two small wheels for legs. Ishiguro's androids have not been able to walk as they have used pneumatic actuators that require a compressor. The ibuki android is a battery-run model with forty-seven degrees of freedom and significantly conveys a childlike aura. It will eventually gain all the abilities that ERICA and other androids have.

Chapter summary

The nonverbal expressivity of robot/androids is rapidly approaching the

human level. Extensive work is needed to make the next-generation robot theatre what Kara Reilly calls "onto-epistemic mimesis," in other
words "mimesis that changes a person's way of knowing and by extension their way of being" (2011, 7).

Verbal expressiveness is the next challenge and will need appropriate
scripts as well as further development in technology as the Hirata-Ishig-
uro type of android is restricted in mobility to an extreme with most of
the focus on the upper body.[13] Due to the limitations of the scientific project objectives, standing or walking was not a requisite of the androids in
Sayonara, Three Sisters, or *La Métamorphose*.[14]

It is time for a new kind of actor-android with both upper and lower
body parts that function. Although such androids already exist elsewhere,
expense may still be an inhibiting factor. Geminoid F alone costs approximately $100,000 and the project's funding from the prestigious Grant-
in-Aid for Scientific Research was approximately $449,690 (¥49,000,000)
annually from fiscal 2011 to 2014 (Kimura 2007). Since the inception of
the Robot Theatre Project, seven robot/android plays have been produced. Is there any possibility for a continuation of robot theatre?

In August 2018, the *Sankei News* reported that Oriza Hirata was to
become the president of a four-year prefectural university, provisionally
called the International Tourism and Arts Professional University, to be
established in 2021 in Toyooka City, Hyogo Prefecture. It aims to develop specialized human resources through practical training in the fields of
theatre and tourism. Hence Hirata may continue to use Geminoid F and
develop new plays as a training ground for communications between
people and next generation service robots.

Whether the uncanny valley is universal or not is not clear yet. However, realistic robots are not always a necessity. As Masahiro Mori pre-
dicted almost fifty years ago and affirmed in 2013 at the International
Conference on Intelligent Robots and Systems, it is possible to create a
safe level of affinity by deliberately pursuing a nonhuman design. Monzaemon Chikamatsu would second him with his own statement, as recorded in *Naniwa miyage* (1738) by Hozumi Ikan (1955, 389): "Art is
something that lies in the slender margin between the real and the unre-
al."

1 Wikipedia, s.v. "Humanoid Robotics Project," last modified November 20,
2019, 10:58, https://en.wikipedia.org/wiki/Humanoid_Robotics Project.

2   Degrees of freedom in this context are basically the same as directions of movement.

3   The family name Inobe comes from *inobeshon,* the Romanization of innovation.

4   The government's effort to contain the coronavirus pandemic in 2020 has probably served to precipitate the shift to telework due to its home quarantine policy.

5   Cf. METI in Sone 2017, 6.

6   Gakutensoku is a 3.2 m (10.6 ft.) automaton, whose name is a precept "Learn from natural law." The present replica can tilt its head, move its eyes, smile, and puff up its cheeks and chest. It can write the word "Osaka" with an arrow-shaped pen and carries a lamp of inspiration—all thanks to a computer-controlled pneumatic servo system.

7   **Chronology of *joruri* puppet development**
    1703   Manipulators become "visible" onstage; but stay behind a translucent curtain.
    1705   Chanter and musicians also become visible onstage when the curtain is removed.
    1727   Puppets are equipped with hands that move and *karakuri* eyes and mouth that open and close.
    1728   Separate platform (*chobo*) for chanter and musicians is installed.
    1733   *Karakuri* fingers become articulated.
    1734   Yoshida Bunzaburo of the Takemoto Ningyo Joruri Theatre devises three-person puppets.
    1736   Takemoto Ningyo Joruri Theatre doubles the height of three-person puppets to fifty-five inches.
    1765   *Joruri* reaches its present form.
    1872   *Bunraku* eventually becomes the popular term for three-person puppetry through the connection with Bunrakuken Uemura (1789–1801) and his Bunrakuza theatre (1872–1963).

8   Oriza Hirata (b. 1962) is a playwright, director, and founder of the Seinendan theatre company. His reputation stands on his highly innovative "contemporary colloquial theatre" and robot/android theatre. As an interdisciplinary academic, he has taught theatre at Obirin University and communication-design and robotics at Osaka University. A global collaborator, he has taken his company on tour to Europe, Asia, Australia, and North and South Americas. He has also produced many foreign plays at his Agora Theatre. He won the prestigious Kishida Drama Prize for his best-known

play, *Tokyo Notes* (1995), and the Montblanc de la Culture Arts Patronage Award in 2006.

9 Hiroshi Ishiguro (b. 1963) is director of the Intelligent Robotics Laboratory at the Graduate School of Engineering Science, Osaka University. An ATR Institute International fellow, he also heads the Hiroshi Ishiguro Laboratories. His idea of the future is a society of human-robot symbiosis, for which his present objective is to "develop technologies for the new generation information infrastructures based on computer vision, robotics, and artificial intelligence." In 2011, he was listed as one of the "15 Asian Scientists to Watch" by *Asian Scientist Magazine*. In 2015, he received the MEXT Prize for Science and Technology and the Sheikh Mohammed Bin Rashid Al Maktoum Knowledge Award.

10 The project's JSPS Grants-in-Aid for Scientific Research ended in 2014, but the project name still appeared in their PR materials as of 2018.

11 **Robot/android theatre chronology**

(Script and director: Hirata; android advisor: Ishiguro)

2006–2007 *Forever* (Itsumademo, trial performance, 5 minutes), featuring Wakamaru

2008 November: *I, Worker* (Hataraku watashi, trial run, 30 minutes), featuring Wakamaru

2010 August: International collaboration of *In the Heart of a Forest, Robot Version* (Robotto-ban mori no oku, premiere, 1 hour 40 minutes), featuring Wakamaru

September: *Sayonara* (premiere, 22 minutes), featuring Geminoid F

November: *I, Worker* (premiere, 30 minutes), featuring Wakamaru

2012 February: *Sayonara Ver. 2* (premiere, 30 minutes), featuring Geminoid F

October: *Three Sisters, Android Version* (Andoroido-ban sannin shimai, premiere, 90 minutes), featuring Geminoid F, Robovie-R3, and elfoid

2013 May: *The Night on the Galactic Railroad, Robot Version* (Robotto-ban Gingatetsudo no yoru, premiere, 60 minutes, for families), featuring Robovie R3

2014 October: International collaboration of *La Métamorphose version androïde* (Henshin, premiere, 90 minutes), featuring Repliee S1

Other robot/android productions involving Hirata and/or Ishiguro

2015 *Sayonara* (film), directed by Koji Fukada

2016 International collaboration of *Stilles Meer* (Silent Sea), composed by Toshio Hosokawa, directed by Hirata, featuring Robovie R3

2018   Soseki Android Theatre *A Letter* (Tegami), scripted and directed by Hirata, with roboticist Takenobu Chikaraishi, featuring Geminoid F.

12 Erato stands for Exploratory Research for Advanced Technology, a research funding program founded in 1981 by the JSTA to promote basic research in science and technology. Cf. https://www.jst.go.jp/erato/en/about/index.html.

13 Stillness in itself is not problematic. If the other characters are moving, the audience is likely to be drawn to a still figure.

14 Ishiguro's Repliee-S1 android featured in *La Métamorphose* was different from the other androids in that it had no lower body, legs or "skin."

Chapter 6

New Media Theatre and Intermedial Theatre

Introduction

Technology's manifest contribution to expanding the potential for visualization and communication in media performance demands attention. Among the many forms that have arisen in recent times, New Media Theatre (NMT) highlights the application of digital technology while retaining theatrical aspects, such as live interaction and verbal exchange, with performers and audience in the same space. NMT is similar to digital theatre but can include analogue as well as digital technology. As a hybrid art, it does not include pure animation, completely nonverbal performances such as pure dance and music concerts.

Media generally refers to various means of widespread communication and theatre is considered a hypermedium—a medium that can include an indefinite variety of other media. According to Freda Chapple, Chiel Kallenbelt, Peter Boenisch, and others, mediality refers to the specific practice, situation, quality, and effects of media use, and the concept of intermediality refers to an integration or entanglement of medial processes. Intermedial theatre is considered to be located at the points situated in-between performers and audience members, and the confluence of media, medial spaces and art forms that are involved.

I will position Binghao Zhao's string-object play *As the Sparrows*

Wended in a Windless Winter within intermedial theatre by tracing the simultaneous transformation of a play being staged and remediated into a hybrid stage-film via live video. String-objects are understood to be already mediatized objects, i.e., entangled combinations of analogue technology and human manipulation that provide an illusion of life. An introduction of the theatre project will be followed by a discussion on how the non-diegetic principles of remediation and intermediality are applied.

6-1 Case study of *As the Sparrows Wended in a Windless Winter*, an international collaborative project by Youkiza with the Théâtre du Rêve Expérimental

Production data

As the Sparrows Wended in a Windless Winter (2017; hereafter *The Sparrows Wended*; Chinese title: Chechydonrai) was written for a "live video and Edo string-object" collaborative project by Youkiza in Tokyo and two principal members of the Théâtre du Rêve Expérimental (f. 2008), located in Beijing—Binghao Zhao,[1] resident playwright, and Chong Wang,[2] artistic director and head of the company. The main translator was Akiko Nobue. The production was staged at Za-Koenji Public Theatre from November 30 to December 3, 2017. (See fig. 6.1 in the color plates.)

Synopsis and analysis

This two-hour, twenty-scene performance features young Shaolin (played by actor Atsushi Sakamoto), who starts working at his uncle's nursing home as a certified caregiver and is amused to find that the elderly residents have the same run-of-the-mill problems (carnal desire, rivalry, complexes, death wish, and so on) as youth do. He eventually becomes disgusted with the endlessly repetitive menial work and begins to despise, and even fear, the residents.

Later on, the thirteen-year-old Chilirenka, who has delusions of being a rabbit, is abandoned at the home by her desperate, burned-out father. She develops a strong attachment to a resident, Yozei, and desires to help him attain his death wish. Out of pity, she generously gives drugs to him and the rest of the residents and then sets fire to the building for good measure. The play ends with a funeral on the razed grounds of the home attended by Shaolin, the doctor, and others.

Fig. 6.1. Youkiza and Théâtre du Rêve Expérimental, *As the Sparrows Wended in a Windless Winter*, 2017, Za-Koenji Public Theatre, Tokyo. Courtesy of Youkiza.

Seven manipulators and one actor perform the fourteen-plus characters. The full list comprising nursing home staff, residents and relatives, and others is provided in the Appendix.

The stage has a huge tree standing far upstage left, from which a thick, sturdy branch extends stage right, almost the full length of the stage with a 12-by-5 m (39-by-16 ft.) screen embedded in it. The final words of Shaolin at the end of the play suggest that the string-characters projected on the branch screen are metaphorically linked with the "sparrows" in the diegetic content (Zhao 2017b, 8).

Application of Alain Badiou's concept of Event

Alain Badiou's[3] Event enables a deep reading of nursing home residents' predicament. According to political theorist Andrew Robinson, Badiou maintains that:

> reality is grounded on a "void" of "inconsistent multiplicity," which is at once void and excess. Normally, the state [...] and dominant ideology cover up this foundation. But it remains present—imprisoned or kettled, so to speak, at the site of the exclud-

ed part. An Event happens when the excluded part appears on the social scene, suddenly and drastically. It ruptures the appearance of normality, and opens a space to rethink reality from the standpoint of its real basis in inconsistent multiplicity. (Robinson 2014)

An Event succeeds in representing a part of reality previously unrepresented. This unfolding of new representations from an Event can produce "truthprocedures" (or new perspectives), "subjects" (processes rather than persons), and new social systems, which yet stay outside the established order of society. Thus, an Event can interrupt the continuity of determinism. Robinson also points out that, "a true Evental calling is completely dismissive of the individual's becoming" (2014). Oliver Feltham[4] notes less dramatically that "events are not so much the emergence of new entities as a tear in the texture of the situation. They establish nothing" (2008, 100–2).

We could say that this Event makes the socially invisible, visible for a short time, but without further human engagement the newly visible will become absorbed back into the void. It is possible to discern two Events: Chilirenka's drug-and-arson maneuver that brings down the whole Home; the other, already a memory, is Shaolin's marriage proposal with fireworks when his explosives led to the death of an old man. Focus will be on the first as it is the climax of the play.

Both Chilirenka and Shaolin are present and active during the last three scenes of the play, which comprise the lead-up, the Event itself, and the aftermath. In Scene 19, the girl visits the bedrooms of the residents upstairs and poisons them one by one, taking particular care with Yozei, who, by this time, seriously wants to die. She then ritualistically lights three matches, and sets fire to the second floor. Shaolin is too sick from the drug-laced alcohol she gave him to stop her. To his shouts, she counters by recalling his fireworks accident, "You set the old man free" (Zhao 2017b). Her statement also references Yozei's plea to Shaolin to kill him in Scene 18: "Save me; you will be saved, too" (ibid., 11). Out of affection for Yozei, she resorts to euthanasia.

Chilirenka also points out that she is stupid, a minor, a mental case, and a "rabbit"; all these signs of powerlessness render her socially invisible. Society could not hold her responsible even if she survived as she is part of "the excluded" and cannot exist as an adult, citizen, nursing home resident, or human being would. Chilirenka's mission has become one of alleviating the unnecessary suffering of the dying and, in her zeal, she takes others with Yozei and herself. Robinson's earlier point that an "Evental calling is completely dismissive of the individual's becoming" applies to Chilirenka in that, like a revolution or tsunami, she embroils others in the surge. Despite her motivation, Chilirenka's surprise action does not seem to "set things right." Could it lead to Badiou's truthprocedures?

Shaolin's response is commonsensical and restorative. Badiou would call Shaolin a Thermidorian reactionary, as he has renounced his former rebellious firebrand antics and learned to acquiesce by becoming a moderate, though with a certain energy fueled "by a subjective experience with the other side" (Pluth 2010, 3). If the authorities are willing to rebuild the home, he is willing to take charge. Hopefully, he will make some improvements within the permissible parameters of the social care system. But one suspects that the chance for any fundamental change may very well slip by.

Neither Chilirenka's nor Shaolin's intentions are negative; but their acts of decreation do not guarantee creation, only repetition. They are minor forces in a longer process of haphazard change and their Event will most likely remain unnamed and sink back into the multiplicity of the void/excess. The play does not, after all, answer the question of how to live for any one individual, but indicates a long view of cumulative social truthprocedures through small gashes in the fabric of social existence.

In the closing scene, Ahon presides over a multi-faith funeral service, after which Shaolin pushes his uncle in a wheelchair around the devastated compound where the trees have been razed and sparrows fled. He speaks of rebuilding the nursing home to live and work there together with his uncle. In the background, Buddhist, Christian, and Islamic chanting gradually mix and turn into a dark chaotic polyphony, as if everything could be heard at once. Suggesting the truthprocedure of Badiou's Event, this scene illustrates the temporary lifting of materiality and the social system. The scorched earth and cacophony represent Badiou's void of inconsistent multiplicity momentarily revealed. The play ends at this point in its macro-level treatment of the human condition in a state of amorphous potentiality.

The following section will focus on the non-diegetic aspects of the play, address its intermedial structure, and continue investigating the visible/invisible and in-between characteristics of the production.

6-2 *As the Sparrows Wended in a Windless Winter* as intermedial theatre

A "visible/invisible" strategy underpinning the intermediality of this play is evident in both the analogue-style handling by humans and the digital live-video mediation. The characters who are represented by the string-objects and the human character Shaolin are totally unaware of the manipulators, the stage hands, the camera crew and their equipment, the video screen overhead, and their virtual counterparts. In contrast, the viewer, in line with the traditional Japanese performance custom of conceptual visibility, has potentially full access to these aforementioned invisible aspects, as well as the unfolding narrative.

With this in mind, we will look at the theoretical basis of New Media Theatre drawn mainly from J. D. Bolter and R. Grusin's groundbreaking concept of remediation (2000) and the expanded views on intermediality by Chapple and Kallenbelt (2006) and Klich and Scheer (2012).

Remediation and intermediality

Remediation refers to the process of changing the material from the source medium into the target medium. According to Bolter and Grusin, the purpose of remediation is "reform, improvement, or reimagining," specially to amend a lack of immediacy in a particular medium (2000, 59–60). In performing-object theatre, such a lack can easily occur when the string-objects are small and the auditorium too large for comfortable viewing with the naked eye.

Bolter and Grusin posit that a double logic of transparency and hypermediacy underlies the remediation process. Succinctly summarized by Kattenbelt, "the first logic aims at making the user forget the medium, whereas the second logic aims at making the user aware of the medium. [...] Ultimately, their aim is the same, which is to exceed the restrictions of representation, in order to intensify the experience of the real" (Kattenbelt 2008, 19–29).

A total acceptance of a given medium will render it "invisible" so that we can transcend the threshold of a proscenium stage, frame or screen, gain transparent immediacy, and enjoy the "real" or "authenticity" of the fictive world. Established representational media like theatre or film enable us to reach this mindful receptivity with ease.

However, the logic of hypermediacy, which draws attention to process rather than product, engages in "multiplying mediation so as to create a feeling of fullness, a satiety of experience" (Bolter and Grusin, 53). In practice, this has often led to a "windowed" style similar to computer screen interfaces, offering heterogeneous information simultaneously. For example, Jay Scheib's Live Cinema work, such as *World of Wires* (2012), uses numerous detached displays like monitors and mirrors to open up access to further diegetic content. The viewer is dazzled by the excess of perspectives and information and struggles pleasantly to keep up with them.

With intermediality, Klich and Scheer note that "the 'inter' of intermediality implies a 'between space,' and the intermedial exists between previously assumed ideas of medium specificity" (2012, 71). Boenisch states that intermediality is "an effect performed in-between mediality, supplying multiple perspectives, and foregrounding the making of meaning rather than obediently transmitting meaning" (quoted in Chapple and Kattenbelt, 103). It includes the pushing and pulling of the two logics of remediation as well as the aspects of intermediality identified at the beginning of this chapter, the "in-between" of performers, spectators, medial spaces, and art forms.

Boenisch adds that intermediality is conducive to a dialectical "perspective of disruption and resistance" (ibid., 115). If we understand this to apply not only to the performance method but also to the content, as meaning is rarely totally abandoned, it takes us back to Badiou's tear in the fabric of dominant society, so that Chilirenka's maneuver can be seen as a more political moment of resistance to the establishment. Finally, it is important to remember that this intermedial effect is captured and processed in each viewer's mind and imagination, and thus can lead to varying responses and interpretations of a production.

Unlike multimedia performances, which, in Japan, tend to invite various discrete media to perform in the same space with little entanglement, cutting-edge intermediality emphasizes interpenetration or entanglement that hybridizes mediality. "Intermedial theatre subsumes media, uniting both live and mediated elements within the frame of performance" (Klich and Scheer, 71).

In this way, remediation often exploits the gap between the viewer's level of immersion in the content and their awareness of mediatedness to encourage an extreme sense of enriched experience, and overlaps with the thrust of intermediality, which also encourages in-between attention-shifting, multitasking, balancing, and a constant evaluation of what/ which might be more important or interesting to watch or know.

Application to *The Sparrows Wended*

From the opening scene with the screen towering over the stage, the production is clearly intermedial theatre as the staging enables a simultaneous view of string-object manipulation and remediation into video from two different angles almost all the time. The logic of hypermediacy dominates and is underpinned by a "visible/invisible" methodology.

The fiction of the play already includes various standard-sized devices for human communication, such as a landline phone and mobile phones, which the miniature characters can see and sometimes use. Shaolin uses a video camera but in a wild, amateurish manner, a striking contrast to the steadiness of the rest of the filming. This initial signaling seems insufficient to establish him as the narrator or documenter of the whole story.

Aside from Shaolin's rather lame attempts at video recording the life of the residents he finds both amusing and annoying, the hypermediacy intensifies exponentially with the "interweaving" presence of two human-sized video cameras, cables, and mobile platforms operated by masked stage hands, all of whom together with the manipulators, are, as noted earlier, conceptually invisible to the small characters. It is clear to the audience that the stage is a site of mediation.

Let us turn now to the live video remediation of the stage action up into the virtual space. Varying framing techniques guide the viewer's attention to modify their reading of the stage action, such as indexing, zooming, bracketing, and tracking. Indexing is to perceptually indicate, and is the equivalent of pointing to something in the frame. An example would be the foregrounding of the Old Lady in the medical questionnaire scene. Zooming usually brings a subject/object closer or farther away from the viewer, as when the video camera zooms in on the electric drill as the sole focus of Yozei's fearful attention on his third suicide attempt. Another memorable moment occurs when Chilirenka lights a match to guarantee the end of Yozei's existential torment. The camera's zoom enabled every spectator seated anywhere in the auditorium to feel frisson at her macabre look seemingly directed right in their faces, an expression usually impossible to see on a 70 cm (2.3 ft.) performing-object from the audience seats.

Bracketing refers to excluding or including certain information in a frame. Unlike the remediation of the string-objects, the manipulators themselves were consistently kept out of view or made difficult to identify as parts of their black uniforms would function as on-the-spot backdrops for individual string-figures—another application of the "visible-but-invisible" strategy—thus greatly promoting a puppet film impression. Tracking shots are commonly taken from a moving dolly of someone/ something often also in movement. In this play, such shots increased in the second half of the play to enhance the filmic quality of transitions in space, time, or culminating action as can be seen in celebrant Ahon's departure with his "multi-religion" suitcase after Shimei and Li Tokusei's open-air wedding-cum-funeral, the temporal shift to a scene from Shaolin's boyhood, and the climactic indoor arson scene.

Overall, high distortion by live video was rare. There was one high ceiling angle used for Yozei's hanging attempt. Most shifts were far more restrained, giving the viewer an uneasy impression of being tested. In the opening scene, "Kiss of Death," the minimally different angles of the cardiogram monitor on the table and its virtual copy on the huge video display above seemed to hint that finer differences needed to be noted between various media throughout the performance. In terms of Badiouian discourse, this would mean "tears or rips" rather than major ruptures in the stage action and that a performative version of his dialectical perspective of disruption and resistance was in effect.

For a few scenes, a very low-distortion live video feed that mainly transmitted stage action enabled the viewer to stay attentive to the action whether onstage or on the screen, without his or her eyes wandering to sneak a peek at the other medium. These scenes focused on the portrayal of character and relationships and provided the viewer periods of media transparency to experience a sense of emotional fullness.

A major example of such transparent immediacy occurs when seventy-five-year-old Li Tokusei and sixty-five-year-old Shimei's mutual affection deepens into a marriage agreement in the two "Happy Times" scenes they have together. He dies from a heart attack in the latter scene and her gentle sorrow, together with her subsequent donning of a wedding dress at his funeral, indicates the depth of her sense of loss. It is worth noting that in Scene 13, the couple is watching a famous Japanese romantic adventure film on TV, but no visual monitor is supplied. Only the voices of the lovers in the movie were heard, and these were quickly superseded by those of the characters, who identified with the filmic lovers. The director carefully calibrated that scene to maintain audience interest in the emotion rather than the visual medium.

Discrepancies between the stage and screen action and pacing grew as the narrative developed. Very fast, smooth scene changes became noticeable. It helps to know that in traditional puppetry, even simple scene or set changes can take much time; a wait of two minutes is not unusual in Youkiza's Edo-era repertory performances. In *The Sparrows Wended*, two sets were often on stage at the same time as the new one was slid in before the other was dismantled. On the video screen, only the new scene was visible while onstage the previous set gradually faded out of sight. Rarely did the live video follow a character's exit as it is time-consuming; the short figure tends to be concealed from view by the taller manipulator, and their departure can anyway be seen quite well from the audience seats.

The highlight in remediation and virtual illusion came in Scene 19 when Chilirenka sets fire to the nursing home. The same video camera that filmed her lighting the match also shot the burning pit with one large performing-object in flames. The mise en scène was anti-climactic in comparison to the amazingly wild effect on the wide screen, where the sense of immediacy was breathtaking. Though actual statistics are not available, it is likely that the frequency of viewers looking back and forth between screen and stage lessened a great deal during the spectacular euthanasia-by-fire, probably an indication that they had accepted the finished production as a puppet film and that the filming process, while challenging in the earlier scenes, was only supplementary and no longer engaging.

Then a totally new remediation happened in the last scene that had the audience metaphorically falling between two medial stools. The film display went dark and the manipulators and video crew vanished. Aside from Shaolin, the characters who appeared—Ahon, funeral attendants, and the Doctor—were now performed by non-masked manipulators in costume (i.e., actors). As if a layer has been stripped off, these actors, who had been "invisible," were in full view for the first time. This effectively changed the medium to "live" drama rather than a play/film about aesthetic performing-figures in a nursing home.

The sudden takeover by human presence added a visceral sense of fleshy embodiment to the staging, unattainable by dainty wooden figures or slick digital images. Unexpected defamiliarization pervaded the mise en scène of enervated humanity shorn of social trappings and deepened the sense of Badiou's evental happening when prevailing human agency is stalled, and a hereto unforeseen reality and disaster erupts. Whether any fundamental, long-lasting social change will arise from this incident is unlikely, as Shaolin seems willing to restore the building and institution without any petition for reform.

Audience reception

Through the live video remediation, the audience's visual reception of the performing-figures and objects was greatly improved. Emphasis was put solidly on the performance art, especially their facial expressions and their props (e.g., the drill) through zooms and bracketing, just as in mask theatre, where masks can evince delicate changes of emotion through subtle movement, like tilting, in appropriate lighting.

Once the audience became acclimatized to the optical illusion of black strings vanishing from the screen, the action on the video screen became glamorous for them. They became increasingly reluctant to watch the mise en scène crowded with manipulators and crew. The magical quality of independent figures seemingly unsupervised by manipulators regained its attraction. In a sense, the video screen rendering took viewers both back to the literal invisibility of traditional marionette operation, when puppeteers were hidden up on tall upstage bridges, and forward to New Media Theatre, in which hypermediacy provides a bevy of larger-than-life performing-figure doubles while also erasing the manipulators.

Chapter summary

From its inception, *The Sparrows Wended* project was to stage together string-objects, "invisible" black-clad manipulators, human actors, and mediatized bodies (virtual performing-objects and actors), thus putting the human figure into an "ambiguous position between an animated agent and a symbol of mediatization" (Wagner 2006, 127). By first entangling two well-known medialities, one analogue and the other digital, then suddenly discarding both, the playwright and director took the audience back to human actors representing characters in the midst of a collapsed social institution. The appalling desolation of this ending is another posthuman landscape divorced from human desire, and echoes the Sayonara image of the empty beach where a lone android recites poetry in requiem.

Queried about his own philosophy of life, Wang gave a surprising reply:

> In late 2017, I moved to a new home in Beijing that I designed. I call it TDT (The De-electrified Territory, 停电亭). There is no electricity or electronics in it. I could only meditate, read, write, or sleep in it. If you visit me in TDT, you will have to hand over your cell phone and I shall put it into a little safe I set up outside the apartment. Plus, I gave up cell phone and social media earlier. These actions sum up my philosophy. (Email correspondence, February 28, 2019)

It has suddenly become difficult to find an appropriate ending to this section. Nonetheless, to close these two chapters on technological innovation and performing-objects on a positive note, it does seem that both robot/android theatre and New Media Theatre will continue to develop exponentially with the assistance of AI-driven technologies providing ever new opportunities for humanoid and virtual expression.[5]

1 Binghao Zhao (b. 1988) has been resident playwright of the Théâtre du Rêve Expérimental in Beijing since 2013. His work has been staged in major global cities like New York, London, Singapore as well as in China. His play *Landmine 2.0* premiered at Festival/Tokyo 2013. He received the 2015 World Sinophone Young Playwright Award in Taipei. His feature film credits include *Tropical Memories*. He is working on his first book, *The Continent Trilogy*.

2 Chong Wang (b. 1982) is the founder, head, and artistic director of the Beijing-based Théâtre du Rêve Expérimental. Wang is one of the new wave of theatre-makers in China. He is known in Japan for his remarkable directing, which he has showcased in *Landmine 2.0* (2013, Festival/Tokyo Award) and *Ghosts 2.0* (2014), where he applied absurd and intrusive live video "surgery" to Ibsen's *Ghosts*. He is in the process of breaking out of live video directing. A recent work of his as director was Nick Yu's *The*

Insane Asylum Next to Heaven in Shanghai in 2019–2020.

3   Alain Badiou (b. 1937) is a French philosopher and founder of the faculty of Philosophy of the University of Paris 8 with Gilles Deleuze, Michel Foucault, and Jean-François Lyotard. Badiou has written about the concepts of being, truth, event and the subject in a way that, he claims, is neither postmodern nor simply a repetition of modernity. He identifies with Maoism and was supportive of the Cultural Revolution. Badiou advocates a return of communism as a political force.

4   Oliver Feltham, an Australian philosopher, is known mainly for his English translations of Alain Badiou. Feltham's own writings include Marxism, critical theory, and the history of metaphysics. His recent work focuses on psychoanalysis and Jaques Lacan. Wikipedia, s.v. "Oliver Feltham," last modified November 26, 2019, 17:47, https://en.wikipedia.org/wiki/Oliver_Feltham.

5   For further documentation on *The Sparrows Wended*, see the Appendix.

PART TWO

Japanese Material Performance in
Translation

Commentary on the Performances

As this study is about performing-objects in Japan, Part Two provides translations of three intracultural productions, all of which have been discussed extensively at various points in Part One. Within the intracultural category, these three plays and their respective playwrights and companies differ clearly from each other in the following four aspects and serve to indicate the rich variety of contemporary performing-object theatre: the human/cultural resources, performance methods, the types and ratios of performers, and the passage of fictional time—calendric, cosmic, social, and psychological time.

The first aspect is the combination of the main contributing human and cultural resources. The production base for Amano's *Heitaro's Yokai Diary* is the I.T.O. Project, which comprises performing-object specialists, with actor-theatre artist Amano offering his unique worldview and whimsical talent for supersaturated adaptation. The production base for Yamamoto's *Choan and the Ripped Umbrella: Heisei Trick Peep Show*, a *kabuki* adaptation, is the Edo Marionette Theatre Youkiza (hereafter Youkiza), with countercultural *angura* artists also enlisted. For Tanino's *Avidya—The Dark Inn*, the four-person Niwa Gekidan Penino theatre company (hereafter Penino), which has no actors, functions as a production team that brings together diverse stage performers and artists to work with their Penino advisor, curator/dramaturg, and technician to turn Tanino's original playtext into a three-dimensional mobile artifact (Tanino 2011). The second aspect is the difference in performance methods. Central to *Heitaro's Yokai Diary* is the dizzying parade of *kimo/ero/gurokawaii* trick objects, multiplying and atomizing on a conventional puppet stage with an upstage screen showing newsreel as well as expanding cosmic space and time. For *Choan and the Ripped Umbrella*, the driving forces are the principle of breaking the conventions of puppet manipulation to instigate rupture and the dazzling multiple-character manipulation by master Magosaburo XII and actor Kushida. What is important in *Avidya—The Dark Inn* is the conjuring up of the uncanny through the subtle use of performing-objects and light and shade so that both human characters and props large and small seem to breathe.

The third aspect is the differing ratios of performing-objects, manipulators, and actors, which give variety to the mise en scène. *Heitaro's*

Yokai Diary has thirty-one types of *yokai* string-objects, some of which are nested like *matryoshka* dolls, nine hidden manipulators, and no actors. Despite the overwhelming number of performing-objects, the use of the stage is more "conventionally magical." *Choan and the Ripped Umbrella* has about fifty performing-figures including *mezashi*[1] policemen, nine visible manipulators, and one actor. *Avidya—The Dark Inn* has two major performing-objects—the homunculus and the inn—plus countless minor ones, a single visible manipulator, and six actors.

The last aspect is the varied flow of fictional time. While the author Amano is known for his subversion of the linear, *Heitaro's Yokai Diary* proceeds according to the calendar for the first ten days in July 1749, after which time accelerates to the end of that month when a Maoo[2] demon appears, signifying a greater cosmic and transhuman hierarchy that rules the universe and its parallel worlds. *Choan and the Ripped Umbrella* covers three years from the doctor's plotting to his final arrest for murder, marked by the societal system of bell ringing in the late Edo period. *Avidya—The Dark Inn* covers an overnight stay at a spa by two traveling performers in the recent past of 2013, intimating a psychologically intense period.

The following chapter will present Tengai Amano and his *Heitaro's Yokai Diary*.

1   Cf. Chapter 1, n. 3, p. 20.
2   Cf. Chapter 7, n.10, p. 199.

Chapter 7

Tengai Amano and *Heitaro's Yokai Diary*

Tengai Amano (b. 1960) is a Nagoya-based playwright, director, film director, illustrator, and collage artist, who founded the Shonen-Ojakan
theatre company in 1982. His broad range of artistic interests and abilities has enabled him to address his fundamental question in life—"Why
am I here?"—in ways that delight his audiences. Known for his playful,
surrealistic theatre of images, said to convey "cosmic nostalgia," he has
brought his considerable talents to material performance since 2004.
Since this successful initiation, Amano has scripted and directed five
more material works for four performing-object groups including the I.
T.O. Project.

Like many visually oriented directors, Amano is not always comfortable with words alone; valuing the illustrations equally with the script,
he sometimes attaches stage directions to the illustrations as well. The
translated script of *Heitaro's Yokai Diary* in this chapter does not include
those illustrations as such a provision would more than double the length
of the play. Priority has, instead, been given to conveying the overall
"look" of the stage through the standard method of adding stage pictures
and flyers. In addition, this translation retains the original Japanese text's
use of the musical symbols (namely, quavers) to indicate sound or music
effects. The published Japanese script, containing all the illustrations, is
available from the publisher Hokuto Shobo in Tokyo.

For further discussion on *Heitaro's Yokai Diary*, refer to the first section of Chapter 2.

Selected Chronology

This lists only the performing-object productions for which Amano has provided scripts, adaptations, and/or direction.

2004 *Heitaro's Yokai Diary* (script/dir.) for the I.T.O. Project; revived 2007, 2008. Amano received the 9th Matsubara & Wakao Memorial Theatre Award for this play.

2005 *Demon Pond* (Yashagaike) (adapt./dir.) by Kyoka Izumi for Musubiza Puppet Company

2012 *Miss Tanaka* (Misu Tanaka) (dir.) by John Romeril for Youkiza

2014 *The Red Demon that Cried* (Naita akaoni) (dir.) by Hirosuke Hamada for Marionette Company Isshiza; revived 2016, 2018

2016 *Golem* (Goremu) (main dir.) by Gustav Meyer for the Japan-Czech International Theatre Collaboration Project with Marionette Company Isshiza; co-director Zoya Mikotover; revived 2017

2018 *The Voyage of Imperial Prince Takaoka* (adapt./dir.) by Tatsuhiko Shibusawa for the I.T.O. Project; revived 2019

Fig. 7.1. Tengai Amano, *Heitaro's Yokai Diary*, 2004, Shizuoka Performing Arts Center. Photo © Noriaki Yamazaki. Courtesy of I.T.O. Project.

Heitaro's Yokai Diary

By Tengai Amano
Translated by Mari Boyd

Cast of Characters

Humans (in order of appearance)
HEITARO, 16-year-old samurai
GONPEI, follower of Heitaro
GONPACHI, 16-year-old samurai
UNCLE, Heitaro and Katsuya's uncle
KATSUYA, Heitaro's younger brother

NARRATOR (voiceover only)

Main *Yokai*

Scene 0. **Giant with bowler hat, white hands**
Scene 1. July 1. Daytime. **Cyclops, big and small one-eyed bonzes**
Scene 2. July 2. Daytime. None
Scene 3. July 2. Night. **Lanterns and flames, faucet, water, fish**
Scene 4. July 3. **Household items, scissor dancers**
Scene 5. July 4. **Butterflies, caterpillars**
　　　　 July 5. **Woman, boobs, tongues**
Scene 6. July 6. **Doppelgängers of Gonpei, Gonpei babies, uncle**
Scene 7. July 7. **Tanabata Star Festival[1] decorations, hands and fingers that multiply fractally, Christmas trees, etc.**
Scene 8. July 8. **Large ear, other body parts like heads on a skewer, large crying face with its eyes pierced by swords, multiple facial expressions on a rotating head, face/ear/voice wannabes, etc.**
Scene 9. July 9. **Holes and fingers, Heitaro doppelgängers, candles, mirrors, dancers, written characters ("eye," "dream," etc.)**
Scene 10. July 10. **Gonpachi doppelgänger, Gonpachi's sword, writing table, stone mortar, *chikuwa*[2]**
Scene 11. July 30. **Gonpachi doppelgänger, strange short man with a long stick**
Scene 12. July 31. **Gigantic hands and feet, Gorozaemon Sanmoto,**

worms, moon with holes

Manipulators
Ayako Bando (JIJO)
Mieko Gomi
koichic Iimuro (Marionette MINOMUSHI)
Hiromi Morita (Dunku)
Aki Nagatsuka (Marionette Theatre Appuu)
Sayoko Nishimiya (Negibozu SAYO)
Kazumi Takenoshita (Omake no omake Puppet Company)
Hazuki Ueda (Omake no omake Puppet Company)
Toshihiko Yamada (Puppet Theatre Cocon)

Lights out. A shabby screen stands centerstage. Visuals are projected.
The white screen has numerous rain-like scratches.

Surtitles: *(♪Click, click, click.)*
Long, long ago
when Japanese men
still wore topknots,
in the land of Bingo,
in the castle town of Miyoshi,
lived a strong, young man
called Heitaro Inao.
He was 16 years old.
His parents have already passed on.
In a house on the outskirts of town,
he lived with his kid brother, Katsuya,
and a follower called Gonpei.
One summer evening,
Heitaro and Gonpachi, his neighbor and friend,
tested their courage
by climbing Mount Hikuma nearby
and touching
a forbidden tomb.
They went back home.
For their foolish deed,
for a full month
at Heitaro's house,
supernatural events occurred one after another.
Night after night,
he was attacked by *yokai*.
But coolheaded Heitaro
did hang in there.
He braved it out without a single shiver.
Long, long ago,
in the summer of 1794,
this *yokai* invasion occurred from July 1 to July 30.
Long, long ago,
when samurai still wore
heavy swords when outside.

When neither radio
nor television had been invented.
When movies like this
had not been invented.

The surtitles stop and the rain-like scars move on the screen.

VOICE: HEITAROOO

♪ *A softer clicking sound.*

The front projector light dies and the back light turns on. Like shadow theatre, many strings, resembling the earlier rain-like distortion, hang down. Black birds on strings fly away. They fly above the frame and go higher. Sound of wings slicing the air—♪ swoosh, swoosh, swoosh.

VOICE: HEITAROOO

In black silhouette, Heitaro on strings appears from below.

HEITARO: Here.

Then the screen falls forwards and the string figure Heitaro appears.
♪ *The play title appears on the screen, letter by letter in upper case:*

HEITARO'S YOKAI DIARY

The projector casts the title across the whole stage, together with clouds floating in a blue sky. The backdrop shows mountains in black silhouette. In the moving clouds, string figure Heitaro keeps rising.

VOICE: Heeeey.

Thud.

Large, white hands appear over the mountain range. A face wearing a bowler hat appears. One hand takes off the hat and withdraws its hand. The other hand is also withdrawn. The face begins to float upwards. The face stops and surtitles appear on the screen. The mountain splits to left and right and simultaneously the set for Heitaro's home moves in from both wings. ♪ A softer clicking sound. Evening lights come on. ♪

Scene 1. July 1

Narration begins during the set change.

NARRATOR: On July 1, when Heitaro is enjoying the coolness of evening on the veranda, pitch-black clouds rise from Mount Hikuma, and a heavy evening shower begins.

Heitaro is sitting on the veranda. ♪ The sound of pouring rain—

NARRATOR: The rain continues till midnight and thunder rolls through the sky.

♪ Sound of thunder—rumble, rrrumble. Flashes of lightning—krack, krack, kra-krahh. A moment of total darkness. After that, a lantern is lit. At centerstage, a futon is laid out—♪ flup, flup. Heitaro is sitting on the futon in the dim light.

HEITARO: I can't sleep with all this thunder.

Right away, a voice is heard from the room stage left.

GONPEI: Hey.
HEITARO: Huh?
GONPEI: Hey, hey…
HEITARO: What?
GONPEI: He-hey, he-hey.
HEITARO: What it is?
GONPEI: He-hey, he-hey, Heitaro. Master Heitaro!! *(Comes flying in from the adjacent room.)*
HEITARO: What's up, Gonpei?

Gonpei trembles and trembles.

149

HEITARO: Why are you shivering like that?

GONPEI: A-a huge giant, a giant!

HEITARO: A giant!

GONPEI: *(Overlapping with Heitaro's last words.)* A giant tried to push me over. Whew-whew. *(Heavy breathing.)*

HEITARO: A giant?

GONPEI: Yes, master.

HEITARO: You must've had a nightmare.

GONPEI: But...

HEITARO: *(Overlapping with Gonpei's word.)* But this darn weather. This wild rain and thunder are getting to you.

GONPEI: Is that right?...

HEITARO: Yes, I am right.

GONPEI: You must be right. Ha-ha. I was so scared.

HEITARO: Now, get back to bed.

GONPEI: Ah yes, thank you, master. Sorry to trouble you.

Gonpei goes back to his room.

NARRATOR: After a while...

A voice is heard from the other room.

GONPEI: No...

HEITARO: Huh?

GONPEI: No, no, no, no, no, no, no.

HEITARO: What now?

Gonpei comes flying in again.

GONPEI: It-t-t-t's a monster, after all!

HEITARO: What the hell are you talking about?!

GONPEI: It's a huge monster with a shaven head!

HEITARO: Absolute nonsense!

GONPEI: But...

HEITARO: You probably just slept with your hands on your chest.

GONPEI: Huh, oh yes. You're right.

HEITARO: It's just a darn nightmare. You only had a frightening dream, that's all. Now go back to bed, for crying out loud.

GONPEI: …Uh…aye, master.

HEITARO: Go.

Dispirited, Gonpei returns to his room. At that moment, ♪ it stops raining.

HEITARO: Oh? The rain's stopped.

NARRATOR: Immediately, a wind blows through the house.

♪ The wind's whistling—hwiiiiiiieeee. The lantern is extinguished and darkness falls.

HEITARO: Oh no. *(♪ A low whistling—phiiiiee.)* So what. The night's always dark anyways. The thunder's died out, too.

NARRATOR: At that moment…

♪ Crackle, crackle, crash. Visuals of a fire are projected on stage.

HEITARO: Oh my god, a fire!!

The next moment, ♪ the visuals disappear. It is quiet again… Insect sounds can be heard—♪ chirp, chirp.

HEITARO: What's going on, eh?

In the low, dim light, a huge hand creeps from the adjacent room to where Heitaro is.

HEITARO: What's this?!

As soon as Heitaro looks that way, the hand withdraws. Simultaneously, another huge hand appears from high upstage.

HEITARO: Uh?!

The huge hand grabs Heitaro's head.

HEITARO: What the hell…

The huge hand pulls Heitaro's head.

HEITARO: Eh? Darn… *(Digs in his heels and hangs in there.)* I'm gonna win this one.

He escapes from the monstrous hand, which immediately disappears.

HEITARO: Reveal yourself, you monster!

*At that moment, on the other side of the shoji[3] paper sliding doors, a
huge eye sparkles and becomes visible.*

HEITARO: Oh no, a Cyclops!!

*When the Cyclops closes its eye, the stage becomes dark, and when it
opens its eye, the stage becomes as bright as day.*

HEITARO: Hey, Gonpei, bring my sword, my sword at once!
NARRATOR: But there is no answer.

*The top of the Cyclops's head cracks open and a little Cyclops appears.
It gives a shrill laugh—♪ heeheeheehee.*

HEITARO: What the hell? *(♪—)*

*Laughing—♪ heeheeheehee—the little Cyclops circles around Heitaro.
Then it vanishes upstage. At the same time, Gonpei stage right screams.*

GONPEI: Aiiiiiiiiiiieeeeeeeeeeeeeeeeeeeee!

Gonpei flees from stage right to stage left, pursued by the little Cyclops.

HEITARO: Hey!
GONPEI'S VOICE: *(From backstage.)* Aiiiiiiiiiiieeeeeeee.

At the same time, as before, Gonpei runs across from stage right to left, pursued by the little Cyclops.

HEITARO: Look here, what's going on?
BIG CYCLOPS: Ho, ho, ho.

Laughing heartily, the big Cyclops vanishes. At the same time, someone knocks hard—♪ bang, bang, bang—on the central sliding doors. Heitaro turns around...

HEITARO: Now what? *(The banging continues. Heitaro grips his sword.)* Enter, you monster.

The banging continues.

GONPACHI'S VOICE: Hey, Heitaro.
HEITARO: Huh?
GONPACHI'S VOICE: Heitaro, it's me. Me.
HEITARO: *(Overlapping with Gonpachi's last word.)* Me?
GONPACHI: No, me. Gonpachi.
HEITARO: Gonpachi?

Gonpachi opens the sliding doors and enters.

GONPACHI: Heitaro, you OK?
HEITARO: They've arrived.
GONPACHI: Who?
HEITARO: The *yokai.*
GONPACHI: So I thought.
HEITARO: Huh?
GONPACHI: I heard you and Gonpei shouting and screaming. I came over in a hurry—as far as your gate…
HEITARO: Yeah…
GONPACHI: From your house, a one-eyed bonze-type *yokai* came trotting out.
HEITARO: That's the one.
GONPACHI: As it passed me, a super powerful beam shot out of its eye.
HEITARO: And?

GONPACHI: I closed my eyes and blindly found my way into this house. Then I tripped over something.

HEITARO: Like what?

GONPACHI: I opened my eyes to find Gonpei lying unconscious on the floor. I gave him some water and left him by Katsuya to sleep off his shock.

HEITARO: Of course! Katsuya, Katsuya. How is he?

Gonpachi looks back beyond the sliding doors.

GONPACHI: Take a look.

Heitaro peers through a crack in the sliding doors.

GONPACHI: He's sound asleep. You can hear his calm breathing. *(♪ zzzzzzzzzz.)*

HEITARO: Thank god.

NARRATOR: Relieved, Heitaro explains in detail what happened earlier.

During the Narrator's lines, Heitaro is talking to Gonpachi.

GONPACHI: I get it. These creatures are the true blue *yokai*.

HEITARO: Yeah.

GONPACHI: The real thing.

GONPACHI & HEITARO: *MONSTERS*.

GONPACHI: But you did a fine job of standing up to them.

HEITARO: Aww, I always wanted to meet up with some *yokai*, you know.

GONPACHI: This must be the payback for our test of courage the other day.

HEITARO: When we messed with that ancient burial mound…

GONPACHI: That's right.

HEITARO: Uh-huh.

GONPACHI: They must have ridden on that black cloud from Mount Hikuma.

HEITARO: They'll come again.

GONPACHI: Yep, sure thing.

HEITARO: I challenge them to come back as much as they like.

GONPACHI: Aha, I'm feeling good about this already.

HEITARO: Ha-ha-ha, my combat arm is itching to take them on.

NARRATOR: As they talk, dawn approaches.

The stage begins to light up.

GONPACHI: You know, Heitaro.

HEITARO: Huh?

GONPACHI: Maybe we should rest.

HEITARO: Yeah, there's no sign of them coming back anymore tonight.

Sounds from the room beyond the sliding doors.

GONPEI'S VOICE: Ahhhh.

GONPACHI: Huh? *(Peers into the room.)* Ha-ha-ha, Gonpei's talking in his sleep. Katsuya is still fast asleep.

NARRATOR: Gonpachi is attached to Katsuya as if the boy were his own kid brother.

GONPACHI: Well, I'll be heading home.

HEITARO: Yeah.

GONPACHI: We'll wipe 'm out together, right?

HEITARO: Yeah, we've gotta win this one.

Talking in this fashion, the two young men pass through the doors and exit. The doors slide shut slowly.

NARRATOR: *(As the doors close.)* Heitaro sees Gonpachi to the front door. Nothing untoward happens after this and Heitaro is able to sleep well till morning.

Lights fade out. On the screen in capital letters:

JULY 2

Scene 2. July 2

As voices are heard, daytime lights come on.

UNCLE: That won't do! You two must leave this haunted house and live with me. Now, get ready at once!

HEITARO: Uncle, please, not so fast.

UNCLE: No time to waste.

HEITARO: But...

UNCLE: If something happened to you, I wouldn't know what to report to my deceased brother.

The Uncle, Heitaro, and Katsuya sit in the living room, while Gonpei is out on the veranda. Gonpei speaks to the audience.

GONPEI: This is Heitaro's uncle and the deceased brother refers to Heitaro and Katsuya's dear father.

HEITARO: Enough, Gonpei, who the hell are you talking to?

GONPEI: Uhh...

HEITARO: You were so scared you went around telling anyone who'd listen about the monsters. Now the whole town is in an uproar. Even Uncle has heard about this.

GONPEI: No one can keep silent about something as terrifying as that.

UNCLE: Whatever. *(To Heitaro.)* You must vacate this house.

HEITARO: But...

UNCLE: And never come back.

HEITARO: No, I will stay here until I uncover the identity of the monsters.

UNCLE: Impossible.

HEITARO: I refuse to leave.

UNCLE: Unacceptable.

HEITARO: I will stay.

UNCLE: No.

HEITARO: I will not move.

UNCLE: *(Overlapping with Heitaro's last word.)* Move you must.

While the two men are arguing, Gonpei turns to the audience.

GONPEI: They go around in circles without ever seeming to reach a course of action.

At that moment, Gonpachi appears at upstage left.

GONPACHI: Hold on, who are you talking to?
GONPEI: Uh.
HEITARO: Hi Gonpachi.

Gonpachi talks to Uncle.

GONPACHI: Uncle.
UNCLE: Eh?
GONPACHI: The *yokai* have only come once. It's not clear if they will come again. So what about we just see how it goes?
UNCLE: Ah, um.
GONPACHI: When something happens, I will be as much help as I can.

Gonpei turns to the audience.

GONPEI: Gonpachi doesn't want Heitaro to leave the neighborhood.
UNCLE: Umm, if the powerful Gonpachi could stay, that would be tremendously reassuring, indeed.

Gonpei speaks to the audience.

GONPEI: Uncle is changing his mind.
HEITARO & GONPACHI: *(To Gonpei.)* Why the heck are you behaving like a commentator?
GONPEI: Ah.
UNCLE: *(His first phrase overlaps with Gonpei's utterance.)* Ah, shall we wait and see what develops?
HEITARO & GONPACHI: Yes, sir.
UNCLE: But Katsuya is still young. I will take care of him at my home.
HEITARO: That would be a great help.
KATSUYA: Big Brother, please take care of yourself.
HEITARO: Thanks, kid.
GONPACHI: *(Delighted.)* Aha, that's settled

Gonpei suddenly sits in the garden and starts to shout: Aaaaaargh!

157

HEITARO & GONPACHI: Hey, now what's up?

Gonpei will not budge from the garden.

GONPEI: I can't accept this!
HEITARO, UNCLE & GONPACHI: What?!
GONPEI: I can't. I am so scared I can't stay in this house anymore! Please let me go. *(Bowing deeply, he rubs his forehead hard against the ground, ♪ scrub-a-rub-rub.)*
GONPACHI: Gonpei.
GONPEI: I'm terrified.
HEITARO: Are you really terrified?
GONPEI: I am, I am.
GONPACHI: Being here in the daytime is all right, isn't it?
GONPEI: Eh?
GONPACHI: It's daytime. Daytime.
GONPEI: Ah, during the day, it's not scary.
GONPACHI: How about this, then? At night you stay at my place, and from morning to evening, you stay in service here with your master, Heitaro.
UNCLE: Uh-huh, that sounds good. Right, Gonpei?
GONPEI: Yes, then as usual, I will work here until dinner time.
HEITARO: That would be a great help, you know.
UNCLE: *(His first phrase overlaps with Heitaro's last phrase.)* You know, that'll work out. Katsuya, you get it?

Uncle takes Katsuya's hand and they stand up. The boy waves to Heitaro.

KATSUYA: Big Bro, get them all.
HEITARO: Right, I'll bust the monsters and come by to pick you up.
KATSUYA: I'll be waiting.

Uncle and Katsuya exit out the sliding doors.

GONPACHI: What about food, Gonpei?
GONPEI: The meal is ready.
GONPACHI: It's getting dark. Let's go to my place.
GONPEI: Yes, sir.

GONPACHI: Well then, Heitaro, I'll see you later. I'll drop by.
GONPEI: Thank you for your consideration. Please take care.
HEITARO: Yeah.

Gonpachi and Gonpei exit upstage left.

HEITARO: They've all gone now, feeling safe and at ease.

Gonpei suddenly shows his face upstage left.

GONPEI: Who are you talking to?
HEITARO: Huh?

Lights fade out. ♪ Sound of insects. Words appear on the screen:

AROUND MIDNIGHT

Scene 3. July 2 cont.

The lantern light fades in. Heitaro and Gonpachi sit facing each other with the lantern in the middle.

HEITARO: Around this time yesterday, the wind blew out the lantern.
GONPACHI: Will they come to haunt us?
HEITARO: Who knows?
GONPACHI: *(Overlapping with Heitaro's last phrase.)* Who knows?

Sound of the wind—♪ whoosh.

HEITARO & GONPACHI: It's here.
GONPACHI: Oh no
HEITARO: What is it?
GONPACHI: The flame.
HEITARO: Huh?
GONPACHI: It's growing.
HEITARO: Oh.

The flame in the lantern slowly begins to grow taller.

GONPACHI: Hey.
HEITARO: …Uh.

Multiplying flames begin to surround the two men.

GONPACHI: What's that sound?

♪ *A zinging sound. A sudden whoosh of wind extinguishes all the flames at once. The stage falls into total darkness and silence.*

GONPACHI: Oh.

Suddenly the whole room is a sea of fire through projection. ♪ *Clang, clang, clang.*

GONPACHI: Oh my god. Fire, fire!
HEITARO: Calm down, Gonpachi. It's just a blind.
GONPACHI: Water, water, water. Heitaro, get some water.
HEITARO: Calm down, I tell ya.
GONPACHI: Water, water!

Suddenly the sliding doors open and a gigantic faucet appears with water bursting out. ♪ *Gush, gush, gush…*

GONPACHI: It is water…
HEITARO: After fire comes water. That's a good one.

From below the room, the water level begins to rise.

GONPACHI: Heitaro! The water is rising.
HEITARO: Never mind.
GONPACHI: Hey, Heitaro!
HEITARO: It's just an illusion. See. *(Crouches down and tries to scoops up a handful of water.)* See, nothing goes through my fingers when I try to scoop some water.

♪ *The sound of water gurgling into the room.*

GONPACHI: Heitaro!
HEITARO: Ha-ha, look at the fish swimming.

Fish are swimming back and forth in the water.

GONPACHI: Heitaro!! I…
HEITARO: What?
GONPACHI: I can't swim!
HEITARO: No big deal. This is fake.
GONPACHI: Then why do I float?!

The water has risen above their necks and their bodies are floating.

GONPACHI: Aaaaaargh!! Glug, glug, glug, glug…
HEITARO: Gonpachi!!
GONPACHI: I'm drowning—glug, glug, glug, glug…

♪ *With a loud roar, the water recedes. The two land on the floor. The lantern is lit.*

GONPACHI: Uuuugh. I'm gonna drown…Glug, glug, glug, glug…
HEITARO: Gonpachi! Look, the water's gone!
GONPACHI: *(Breathing hard.)* Hwooooooo Hwaaa Hwooooooo Hwaaa—aaaa…
HEITARO: See, nothing's wet, the lantern's on, and no fish.
GONPACHI: I got screwed.
HEITARO: Gonpachi, I didn't know you couldn't swim.
GONPACHI: I'm really ashamed of myself.
HEITARO: We all have weak points, you know. *(Gonpachi doesn't answer.)* Gonpachi, you're very pale.
GONPACHI: Ha-ha. I'm OK. Completely OK.
HEITARO: This is probably it for tonight.
GONPACHI: Right…
HEITARO: Let's get some sleep.
GONPACHI: Right, sleep…
HEITARO: Good night.

GONPACHI: 'Night. *(Opens the sliding doors, taps one side of his head near his ear to release water, and exits.)*

HEITARO: ...Fire and water... What a ruse. Those wily *yokai*. Hm. *(Lies down.)*

NARRATOR: As soon as Heitaro lies down, he falls asleep. (♪—)

Lights fade out. Words appear on the screen:

JULY 3 NIGHT

Scene 4. July 3

Lights come on. Gonpachi enters from stage right.

GONPACHI: Hey, Heitaro...

HEITARO: Hi, Gonpachi, last night was quite something... *(Gets up from the veranda where he was snoozing.)* What's that thing?

Gonpachi is wearing a swim ring.

GONPACHI: Ha-ha, with this, I won't be fazed by any water attack.

HEITARO: I can tell you've given it some thought, Gonpachi.

GONPACHI: I am really embarrassed about that bad blunder, yesterday.

HEITARO: Please come in.

GONPACHI: Thanks. *(Enters the room.)*

HEITARO: Do you think they will come tonight, too?

GONPACHI: Ha-ha-ha, I'm ready for them. Come one, come all.

He slaps the swim ring. At the same time, a heavy sound is heard —♪ BOOOOOOOM.

GONPACHI: Wow—

The two young men jump up. The ground rumbles and roars.

HEITARO: The earth is sh-shaking.

GONPACHI: Heitaro.

HEITARO: Huh? *(Looks at Gonpachi who is suspended in midair.)*
GONPACHI: Ah. I can't get down on my own two feet. *(Struggles.)*
HEITARO: Gonpachi!

The rumbling stops. Gonpachi becomes subject to the normal pull of gravity again and falls down hard on the floor—crash.

GONPACHI: Ouch, ouchieeee.
HEITARO: Back to normal.
GONPACHI: Ouch. Ha-hah… Huh?

From the stage left wing, a broom, teacups, rice bowls, and a low table come floating in leisurely.

HEITARO: Oh.
GONPACHI: What the hell is this?

The household items disappear from the stage right wing. At that moment, a sharp ♪ ♪ slicing sound is heard—♪ shah-kiiiin.

HEITARO & GONPACHI: What now?!

♪ To a graceful rhythm of shah-kin, shah-kin, shah-kin, a pair of scissors conduct a ballet from stage left to right.

HEITARO: Scissors.
GONPACHI: The scissors are dancing.

The two are just staring when a loud ♪ shah-kiiiin is heard, and an out-sized pair of scissors appears downstage center opening and closing its blades. At the same time, from stage right, another pair moves towards Gonpachi also opening and closing its blades.

GONPACHI: Argh, argh… Oh no… Hey you, stop that!

The scissors aim at Gonpachi's strings.

GONPACHI: Hey, if you cut my strings—hey, that's not funny, eh.

♪ *Shah-kin, shah-kin.*

GONPACHI: STOP IT!

The scissors slice through Gonpachi's left-hand string. ♪ *SNIP...*

GONPACHI: Nooooo!!
HEITARO: Gonpachi!
GONPACHI: My hand! My hand won't move! *(His left-hand dangles by his side.)*
HEITARO: You fucking monsters!! Come on! *(Draws his sword.)*

The scissors challenge him. Heitaro swings his sword—♪ *swish—one of the scissors' strings snap.* ♪ *Waltz music. Dancing with a limp, the scissors move off stage right—*

HEITARO: That was dangerous. Gonpachi, you OK?
GONPACHI: Ha-ha... No problem, no problem...
HEITARO: But...
GONPACHI: This is nothing to worry about. I'll get this fixed in no time. *(Guarding his left hand, he exits through the central sliding doors.)*
HEITARO: Gonpachi... *(Seeing him off, he touches his own strings.)* Isn't it cowardly to target these strings?
NARRATOR: Monsters don't care about cowardice or any other dicey things.
HEITARO: I guess you have a point there. Well, I'd better be careful. Phew... *(Yawns.)* Oh I'm wiped out. Gotta get some shuteye.
NARRATOR: Heitaro falls asleep again as if he has no troubles in the world.

♪ *Lights fade out. Words appear on the screen:*

JULY 4 NIGHT

Scene 5. July 4

GONPACHI: Heitaro.

♪ *Music stops. Lights come on. Gonpachi is at stage right.*

HEITARO: Hey there, Gonpachi. *(Gets up from the veranda, where he was sleeping.)* Ah.

A bandage indicates that the string for Gonpachi's left hand has been fixed.

GONPACHI: Ha-ha, I'm OK now. *(Moving his left hand vigorously.)*
HEITARO: Ha-ha, great. Your bandage looks like a butterfly.

At that moment, a white butterfly passes from stage right to left.

HEITARO & GONPACHI: Oh, a butterfly.

At once, hundreds of butterflies flitter around. Then a projection of white butterflies on stage follows—♪ flutter, flutter.

HEITARO & GONPACHI: Wow!!

In a flash, they all disappear and the mise en scène returns to normal. ♪ Music ends. At the same time, three green caterpillars in bandages and with Cleopatra-style bangs crawl in from stage right.

HEITARO: Green caterpillars.
GONPACHI: They're yucky.

The three caterpillars turn towards Heitaro and Gonpachi.

VOICE: What was that?!

At the same moment, the "White Butterfly Samba" plays. Also, the central sliding doors open and a girl in white against a backdrop of a huge, white butterfly ribbon enters.

165

HEITARO & GONPACHI: What's this?!

To the ♪ music, the girl in white turns 180 degrees and transforms into a girl in a floral-patterned dress. Then her head falls out of the dress to reveal a green caterpillar in bandages. It pops out of the dress, which slides down to the floor. The four green caterpillar girls' bandages are pulled to right and left and begin to turn. In unison with the revolving, their tiny powdery scales become airborne.

The four caterpillar girls all stretch their wings and metamorphize into butterflies. The projection visuals overlap with the caterpillar girls and when the ♪ music ends, they all disappear—♪ flutter, flutter, flutter.

Gonpachi is coughing a great deal.

HEITARO: Wow, tonight's *yokai* are beautiful. Don't you think, Gonpachi?

Gonpachi has an attack of deep, wet coughing.

GONPACHI: Goff, goff, goff. Goff.
HEITARO: Gonpachi!
GONPACHI: Yuck, I feel sick. Geoff.
HEITARO: Are you OK?
GONPACHI: The butterfly powder has got at me. Heitaro, I think I'll call it a night.
HEITARO: Yeah, sure thing. Take care of yourself.
GONPACHI: Aah, Goff, goff.

Gonpachi exits through the sliding doors. Heitaro sees him off…

HEITARO: Gee, hope he's OK.
NARRATOR: Though worried about Gonpachi, Heitaro manages to have a good night's sleep again.

♪ Music fades in. Lights fade out. Words appear on the screen:

GONPACHI HAS A DANGEROUSLY HIGH FEVER FROM THAT NIGHT ON AND IS FORCED TO STAY AT HOME.

JULY 5

Scene 5 cont. July 5

Lights fade in. Heitaro sits on the veranda in a vacant mood.

HEITARO: Gonpei doesn't come over at all, either. I am finally alone now.

At that moment a woman's voice with a built-in echo is heard.

VOICE: So lonely.
HEITARO: Huh?
VOICE: So lonely.
HEITARO: Who are you?
VOICE: Me.
HEITARO: What?
VOICE: It is me.

A gigantic woman's face appears over the transom.

HEITARO: Whoa.
VOICE: I'll give you a blow job. Oooooopen. *(She opens her mouth as wide as possible.)*
HEITARO: What an enormous mouth!

Her tongue sticks out and starts licking him.

HEITARO: Cut it out. This is really disgusting.

The tongue continues to lick him—slurp, slurp.

HEITARO: Fuck. I'll pull it outa your face. *(He pulls the long tongue from her mouth and throws it to stage left wing.)*
HEITARO: Howzat?

167

VOICE: Waaaaaaah.

The woman's hands appear on the transom and climb down to the floor.
Two boobs with bodies appear and start walking and clinging to Heitaro.

VOICE: Waaaaaaah. Waaaaaaah.
HEITARO: Git going!

The hands and boobs flee stage right crying.

HEITARO: Filthy, disgusting stuff.

The gigantic woman is opening and closing her mouth.

HEITARO: You can't talk 'cause you don't have a tongue anymore.
  Serves ya right!

The voice comes from above...

VOICE: Waaaaaaah. *(The tongue enters stage in tears.)*
HEITARO: Oh.

The tongue stops, conducts a military salute, and pops into the gigantic
woman's mouth.

HEITARO: Oh no.
VOICE: Ha-ha-ha...I can talk—Howzat? ...Hohohoho.

The gigantic woman disappears with a roar—♪ booooooom.
When the roaring ends, everything goes back to normal.

HEITARO: Phew... But what was it? Aaaah, I'm so tired all of a sudden.
  (Lies down to sleep.)
NARRATOR: Heitaro falls asleep as soon as he lies down.

Lights fade out. ♪ Words appear on the screen:

JULY 6

Scene 6. July 6

During the blackout, there is heavy knocking on the sliding doors—♪ thud, thud.

GONPEI'S VOICE: Master Heitaro?
HEITARO'S VOICE: Huh?

♪ Thud, thud.

GONPEI: Master Heitaro?
HEITARO: What is it?

Gonpei lights the lantern, opens the sliding doors slightly, and shows his face.

HEITARO: Yo, Gonpei.
GONPEI: Master Heitaro
HEITARO: You haven't come by here for quite a while.
GONPEI: *(In the vocal and gestural style of comedian Sanpei Hayashi-ya's signature line "So sorry.")* So sorry.[4]
HEITARO: What?

For a moment, the projector emits distortion—zhaaaaa.

GONPEI: *(As his usual self.)* I am very sorry.
HEITARO: You're Gonpei, right?
GONPEI: I'm Sanpei. *(In Sanpei style.)* So sorry.
HEITARO: Really?

For a moment, the projector again emits distortion—zhaaaaa.

HEITARO: Who the heck is Sanpei?
GONPEI: Master, what are you saying? I am Gonpei.
HEITARO: So sorry. My ears are playing tricks on me.
GONPEI: I have also been afflicted by bad health for a while.

HEITARO: That's too bad. What's wrong?
GONPEI: *(In Gonpei B's voice.)* My head.
HEITARO: Huh?
GONPEI: *(In Gonpei C's voice.)* My head.
HEITARO: Your head hurts?
GONPEI: *(In Sanpei style.)* My head. *(Then as Gonpei D and A.)* My head. *(Then as Gonpei D, A, and B.)* My head. *(As Gonpei D, A, B, and C.)* My head. *(As Gonpei D, A, B, and C.)*
HEITARO: *(Overlapping with Gonpei's last two words.)* Your head. What happened to it?

Gonpei's voice doubles and trebles.

GONPEI: My head hurts.
GONPEI B: Hurts.
GONPEI C: Hurts.
GONPEI D: *(In Sanpei style.)* Hurts.

Gonpei's head snaps open and, with each word Gonpei says, a new head pops up like a matryoshka.

HEITARO: Hey you lot!
GONPEI A–D: My head hurts.
HEITARO: You monsters!
GONPEI A–D: That's insulting! We are not monsters.
HEITARO: You are *yokai* monsters plain as day.
GONPEI A: YO—
GONPEI B: KAI
GONPEI C: MON—
GONPEI D: STERS
GONPEI A–D: *(In Sanpei style.)* Monsters are like this.

For a moment the projector emits distortion—zhaaaaa. When it ends, instead of Gonpei A, B, C, and D, Gonpei with a gigantic face is standing there.

HEITARO: Wow. That is an enormous head.
GONPEI: My head…

HEITARO: What about it?

GONPEI: My head…my head…my head…my head…

HEITARO: *(Coming in on Gonpei's last "head" phrase.)* …Head. So what?

GONPEI: My head is cracking up.

Gonpei's head cracks open and many baby Gonpeis come crawling out.

HEITARO: Oh no.

BABY GONPEIS: Toddle, toddle, toddle, toddle. *(They toddle around.)*

HEITARO: Makes me want to puke.

The baby Gonpeis speak one after another. The effect is created by a voice multiplier with one person's voice.

BABY GONPEI: Big Bro, I'm hungry. Yo, pat my head. Yo, Big Bro, yo Big Bro, Big Bro.

HEITARO: I'm not your big brother! Get out!

They all stop at once. The next moment, they all cry together.

BABY GONPEIS: Wooh, waaaaaah. Waaaaaah, waaaaah. *(Crawling in circles around Heitaro.)*

HEITARO: Shut up!!

Again, they all stop at once. The next moment, they all cry together. Crying, they exit from the wing—Waaaaaah, waaaaah, waaaaaah, waaaaah.

HEITARO: …Phew…

Suddenly, the projector emits distortion—zhaaaaa. Then, where the Gonpeis were, now the uncle stands with only a loincloth on.

UNCLE: Stop that at once!

HEITARO: Uncle what are you doing in the nude?

UNCLE: Heitaro, you know you shouldn't make cute babies cry.

HEITARO: But…

UNCLE: Are you really a man? Are you really a samurai?

HEITARO: Uhh…
UNCLE: Such little…such little…such little…such little…such little…

Uncle's voice quickly becomes like a baby's.

HEITARO: U-Uncle?
BABY UNCLE: Abababa.
HEITARO: What?
BABY UNCLE: Abababa *(His upper body ♪ pops off and the lower half turns into a baby wearing a long bib.)* How dare you bully a little baby like me!
HEITARO: Another baby?!
BABY UNCLE: So what? What's wrong with a baby?
HEITARO: It's plenty wrong.
BABY UNCLE: What?
HEITARO: Get out!
BABY UNCLE: …Waaaaah, waaaaah. *(Starts to cry, walks a few steps, stops, and looks at Heitaro, and then starts to walk towards the wing.)* Aaaaaan, waaaaan, Heitaro's a bully. Waaaah. *(Stops again and glances at Heitaro, and then walks toward the wing again.)* Aaaaaah, waaaaanh, waaaaah. *(Exits stage right.)*
HEITARO: Phew…exploiting babies and even my uncle. These cunning *yokai* methods are disgusting and leave a bad taste in the mouth.

The night sky begins to lighten.

HEITARO: Now to forget the bad stuff and get some shuteye.
NARRATOR: Heitaro slept deeply that night as if nothing had happened.

Lights fade out. Words appear on the screen:

JULY 7, TANABATA STAR FESTIVAL

Scene 7. July 7

NARRATOR: From evening, it rained.

♪ *Sound of rain. Lights fade in. Heitaro is on the veranda dangling his legs over the edge.*

HEITARO: The Tanabata Star Festival is spoiled by this rain.
NARRATOR: But at night the rain stopped.

♪ *Sound of rain fades out.*

NARRATOR: The evening shone with a star-studded sky.

♪ *Insects are chirping.*

HEITARO: Yay, the stars are gorgeous.

At that moment, the distant buzzing of cicadas overlaps with the other insect sounds.

HEITARO: Strange. Cicadas at night?

The cicada sound grows louder—♪ miiiin, miiiin—and a shower ensues. The sliding doors slowly open, lights fade out, and beyond the doors a clear blue sky appears. Heitaro turns around.

HEITARO: Huh? It's nighttime now, isn't it? (♪...)

Thunderhead clouds are rising slow and thick into the blue sky. Suddenly like shadows, numerous fingers crowd in from below the blue sky for just a moment. The sliding doors slam shut. ♪ A wind bell rings—♪ tinkle, tinkle.

HEITARO: What's up now?

A wall softens and, forming hands and fingers, stretches out and shrinks back. Then a small hand jumps out from the upstage left wing.

HEITARO: Huh?

When Heitaro looks at the hand, it withdraws, and when he looks away,

173

it reappears and then disappears.

HEITARO: What the heck. Stop that peekaboo game. If you're coming out, just do it.

At once, small hands of fractal dimensions enter at a tremendous rate.

HEITARO: Oh my god, what's going on?

Watching the hands pass by, he notices an outsized hand come in at the end. He slices it at the root with his sword.

HEITARO: Yah!

♪ Pop! The fractally growing fingers disappear stage right. The outsized hand's root beckons them back. From stage right, another outsized hand with only three fingers appears. Heitaro notices it.

HEITARO: Not enough fingers.

At once, the hand stage left pulls off the surface of the three-fingered hand stage right. A six-fingered hand is revealed.

HEITARO: Too many fingers now.

At that moment, visuals of numerous fingers swarming are projected on-stage. ♪ Hurry-scurry… When the stage returns to its norm, the sound of a bell is heard from afar—♪ tinkle, tinkle.

HEITARO: Huh?

At once, ♪ Christmas songs come on loud. Simultaneously, the projector provides visuals of snowfall across the stage. In addition to snow, Christmas trees stand on two revolving stages. At the same time, snow crystals that increase fractally are projected on stage.

HEITARO: Wrong! Today is the Star Festival!

At once, a visual of the stars breaking up, followed by a return to normalcy. At the same time, from both wings, bamboo grass branches with many paper finger decorations appear. ♪ Music begins.

HEITARO: Right…today is the Star Festival.

The Star Festival decorations on the wings disappear.

HEITARO: I can't tell whether it's night or day, summer or winter anymore. These darn *yokai* monsters resort to so many tricks.

The night begins to lighten up. ♪ Sparrows begin to chirp.

HEITARO: Dawn? Oh, then the Star Festival is over.
NARRATOR: Heitaro falls into a deep sleep until noon.

Lights fade out. Words appear on the screen:

JULY 8

Scene 8. July 8

Tap, tap—low-key knocking.

HEITARO'S VOICE: Mumble, mumble.

The tapping continues.

HEITARO'S VOICE: Mm…mumble, mumble…

Lights fade in. Heitaro is sleeping in his futon.

NARRATOR: Heitaro must be exhausted. Tonight, he's gone to bed early.
VOICE: A lot, a lot, a lot. Here.
HEITARO'S VOICE: Uhhhhh… *(He is still asleep.)*
VOICE: Here, here, a lot, here.

From stage left, an enormous ear is listening.

VOICE: Sneaky-sneak. Psst, psst. A lot here. Here, here, wanna be here. Wanna be here.

The voice slowly gets louder, and Heitaro wakes up.

HEITARO'S VOICE: Huh?
VOICE: Wanna be, wanna be, wanna be, wanna be here.
HEITARO: You want to be…here? Oh, so you're not going to let me sleep tonight again, you monster of a *yokai*.
VOICE: Wanna be here, wanna be, wanna be, sneaky-sneak.
HEITARO: Shut the fuck up, sneaky-sneak.
VOICE: Wanna be, wanna be here.
HEITARO: Stay if you wanna.
VOICE: Wanna.

With that, the doors slide open and a gigantic face appears. Simultaneously, the ear stage left disappears.

HEITARO: Oh.

The face, now with swords growing out of its eyes, is crying.

FACE: It hurts, it hurts.
HEITARO: *(Growling.)* It really does look painful.

♪ *A sword grows out from between the eyebrows of the face, and slides straight down its face.*

FACE: Hurts, hurts.

The sword having slid down the center, the face breaks up into two parts.

FACE: It HURRRRRTS.

At that moment, ♪ teen beat music or overpowering tango is heard. At the same time, the hanging scrolls in the alcoves of the revolving stages sud-

denly go up in flames. The upstage area behind the cracked face also burns. In addition, a huge watermelon splits in two.

At once, a blackout, during which the sliding doors close.

Men appear in each alcove. Each pulls out his head; another head grows immediately; and the heads pile up on top of each other making a long skewer of faces. At the same time, another skewer of faces hops across the stage saying, "It hurts, it hurts."

Following that, a face caught between two skewered pieces of oden[5] *is hopping around. After that,* yokai *V, W, X, Y, Z, etc. pass by repeating, "It hurts, it hurts." Simultaneously, in a blackout flash, in the alcoves appear* yokai *A and B. At the same time, the sliding doors open and, against a spiral backdrop, a* yokai *appears whose head is spinning around and whose facial expression keeps changing—like flickering lights. The* yokai *lets off a cacophony of "It hurts, it hurts" and "Wanna be here."*

HEITARO: So I said, stay if you wanna!
YOKAI: *(All together.)* What?!!

Right away, ♪ the projector emits distortion—zhaaaaa. Simultaneously, ♪ the lights come back on. Leaving Heitaro, all the yokai *disappear.*

HEITARO: …Now what? *(♪ Tiiiiinkle.)*

Heitaro looks around.

HEITARO: But…tonight, they were even more festive than usual. *(A beat.)* Now, how much longer is this gonna continue. Ahhhhh. *(Yawns.)* They woke me up. Gotta get more shuteye. Whewwww. *(Gets into his futon.)* Night-night.

Lights fade out. ♪ During the fadeout, the yokai *peek in from the wings and look leisurely at Heitaro.*

YOKAI: *(In unison in a low tone.)* Night-night.

Blackout. Words appear on the screen:

JULY 9

♪ *Fade out.*

Scene 9. July 9

The lantern lights up, and Heitaro is reading a book. Insects are chirping.

HEITARO: ...It's quiet. They partied so much last night, they must be into rest and recovery today... *(Putting his book down, he goes to the veranda and looks up at the sky.)* Even the moon is on holiday today... It's pitch-dark outside.

At that moment, Heitaro happens to look at the wall stage left.

HEITARO: Uh-uh. *(Approaching the wall, he sees a hole.)*

Something like a finger jumps out and immediately jumps back in.

HEITARO: Huh?

Fingers jump in and out of other holes as well.

HEITARO: What's going on? *(Tries to pick up a fingerlike creature but can't.)* Darn.

Like the whack-a-mole game, fingers pop up and down.

HEITARO: Uhhhhhh.

One of the holes begins to move loosely.

HEITARO: Now, a hole is moving...

The hole continues to move and finally drops into another hole.

HEITARO: Eh?

At the same time, fingers emerge from all the holes.

HEITARO: Hey! *(Catches one finger.)* Gotcha. *(Pulls at the finger.)*

The finger stretches and stretches. Heitaro keeps pulling at it and ends up disappearing into the stage right wing. After a while, he reappears from the stage left wing still pulling the finger.

HEITARO: This is really weird. *(Lets go of the finger.)*

The finger creeps from the stage right wing towards its original hole. A Second Heitaro enters with his own fingers pinching the tip of a finger. This Second Heitaro's voice is the same as the first. Use a recording.

HEITARO: Oh no.

The Second Heitaro lets go of the finger, which creeps back into its own hole.

HEITARO & SECOND HEITARO: Who the heck are you?

Use ♪ a simultaneous voice multiplier. Both speak in unison.

HEITARO & SECOND HEITARO: I am Heitaro… What?! I am Heita-ro. What's that?

They are mirror images of each other.

HEITARO & SECOND HEITARO: Don't copy me… Wha–? You're telling me not to copy you… Oh, no…there's no end to it.
SECOND HEITARO: Anyways, I am Heitaro.
HEITARO: I AM HEI-TA-RO!!

At that moment, a third voice comes from the other side of the sliding doors.

THIRD HEITARO: I am the real Hei-ta-ro.

Heitaro and Second Heitaro look toward the sliding doors.

HEITARO & SECOND HEITARO: What?!

The sliding doors open to reveal the gigantic face of Heitaro, a screen projection.

THIRD HEITARO: I am the authentic Heitaro
HEITARO & SECOND HEITARO: My face is not so big.

Then the Fourth Voice speaks.

FOURTH HEITARO: Then, I am Heitaro.

The screen disappears and the Second Heitaro is standing there.

HEITARO & SECOND HEITARO: It's me again!
FOURTH HEITARO: I am the real one.
HEITARO: Oh no, one after another. All you disgusting specters, just get lost, will ya.
SECOND & FOURTH HEITARO: You're the ones going somewhere.
HEITARO: No, it's you lot! Just vanish, will ya!!
SECOND & FOURTH HEITARO: Vanish?
HEITARO: Right, vanish.
SECOND & FOURTH HEITARO: Then…let's vanish together.
HEITARO: What?!

Then the Fourth Heitaro's face turns 180 degrees to reveal a black hole—♪ ROAAAAAAAAR. At the same time, within the hole, a dark hole is growing larger and larger. In the end, it envelops everything. Use a projector for this.

Darkness.

HEITARO: Oh no.

♪ *Music and sound cut out. Quietude.*

HEITARO: It's dark. Really dark… Hey…I don't seem to exist anymore.

From afar, a woman's low, smooth, cool voice is heard.

VOICE: I live in the darkness of the blink of a human eye.
HEITARO: What?

At the same moment, ♪ waltz music is heard. The stage brightens up (with candles). The alcoves on both sides of the stage have turned into mirrors with numerous candles in front. The alcove floors are also covered with mirrors and miniature dancers are twirling (an effect achieved using magnets). The upstage side of the sliding doors is brightening up. When the doors open, mirrors with many candles in front of them become visible. The candles are mushrooming out of the floor.

HEITARO: What's this? *(Looks vacantly at the set.)* Who the hell are you, you *yokai*?

From the other side of the transom, the word "I" can be seen.

HEITARO: I?

The word is followed by a huge face of Heitaro with eyes closed—♪ Pera-pera.

HEITARO: What's this about?

The right eye opens. In that eye, the hiragana[6] *rendering of the word for "eye" (me, め) can be seen.*

HEITARO: Eye?

Next, the left eye opens. In it, the kanji *character for "eye" (目).*

HEITARO: Eye?

The character "eye" (目) jumps out of the visual eye and combines with the katakana *for "I" (ワ タ シ) to become "dream" (夢), which is pronounced "yume". At the same time, from stage left, the* hiragana *character "yu" (ゆ) walks across stage. Likewise, the "eye" (め) jumps out of the visual eye and follows after the* hiragana *character "yu" (ゆ), also making the word* yume, *which means "dream." Simultaneously, the sliding doors close. On each of the paper panels of the doors are visible the characters "yu" (ゆ) and "eye/me/I" (め) are visible.*

HEITARO: *Yu...me...* Is this a dream? Am I in a dream? You...me?

A human shadow is perceptible on the other side of the sliding doors. Simultaneously, the shadow knocks heavily on the doors—♪ THUD, THUD. Gonpachi's voice is heard...

GONPACHI'S VOICE: Hello there, hellooo... *(♪ THUD.)* Heitaro. You still asleep, eh? *(♪ THUD, THUD. ♪)* Get up, get up, Heitaro.
HEITARO: Is that you, Gonpachi?
GONPACHI'S VOICE: Are you still asleep? Hallooo. Get up. *(♪ THUD! ♪)*
HEITARO: Got to get up... But how am I gonna to get up?... I'm asleep right now... Oh, I get it. I need to get back to sleep again. That's it, that's it... All right, let's get some more lovely shuteye. Ahhhhhh...

Amid the loud knocking, dancers' waltzing, and the candlelight, Heitaro lies down. At the same time, the projector's distortion comes in—♪ zhaaaaa—and the rooted candles exit, the dancers exit, the alcove floor flips back to its usual side. Heitaro alone stays in the same position while the floor slides so that the straw mats come back up. At the same time, the Narrator speaks.

NARRATOR: Heitaro falls asleep in his own dream.

Blackout. Words appear on the screen:

JULY 10

Scene 10. July 10

At the same time, on the lower screen, letters appear at the top and bottom. The date jumps up and down, as if slightly askew. Simultaneously, Heitaro's gigantic face and the Japanese characters for "dream" disappear. The sliding doors with "dream" on them open, and the doors then return to normal. The doors open again for Gonpachi's entry.

GONPACHI: Heitaro, Heitaro.
HEITARO: Hm…
GONPACHI: Heitaro!

Heitaro opens his eyes and raises his upper body. All at once, the doors close, ♪ the waltz music ends, the letters disappear, and the daytime lights come on. ♪ The cry of cicadas—miiiiiin, miiiiiin.

HEITARO: Oh.
GONPACHI: Heitaro, get out of bed.
HEITARO: Gonpachi?
GONPACHI: It's noon already, for crying out loud.

Heitaro looks around.

HEITARO: Yeah… *(Turning to Gonpachi.)* Say, are you the real Gonpachi?
GONPACHI: Huh?
HEITARO: Are you the real thing?
GONPACHI: You're still half asleep, Heitaro.
HEITARO: No, I've been deceived by them too many times.
GONPACHI: You are still going through a really rough time.
HEITARO: Yeah. Every night, every night… So are you the real thing?
GONPACHI: Of course, I am. Anyways, it's daytime right now.
HEITARO: Oh yeah. Hey, how are you? Have you recovered?
GONPACHI: Yep, I've somehow managed to get over it.
HEITARO: Great.
GONPACHI: There's more important things than that, Heitaro.

HEITARO: Oh yeah?
GONPACHI: Look at this. *(Takes out a short sword from his side.)*
HEITARO: Ohh.
GONPACHI: This is a family heirloom, the "sword that destroys evil." It can destroy shapeshifting foxes, raccoons, and *yokai*.
HEITARO: Fantastic.
GONPACHI: This'll take care of specters in no time. They'll beat a hasty retreat.
HEITARO: They might foam at the mouth once and drop dead.
GONPACHI: I'll make 'm foam twice or 100 times.
HEITARO: ...Hold it...
GONPACHI: Hm?
HEITARO: What's going on?
GONPACHI: Huh?
HEITARO: The writing desk is...behaving strangely.

The legs of the low table are growing longer.

GONPACHI: ...In broad daylight.
HEITARO: The legs are getting longer.

The low table rises as far as the top of the backdrop stage left. The two men look up at it. After a while, the table descends with a strange white object that bubbles and foams.

HEITARO: It's foaming.

♪ *Bubble, bubble. Then, a face appears slyly from out of the bubbles, making a big noise—GURGLE, GURGLE.*

GONPACHI: There you are, ya monster!! Take this!

Gonpachi slashes at the monster's face. With a metallic keening sound, sparks fly. His sword breaks in two and flies apart.

GONPACHI: Oh, no...

A momentary blackout. ♪ A ROAR of laughter. The next moment, the head of foam has turned into a stone mortar.

HEITARO: Oh, that's the stone mortar from the kitchen.
GONPACHI: No…no, no, no.
HEITARO: Huh.

Gonpachi, looking at the sword tip, shakes.

GONPACHI: NOOOOOOO.
HEITARO: What's happened?
GONPACHI: It's broken. *(Collapses weak-kneed to the floor.)* Oh…
HEITARO: Don't lose heart, Gonpachi.
GONPACHI: The sword…the sword.
HEITARO: That's a real disaster. Your precious family heirloom has been ruined.
GONPACHI: Actually, I took it out of the house without my father's permission.
HEITARO: What?! Your father doesn't know?!
GONPACHI: I cannot bear to live anymore.
HEITARO: Don't talk like that…
GONPACHI: This sword was a gift from the Lord to my ancestors for their courage in the final Battle of Sekigahara.[7] I cannot face my great Lord, my brave ancestors, or my honorable father.
HEITARO: What the hell are you saying? You didn't use the heirloom as a joke. You were concerned for my safety…

Gonpachi points the broken sword toward his abdomen.

GONPACHI: Nothing else can be done.
HEITARO: Hold it!!
GONPACHI: Forgive me.

He plunges the sword hard into his abdomen—♪ doshyuuu ♪.

HEITARO: No!!
GONPACHI: Ughh!
NARRATOR: Gonpachi pushes the sword straight across his abdomen.
GONPACHI: Uuuuugghhh!!

Gonpachi withdraws the sword from his abdomen.

NARRATOR: With the blade, he now pierces his own throat.

♪ *Sssinkh. Fresh blood sprays the sliding doors. Gonpachi totters in the direction of the doors, hits them, and falls down.*

HEITARO: Gonpachi!!

♪ *Music ends.*

NARRATOR: Gonpachi dies right away.

Heitaro runs over and shakes him to no avail.

HEITARO: This is terrible. Oh god, the *yokai* have killed him.

NARRATOR: Even the fearless Heitaro is suddenly struck down in dejection.

HEITARO: I let a precious friend die... Oh no...

NARRATOR: Overwhelmed by feelings for his old friend, Heitaro sits down absent-mindedly.

HEITARO: Ahh, this is mortifying.

NARRATOR: Bringing his hands together in prayer, he has a sudden thought.

HEITARO: How shall I explain all this to everyone? Gonpachi mistook a stone mortar for a monster and slashed it with his sword. The blade broke, and in atonement, he committed ritual disembowelment... Who would believe such a statement? *(At that moment, he looks at the stone mortar.)* Oh my god.

The stone mortar has turned into a gigantic chikuwa.

HEITARO: It's a *chikuwa*!! I am even more confused about what I should say. Gonpachi slashed a *chikuwa* and broke his sword. So, he committed ritual disembowelment. Oh no, at this rate, I will be accused of killing him.

NARRATOR: Heitaro is sick at heart.

HEITARO: Even if they don't accuse me of murder, they will want to know why I didn't stop him when I was right by him.

NARRATOR: His thoughts head at great speed towards despair.

HEITARO: Wha…

The area where Gonpachi's corpse is laid out is lighting up hazily. A transparent Gonpachi rises leisurely. The projector remains in the same position. Above the transom, the Japanese character for "funeral" (弔) appears.

HEITARO: Are you undecided, Gonpachi?

The ghost of Gonpachi stands in the hazy light.

HEITARO: You may be mortified, but without any hesitation, go to the eastern paradise.

GONPACHI: *(Mumbles.)* It's galling. There are so many things I wanted to do. I shouldn't have brought that sword with me. Oh my god, it's broken now. I am broken…

HEITARO: Gonpachi…

GONPACHI: I hate the monsters that killed me. *(Looks at Heitaro sharply.)* I hate you for attracting the *yokai*.

HEITARO: Hey, Gonpachi.

GONPACHI: I hate you, I do. I'm mortified. This is hopeless.

HEITARO: Hate me… Go ahead and hate me.

GONPACHI: I curse you… I curse you to death.

HEITARO: Ahh, kill me. Go ahead and kill me.

GONPACHI: I hate you for being so calm and collected. It's galling… I know, I'll curse your brother. I'll curse him to death.

HEITARO: My brother?

GONPACHI: I'll kill Katsuya.

HEITARO: No!! Don't do such a stupid thing!

GONPACHI: At the dead of night.

Above the word "funeral," a clock face appears. The hour, minute, and second hands move.

GONPACHI: Before two o'clock in the morning, I will curse him to death.

The clock hands stop at 1 o'clock, 55 minutes and 40 seconds. At the same time, the hands slide over the clock face to the "funeral" character (弔) and by adding three strokes transform the character to "younger brother" (弟).

HEITARO: Stop that! Take me instead. I'll die.
GONPACHI: Will you die?
HEITARO: Yeah, I will. I don't care about my own life.
GONPACHI: You don't?
HEITARO: I don't.
GONPACHI: In that case, commit ritual disembowelment as I did!
HEITARO: Right, I will commit ritual disembowelment.
NARRATOR: Saying this, Heitaro sits formally for the ritual.
HEITARO: I can't stand outliving Gonpachi anyway, as that would be a terrible disgrace. This must be my destined lifespan.
NARRATOR: Heitaro, in preparation for suicide, places his hand on his short sword when—

The sound of hard knocking on the door—THUD, THUD.

GONPACHI'S VOICE: Heitaro… *(THUD, THUD.)* Heitaro, Heitaro.
HEITARO: Don't rush me, Gonpachi.
GONPACHI'S VOICE: HEITARO!!

♪ Zhaaaaa! The bloodied doors open and then return to their normal white appearance. The living Gonpachi shows his face. At the same time, the clock, the character for "younger brother," chikuwa, and Gonpachi's corpse also all return to normal. ♪ The music stops. Lights return to normal (i.e., to nighttime).

GONPACHI: Hey, Heitaro, what are you up to?
HEITARO: I'm gonna do it.
GONPACHI: Don't do anything stupid.

Gonpachi runs over to Heitaro and grabs his short sword.

HEITARO: Oh…
GONPACHI: Why are you doing this? *(Takes the short sword.)*
HEITARO: Why? Well, you died 'cuz of me.
GONPACHI: Who does "you" refer to?
HEITARO: What do you mean by "who," Gonpachi? Wait a moment. *(Looks at where Gonpachi's corpse was.)* He's not there.
GONPACHI: Who isn't?
HEITARO: Gonpachi.
GONPACHI: I'm here.
HEITARO: I mean the corpse.
GONPACHI: Corpse?
HEITARO: And the *chikuwa.*
GONPACHI: What's this about?
HEITARO: *(A beat.)* I was duped again. Oh hell.
NARRATOR: Heitaro explains what happened to Gonpachi.
GONPACHI: Just as I thought.
HEITARO: Huh?
GONPACHI: The dream I had while I was feverish was just like what you said. I got worried and came over here in a hurry.
HEITARO: I'm sorry, Gonpachi.
GONPACHI: That was a close call.
HEITARO: The next one will be the decisive battle.
GONPACHI: The monsters have moved on to targeting our lives.
HEITARO: Yeah, seems that way…
NARRATOR: Belated, Gonpachi feels shivers up and down his spine.
GONPACHI: Wait, Heitaro, aren't you afraid?
HEITARO: No way.
GONPACHI: Ha-hah. You are invincible, Heitaro.
HEITARO: I won't ever be duped again.
GONPACHI: That's the spirit. That's the spirit.

The night sky begins to lighten up. ♪ *Chirp, chirp. Lights indicate dawn.*

GONPACHI: It's dawn.
HEITARO: Until just a while ago, I thought it was broad daylight.
GONPACHI: Better get some sleep.
HEITARO: Right you are.
GONPACHI: Well, then, I'll head back. You take extra care and be on

guard now.

HEITARO: You, too, Gonpachi.

GONPACHI: Yeah, good night.

HEITARO: Good night.

Gonpachi opens the sliding doors and exits.

HEITARO: Whatever happens, I won't be surprised. Whaoooo. I am so sleepy. I feel as if I haven't slept in days. Now to sleep. *(Lies down.)*

Lights fade out. ♪ Fade in.

NARRATOR: Calculations show that 20 days have passed since the holes in the wall moved.

At the same time, large words appear on the screen:

JULY 30

Scene 11. July 30

Lights fade in. Heitaro is sitting absentmindedly on the veranda. ♪ Fade out. ♪ Insects chirp.

HEITARO: For some reason, my chest itches. July will be over tomorrow… Summer…will be, too.

From afar, ♪ clatter, clatter…

HEITARO: That's a sad sound.

From afar, a voice calls out, "Yoo-hoo."

HEITARO: On an evening like this, many thoughts run through my mind. What am I going to do after this? Where on earth am I, right now? Where on earth am I going?

The area darkens swiftly.

HEITARO: Ah, they've arrived.

In the dark, the sliding doors open, and a visual of a long train passing through is projected.

HEITARO: What the hell is this? *(Watches for a while.)*

In front of the passing train, a robot walks by making mechanical noises—♪ metallic shuffle, shuffle, whirr-whirr. The train passes through and now the silhouettes of boys and girls playing with hula-hoops are projected like a shadow play—sparkle, sparkle, shimmer, shimmer. Heitaro watches for a while.

From the bottom of the screen, a cityscape rises up, and an airplane flies overhead—♪ VOOOM.

From afar, a voice calls out, "Heitaro." The screen disappears and a short man with a stick stands in the spotlight.

SHORT MAN: *(In a high voice.)* Heitaro.
HEITARO: What?
SHORT MAN: Aren't you lonely?
HEITARO: Huh?
SHORT MAN: Aren't you lonely, Heitaro?
HEITARO: No, I am not.

At once, the short man disappears and from above a strange-looking giant of a short man with a huge stick appears.

GIANT SHORT MAN: Don't you feel lonely?
HEITARO: Huh?
GIANT SHORT MAN: Come on, don't you feel lonely?
HEITARO: Oh…
GIANT SHORT MAN: Heitaro, where are you?
HEITARO: *(A beat.)* Here.
GIANT SHORT MAN: *(A beat.)* Heitaro, where are you going?

191

HEITARO: Where?
GIANT SHORT MAN: Don't you feel lonely, Heitaro?

Heitaro is silent.

GIANT SHORT MAN: Look, Heitaro…I'll show you the future.
HEITARO: What?
GIANT SHORT MAN: Here we go.

He waves his stick. At the same time, the strange, giant short man disappears. On the screen, "The History of the Human Race" is projected with tremendous speed. Heitaro watches it. In the end, the earth cracks up into pieces. At the same time, powdery bits fly about the whole screen. ♪ Glitter, glitter. In the dark, tiny, shiny things float around.

HEITARO: They're like glowworms or stars…

In the dark, tiny stars join together and separate, making numerous shining shapes…

HEITARO: Something…somehow…my chest itches.

In a flash, everything disappears with a ♪ swoosh. The set returns to how it was at the beginning of Scene 11. Heitaro is sitting absentmindedly on the veranda. ♪ Insects chirp. ♪ Scarab beetles let off low, booming sounds.

HEITARO: Somehow…it's doubly sad. I feel helpless. *(Coming back to himself.)* No, I mustn't be like this… Those horrible monsters are trying to make me feel lonely and depressed. This is their scheme to destroy me. *(Standing up on the veranda.)* No, no. Feeling helpless is the most dangerous. I must pull myself together.

The scarab beetle's boom-boom grows louder. Lights fade out.

NARRATOR: The following morning, Heitaro could not recall what he had seen the night before.

Words appear on the screen:

JULY 31

Scene 12. July 31

Heitaro is standing on the veranda.

HEITARO: A whole month has passed. Today's the last day of July. Those frigging monsters, how long are they gonna keep this up? I'd better bust them good and proper soon.

Heitaro holds his sword in front, pushes the sheath to one side, and looks at the weapon. A loud noise—♪ BANG. Then—♪ CRASH, ♪ CRASH. Huge feet enter from above, below, and the wings—then disappear. Huge hands also appear in a similar way. The sliding doors open and another hand appears. The three hands aim to catch Heitaro in their grasp. The projector is clicking.

HEITARO: You've come. Yahhh!!

Heitaro attacks them with his sword. The three hands hurriedly withdraw behind the doors, which close after them.

HEITARO: Don't run away!

Heitaro places his hands on the sliding doors when there is another loud noise—♪ BANG. At the same time, a shout with rising intonation echoes. Old, damaged film must be used here and whenever Sanmoto speaks.

SANMOTO'S VOICE: I COMMAND YOU TO STOP!
HEITARO: Huh?
SANMOTO'S VOICE: I have arrived.
HEITARO: Very well. You may enter.
NARRATOR: Heitaro instinctively understands that the voice belongs to the boss of the *yokai.*

193

Heitaro steps back, faces the sliding doors, and gets into position to fight. After a short time, the doors slide open and a dignified man of around 40 years of age, wearing a light blue ceremonial outfit with a floral kimono garment and two swords at his side, enters quickly and sits down quietly.

Heitaro immediately attacks him.

HEITARO: Yah!

For a moment the projector clicks. The seated man disappears in a flash behind the doors.

HEITARO: Oh my god.

The next moment, the man is back in his seated position. Heitaro attacks him again. The projector is clicking.

HEITARO: Yahhh.

Again, the man disappears in a flash behind the doors.

SANMOTO'S VOICE: *(From behind the doors.)* You are wasting time.

The doors slide open and the same man, now double his former size, enters lightly.

HEITARO: Hm.
SANMOTO: You cannot kill me with human power. I came to deliver a message. SHEATHE YOUR SWORD and QUIETEN YOUR HEART and MIND.

Putting away his sword, Heitaro speaks.

HEITARO: I will listen with all my heart.

Sanmoto sits calmly and, retaining his seating posture, teleports in front of Heitaro. Use projection of old, damaged film.

SANMOTO: Though still young, you are highly commendable.

Projector stops.

HEITARO: What's that?
SANMOTO: Ha-ha, you are quite a personage, Heitaro.
HEITARO: I am not happy to receive praise from a monster. Who the hell are you?

Projection of damaged film begins.

SANMOTO: My name is Gorozaemon Sanmoto.[8] My last name is written Yamanmoto but pronounced Sanmoto.

Projector stops.

HEITARO: You cannot be a human being. Are you a fox or a raccoon?

Projection of damaged film starts.

SANMOTO: I do not belong to the lower species like foxes and raccoons.

Projector stops.

HEITARO: Then are you a *tengu*?[9]
SANMOTO: NO, I am not a *tengu*.
HEITARO: Then what are you?
SANMOTO: I belong to the Maoo demons who live in the universe of 3,000 worlds, comprising all time and space, and I live in the time-space of the blink of a human eye. I am a member of the Maoo demons.[10]
HEITARO: Maoo
SANMOTO: YES.
HEITARO: What is a Maoo like?
SANMOTO: You will soon learn.
NARRATOR: Saying this, Sanmoto grinned.

The sound of something being boiled down and other noisy sounds, too, are heard.

HEITARO: Hm?

Worms come pouring out in the thousands from below the tatami *matting, the gaps at the top, bottom, and sides of the walls, and the chinks in the sliding doors, and then rush toward Heitaro.*

HEITARO: Nooo! *(Freezes on the spot.)*
NARRATOR: There is only one thing that Heitaro is afraid of—worms.
HEITARO: Aaaaargh.

Worms reach his feet and start to climb up his legs—♪ shinny-shinny, slimy-slimy.

HEITARO: *(Still glued to the spot.)* I won't be defeated by these creatures. Ahhhhhhhhhhhhhh…
NARRATOR: Sweat pours off his whole body. All he can do is to push his feet firmly into the *tatami* floor in order to stay conscious.
HEITARO: Let dawn come. Then all this will fade into oblivion. I won't be defeated.
NARRATOR: Heitaro clenches his teeth and perseveres.

The projector's sandstorm flashes on—♪ zhaaaaaaa. The next moment, the worms vanish.

HEITARO: Ooooooh…
SANMOTO: Ha-ha-hah.

Heitaro is furious and glares at Sanmoto.

SANMOTO: You persevered well. Your bravery and endurance are second to none. HOWEVER—
HEITARO: What now?
SANMOTO: There are matters in this world that human power cannot control.

HEITARO: You were trying to show me that?

SANMOTO: Exactly. Depending only on your own strength without acknowledging fear, the work of the Maoo will continue.

The projector screens the ferocious explosion of a hydrogen bomb—♪ KEBOOOOOOOOOOOOOOOOOOOOOOOOM.

HEITARO: Ohhh.

SANMOTO: Now I must move on some 210 years.

For a moment, the projector screens in reverse rotation—♪ whirr, whirr...

SANMOTO: Hereafter, nothing mysterious will ever occur in this house again. Gonpachi will recover his health, and Gonpei and Katsuya will return.

HEITARO: Is that true?

SANMOTO: You did not falter under the sustained barrage of terrifying threats. I have overstayed my visit here. I have never met a human like you.

Projection of damaged film starts.

SANMOTO: Well, this is the end of my sojourn. I thank you. *(Bows to Heitaro.)*

Heitaro bows involuntarily. Projector stops.

HEITARO: Are you departing?

Projection of damaged film cuts in.

SANMOTO: I am about to leave. Oblige me by seeing me off.

Sanmoto opens his kimono wide to show a very large hole in the middle of the cloth and himself. At the same time, the sliding doors open slightly and the round moon moves through the large hole towards Heitaro. It then goes back through the kimono hole and rises above Sanmoto's head. At the same time, a gigantic Sanmoto enveloped in smoke rises above the transom, catches the rising moon and throws it into his mouth. At the same time, the alcove floors flip over, the sliding doors open wide, and some of the matting flips over. All the yokai *that had haunted the house make a final appearance.*

Behind Sanmoto is the huge moon. At the same time, the Sanmoto below vanishes.

HUGE SANMOTO: I inhabit multiple places. Farewell. No more shall I visit you.

At that moment, the sliding doors close, the tatami *mats flip back, the huge Sanmoto disappears. At once, the small Sanmoto on the other side of the transom jumps into a hole in the moon, is sucked in, and vanishes. Immediately—♪ schlip, schlip, schlip—the huge moon sinks under the horizon. In the quiet aftermath, Heitaro stands alone.*

HEITARO: They have gone. This cannot be a dream…
NARRATOR: No further weird happenings ever occurred.

Heitaro turns leisurely toward the audience.

HEITARO: The sense of helplessness that overwhelmed me on that day has transformed into a sad yet pure feeling. Is this because it is autumn? Once is enough for such an experience. But in my heart, I am tempted to say, "Sanmoto Maoo, if you like, please visit again."

At the same time, the projector shows something flying through the air—♪ flutter, flutter, flutter. Then piercing rays from the setting sun seem to cancel out the fluttering and envelop all that is around—♪ soft clicking sounds. The colors intensify and then suddenly the sky turns dark.

Only the moon is hanging in the sky—♪.

THE END

1   On July 7, the weaver star and cowherder star are said to traverse the Milky Way to renew their ancient bond of love. In Japan, the starry lovers are celebrated during the Tanabata Star Festival with lively decorations and wishes written on strips of colored paper. "Tanabata (Star Festival)," Nippon.com, July 4, 2015, https://www.nippon.com/en/features/jg00097/tanabata-star-festival.html.

2   *Chikuwa* is a fish paste product shaped like bamboo. Wikipedia, s.v. "Bon Festival," last modified August 7, 2019, 10:53, https://en.wikipedia.org/wiki/Chikuwa.

3   A *shoji* is a sliding door or divider with paper over a wooden lattice.

4   Sanpei Hayashiya (1925–1980) was a famous *rakugo* comedian. His signature line was "So sorry," which was said with his hand against his forehead.

5   *Oden* is a winter hotpot dish with chunky ingredients sometimes on skewers. Wikipedia, s.v. "Oden," last modified October 11, 2019, 03:45, https://en.wikipedia.org/wiki/Oden.

6   *Hiragana* is one of the three syllabaries used in written Japanese. Wikipedia, s.v. "Hiragana," last modified December 15, 2019, 08:21, https://en.wikipedia.org/wiki/Hiragana.

7   The Battle of Sekigahara was a decisive battle in 1600 that preceded the establishment of the Tokugawa shogunate. Wikipedia, s.v. "Battle of Sekigahara," last modified December 6, 2019, 05:35, https://en.wikipedia.org/wiki/Battle_of_Sekigahara.

8   Gorozaemon Sanmoto is an original character without any legendary connections. Manipulator koichic Iimuro's features were used for Sanmoto's face.

9   *Tengu* are *yokai* associated with dogs and birds of prey. They are both protectors of nature as well as troublemakers who trigger natural disasters and war. Wikipedia, s.v. "Tengu," last modified December 2, 2019, 11:53, https://en.wikipedia.org/wiki/Tengu.

10 In Buddhism, the Maoo or the Demon King of the Sixth Heaven, is believed to interfere in a Buddhist devotee's practices. But if the devotee perseveres in his devotion, the Maoo's interference can become an opportunity for spiritual growth. Wikipedia, s.v. "天魔," last modified September 25, 2018, 11:47, https://ja.wikipedia.org/wiki/天魔.

Chapter 8

Kiyokazu Yamamoto and *Choan and the Ripped Umbrella: Heisei Trick Peep Show*

Choan and the Ripped Umbrella: Heisei Trick Peep Show was commissioned by Youkiza and premiered in December 2008 at Theatre Tram. The scriptwriter and director Kiyokazu Yamamoto (1939–2010) was a founding member of the Theatre Center 68/69, which became the 68/71 Black Tent Theatre and is now called the Black Tent Theatre. They are notable Brechtian and experimental companies. Together with Makoto Satoh and Tadashi Kato, Yamamoto was a main resident playwright and director in these groups. In 1983, he won the prestigious Kishida Drama Prize for *Pinocchio Jambalaya* (Pinokio janbaraya, 1982). Well-known among his Brechtian adaptations are *Hazama and Sumi* (Hazama to Sumi-chan, 1993), based on *The Good Person of Setzuan*, and *Mother Courage in the Hidden Fortress* (2002). The present Youkiza head, Magosaburo XII, began his own experimentations in the 1970s, when he collaborated with Theatre 68/Black Tent practitioners like Yamamoto and Kazuyoshi Kushida, the sole actor in Youkiza's production of *Choan and the Ripped Umbrella*.

The play is about an Edo doctor who stops at nothing to satisfy his greed for money and what it can buy. He tricks, exploits, extorts, and kills his way to riches. The themes of greed, cruelty, and defiance of civil order are universal and connect well with similar problems in the twenty-first century, while the allusions to Confucian ethics in the original are toned down. Modernization of the performance text includes sufficient modification of the Edo speech patterns so that contemporary Japanese viewers can understanding the dialogue yet enjoy the premodern flavor of the language. For further discussion on this play, refer to the third section of Chapter 3.

Selected Chronology

This lists only the collaborations between Kiyokazu Yamamoto and Youkiza.

2006 *A Restaurant of Many Orders* (Chumon no ooi ryoriten) (adapt., script, dir.) by Kenji Miyazawa for Youkiza at Theatre Tram, Tokyo

2008 *Choan and the Ripped Umbrella* (adapt./dir.) for Youkiza at Theatre Tram

Fig. 8.1. Kiyokazu Yamamoto, *Choan and the Ripped Umbrella: Heisei Trick Peep Show*, 2008, Theatre Tram, Tokyo. Courtesy of Youkiza.

Choan and the Ripped Umbrella: Heisei Trick Peep Show

Adapted by Kiyokazu Yamamoto
Translated by Mari Boyd

Cast of Characters (in order of appearance)
MOMO, broker's wife
MAN, young woman from the poultry shop
GENTA, greengrocer's boy
KAN or **OKAN,** assistant at the Murai clinic
CHOAN MURAI, a quack doctor
DOJURO FUJIKAKE, former samurai
JUBEI, farmer and Soyo's husband
SOYO or **OSOYO,** Choan's sister
CHUZO OF KAIZUKA, an employment agent
GUNZO SASAGAWA, Edo city magistrate
RIYO or **ORIYO,** wife of Dojuro Fujikake
SADA, widower, manservant at the Murai household
SENTARO, adopted son of Gohei
SANJI, played by the Choan actor, blood brother to Choan
DOLL SANJI (a stringless puppet), same as above
YOSUKE, shop attendant at the Iseya Pawnbroker's shop
KIYOSHICHI, shop attendant at the Iseya Pawnbroker's shop
GOHEI, master of the Iseya Pawnbroker's shop
KYUHACHI, head clerk at the Iseya Pawnbroker's shop
ROKUEMON, Kyuhachi's uncle
MINOMATSU, baby son of Dojuro Fujikake
DONOSUKE, older son of Dojuro Fujikake
ROJIEMON, pallbearer
IDOROKU, pallbearer
ICHIROBEI, widower
CORPSE, Fumi, wife of Ichirobei
YOUNG MAN, Yosuke at a Yoshiwara tea house[1]
GOROBEI, landlord
GUZUICHI, Chuzo's follower
HAGEMATSU, Chuzo's follower

In the Youkiza production, Magosaburo XII would manipulate the string objects Sada, Jubei, Dojuro, Soyo, Gohei, Fumi, Rokuemon, and Gorobei. Chie Youki would manipulate Kan, Kyuhachi, Guzuichi, and Sayoginu. Ikuko Youki would handle Riyo and Minomatsu, while Kazuma Youki would handle Genta, Donosuke, and Yosuke. Kazuyoshi Kushida would play Choan as a regular human actor interacting with the performing-objects.

The setting. The backdrops of Akabanebashi Bridge and Nihonzutsumi embankment provide the original cityscape. Either one should be visible throughout the play. Each scene is built with simple props representing these locales.

Scene 1. Dr. Choan Murai's Kojimachi Residence in Edo

The ambience of a general practitioner's office should be conveyed by the entrance to the residence. Momo, Man, and Genta are waiting for their medicine.

MOMO: You know, our doctor is still single. I'd like to introduce him to a nice lady.

MAN: That's so like you—always matchmaking, always up to a thing or two.

GENTA: Your aim's to saddle him with a wife, get a money gift out of him, and use it to pay for the medicine.

MOMO: What with this bad cold sweeping through town, medication costs are no joke. The doctor must be full of glee.

GENTA: Dr. Murai's not the only one. All the doctors are grinning like monkeys.

MAN: Then doctors should pray to the Divine Wind rather than the Divine Farmer.

MOMO: Really, you have a nasty tongue in your pretty face.

The three laugh. Kan enters with medicine in envelopes.

KAN: Here's your medicine, folks. One for the girl from the poultry shop, one for the greengrocer's boy, and one for the broker's missis. When people come for medicine one after another like this, I get no rest. I need a raise.

A bell rings.

GENTA: It's evening already.
MAN: Dark clouds are filling the sky.
MOMO: I bet it's going to rain.
GENTA: Yikes, better get going before it rains.

MOMO: Thank you…
GENTA, MAN & MOMO: …Very much. *(They head for the front gate downstage right.)*

Man opens the sliding door and exits. The others follow and exit stage right.
The sound of flint stones being struck.

KAN: It's evening already. I'll light a lantern.

Kan brings out a lantern and lights it. Revealed is Choan himself in a black haori *coat worn casually in townsman style.*

CHOAN: With this flu raging in town, even I have been busy since morning. Now most of the patients are gone. *(Spotting Kan.)* Ah, Okan. If you've finished, you can go on home.
KAN: Thank you, Doctor.

Heavy rainfall is heard. Kan looks outside from the entrance.

KAN: Oh, it's begun to rain. I'll borrow an umbrella.
CHOAN: Right, help yourself.
KAN: Well, sir, I will come again tomorrow.

Kan opens the umbrella and exits stage left. The sound of rain. A bell rings. From the hanamachi,[2] *Dojuro, a masterless samurai, enters dressed casually in a* haori *coat with two swords at his side. Wearing clogs, he holds a white umbrella with a wellhead frame and wisteria pattern.*

DOJURO: Excuse me, is Dr. Murai at home?
CHOAN: Well, Dojuro, is it? Take your shoes off and come on in.
DOJURO: Thank you, I will.

Dojuro leaves his umbrella at the entrance and steps up into the reception room.

CHOAN: The maid has gone home, so I can't even offer you tea.

DOJURO: Not to worry. Thanks to your treatment, I have recovered completely and wanted to let you know in person. Thank you very much, Doctor.

CHOAN: That is very gratifying. I am surprised myself at how quickly you have recovered. The medication I concocted must have been just right for you. It goes without saying that medicine is a caring profession. As you can tell, I am rock-bottom poor, but when it comes to treatment, I put profit aside and provide the best.

DOJURO: I admire your attitude to life.

CHOAN: I have never come across a patient with chest pains like yours. You must have had many troubles in life.

DOJURO: Yes, I became a drifting samurai due to circumstances. Many years have passed. The long-term stress has done me in.

CHOAN: I see. But as they say, "If at first you don't succeed, try, try again." Good luck will come your way eventually.

DOJURO: Yes… Oh yes, I've run out of medicine. Could you replenish my supply for the way home?

CHOAN: Certainly, I will prepare some for you. Please wait a while.

Choan stands and goes upstage to another room. Dojuro smokes. Jubei, a farmer, enters from the hanamichi. *He is barefoot and wears a woven hat.*

JUBEI: I hoped to return from the Yoshiwara pleasure quarters to Kojimachi before sundown, but a sudden shower prevented me. *(Entering the terrace housing.)* At last, I'm back.

Choan has just appeared with Dojuro's medicine.

CHOAN: There you are, Jubei. How'd it go?

JUBEI: Right, everything went fine as you'd already prepared the way. From Oume's ransom, three gold coins[3] were deducted to cover her costumes and accessories. Five gold coins went to a guarantor called Sanji. So I had to pay out a total of eight gold coins.

CHOAN: The conventions of selling someone into bondage require that much. Did you secure the remaining 42 gold coins?

JUBEI: Yep, I concealed it in my bellyband and tied that securely to my waist.

CHOAN: That's the price of your daughter's body. Take good care of that cash.

JUBEI: Of course, I will. She worried that if she were not around, there'd be no one to take care of her mom and dad. She didn't resent me but was devoted to the last. To sell such a daughter into harsh servitude is an evil deed.

CHOAN: The poor girl. She is my niece after all. I would like to do something for her, but the affliction called poverty prevents me. I feel mortified, but it's not as if she has died. When the term of service ends, she will be able to return home to her parents. Just wait it out.

JUBEI: Thank you. Thank you. *(Sobs.)*

CHOAN: *(Realizing that Dojuro has been waiting all this time.)* Goodness, I've kept you waiting. Please excuse me. *(Noticing the medicine.)* I almost forgot to give you your medicine.

DOJURO: Thank you. *(He puts the envelope in a small wrapping cloth.)* You seem to be in dire circumstances.

CHOAN: Dojuro, you've had your share of troubles, so has this Jubei here, too.

JUBEI: Choan, don't share my hard luck story with strangers.

CHOAN: You know, as I see it, tearjerkers are a way of making fortunate connections.

JUBEI: In that case, I will tell my story. My brother-in-law here was a farmer from Fujikawa in Mikawa province.

CHOAN: I have a younger sister.

JUBEI: Choan wasn't physically strong enough to be a farmer. When his parents passed on, he called me over right away from a nearby village and gave me his sister Soyo for wife and had me adopted as the family head.

CHOAN: I went to the capital, studied medicine, and managed to become a doctor. As you see, I barely make a living…

JUBEI: As for me, my wife and I were soon blessed with a baby girl. But life has its ups and downs and both of us came down with prolonged illness. Bad harvests continued over the years but we got by, borrowing money with our land as collateral to pay our taxes, Finally, this year we were unable to pay the debt and lost our farm. Hearing this, my wife fell ill again.

CHOAN: My sister's illness can be cured with ginseng and powdered rhino horn drinks. I knew that well, but the costs are immense.

JUBEI: My daughter asked to be sold to a house to pay off the debts. I was adopted into the family. If the land passed out of my hands, both our ancestors as well as the world would badmouth me. Without telling her mother, I brought our daughter to the capital and, through my brother-in-law's connection, I buried my girl in the world of torment called Yoshiwara today. *(Sobs.)*
DOJURO: I see.

The three sink into melancholy thoughts.

CHOAN: We have talked too long about private matters.
DOJURO: I have overstayed my welcome. I should take my leave.
JUBEI: Ahh, I will leave for home, tomorrow.
DOJURO: Take care on the road.
CHOAN: I'll get a lantern for you.
DOJURO: Oh, please don't bother.
JUBEI: It was good to talk, sir.
DOJURO: *(To Jubei.)* If karma allows, we will meet again.
CHOAN: I will see you again.

Music. Dojuro exits via the hanamichi *with the lantern.*

JUBEI: *(Looks at the umbrella.)* Oh, this umbrella…
CHOAN: Oh, that's Dojuro's. He must have forgotten it as the rain stopped.
JUBEI: Should I go after him?
CHOAN: No, I can deliver it tomorrow.
JUBEI: I will take this money to the wife and make her happy. I'll leave at the morning bell tomorrow.
CHOAN: Why don't you take it easy tomorrow and rest?
JUBEI: No, I want to hurry home with this cash, get my farm back, and buy some ginseng and powdered rhino horn for my wife. I will leave tomorrow morning.
CHOAN: My sister is lucky to have a kind husband like you. If you are leaving at the morning bell, you should rest now.
JUBEI: I'll follow your advice and excuse myself. *(Exits.)*
CHOAN: Take good care of that cash.
JUBEI: It's in my bellyband tied around my waist.

Music.

JUBEI: Well then…
CHOAN: I can wake you up at the sixth bell,[4] if you like.
JUBEI: That's very kind of you.

Jubei exits. The sound of heavy rain is heard.

CHOAN: It's coming down again.

Choan goes to the entrance and picks up Dojuro's umbrella.

CHOAN: This umbrella has a wellhead frame and wisteria pattern. Dojuro left it behind. Ahh, what a find! Plotting is more useful than a doctor's measuring spoon.

Loud noise comes from upstage.

CHOAN: Whazzat?! The sound of a rattrap to hell? *(Clicking his tongue.)* That spooked me good and proper.

Scene 2. Akabanebashi Bridge

A large prop of Akabanebashi Bridge faces the audience. An official notice board stands downstage right. Sound of rain. A towel over his head and jowl, kimono hem tucked up, and with a single blade, Choan runs in barefoot holding Dojuro's umbrella over his head. Looking behind, he hides in the shadow of the notice board. Jubei, with a woven straw hat and a double straw mat thrown over him, enters swinging an Odawara lantern. Piano music. Thunder and lightning.

JUBEI: Never thought it would rain so wild. And daybreak is still far off.

Bell rings.

JUBEI: *(Counting.)* That was only the seventh bell.[5] Another hour till daybreak. When I left Kojimachi, it was only the eighth bell.[6] I was sent off too early!

Choan is watching from behind the notice board. The sound of heavy rainfall. Choan draws his blade and cuts down the lantern. Jubei starts to scream in surprise but is struck down from behind.

JUBEI: Arghh—murder, murder, murder!

Jubei's straw hat cord snaps as he tries to escape. Choan chases him around slashing left and right. Choan finally grabs Jubei, covers his mouth, and stabs him in the side. Bleeding profusely, Jubei tries to escape, but falls suddenly.

Choan straddles him and gives him the final blow. He wipes the white blade and returns it to its sheath. He feels about Jubei's waist and pulls out the bellyband. Groping inside, Choan grins wide.

Music begins.

Choan chants.

CHOAN: The hour of the tiger.[7]
Tonight's torrential rain
Kept people indoors
Under the veil of night, I was able to kill
For a scanty 50 gold coins.
To this man, my sister's husband,
I have filial obligations,
But Money must come first.
A harsh remedy requiring bloody hands.
Money's the driving force behind cruel murder.
If you hold a grudge, complain to Money.
(Taking the umbrella.) It's damn cold. I'm drenched. A false charge.
The blame will fall on the owner of this bamboo umbrella. *(Puts it by the corpse.)* Clever me. If you hold a grudge, complain to Money.

Exits.

Scene 3. Kojimachi, Hirakawacho Tenjin Rear Gate

The notice board flips and turns into the rear gate of Hirakawacho Tenjin.

From stage left, Choan runs in drenched.

CHOAN: Fuck. This goddamned rain never stops. I'm soaked to the skin without that umbrella. Well, I've put in enough distance to be pretty safe. *(He wrings out his sleeves.)*

A toy dog barks from behind the gate.

CHOAN: Shush. Hey, you bastard. Shut up. *(The dog continues to bark.)* I'll take care of you, too.

Choan draws his sword and slices the dog in half. It dies.

CHOAN: That's a dog's life for ya. *(Laughs.)*

Choan wipes the blood off his blade with a towel and sheathes it.

From stage right, Chuzo of Kaizaka, in a short raincoat with kimono hem tucked up and wooden clogs, holds a paper umbrella with a bull's-eye design in one hand and an Odawara lantern in the other. The two men come face to face on stage. Choan quickly tries to back off stage right, but Chuzo raises his lantern and speaks.

CHUZO: Huh? I've seen that face before somewhere.

Choan throws gravel at the man and lies flat on the ground. Chuzo drops his lantern, which goes out.

Music. Guards bring Jubei's corpse on a stretcher and lay it down.

Scene 4. Akabanebashi Bridge Guard Station

A backdrop of wooden boards is flown in, facing the audience. The set turns into a guard station. From upstage enters the magistrate, Gunzo Sasagawa. Choan enters and stands by the side of Jubei's corpse. From stage right, a guard brings in Dojuro, informally dressed in a haori *coat.*

GUNZO: Address Kojimachi 3-chome Kyubeidana. Name, Dojuro Fujikake. Is that you?

DOJURO: That is I, Your Honor. What is your business with me?

GUNZO: Is this your bamboo umbrella?

The guard places the umbrella in front of Dojuro.

DOJURO: It is indeed.

GUNZO: Are you sure it is yours?

DOJURO: Yes, Your Honor.

GUNZO: Bring Dr. Choan Murai over here.

GUARD: Choan, come at once.

Choan comes forward.

GUNZO: *(To Dojuro.)* Last night at Akabanebashi Bridge, Dr. Murai's sister's husband, Jubei, a Fujikawa farmer from Chishun region, was killed and 50 gold coins, stolen. You are the suspect.

DOJURO: What? I didn't do that. Why do you suspect me?

GUNZO: The umbrella, you said is yours just now, was found near Jubei's dead body. This murder must lie at your door. Dr. Murai agrees.

DOJURO: No, that umbrella I took with me to Dr. Murai's to thank him for my full recovery. By the time I left his house, the rain had stopped and I forgot my umbrella there. How did it end up by a corpse?

GUNZO: Listen, Dr. Murai, Fujikake says he forgot his umbrella at your house...

CHOAN: That is a lie.

GUNZO: What did you say?

CHOAN: When Dojuro came to my house, the rain had already stopped, so he didn't have an umbrella with him. If he says he forgot it at my place, he lies.

DOJURO: How dare you accuse me of lying! You watched me stand it up in the corner of your entrance. You are the one who lies about my not bringing an umbrella.

CHOAN: Now that is an outright lie! You forget that I cured your illness and instead of gratitude, act in ill will. What a monster! I never thought you were like that. My fault was to talk about Jubei going home the next morning with the cash he got from selling his daughter. You must have followed the man, killed him, and snitched the cash.

DOJURO: I know nothing about that.

CHOAN: That's a barefaced lie. What a monster!

DOJURO: You keep calling me a monster. *(Stands up.)*

GUNZO: That is enough, both of you. Fujikake's umbrella was found at the scene of the crime and is definitely a piece of evidence.

DOJURO: Killing someone and stealing his money. Would such a vicious robber leave behind things that could become evidence later on? Please consider this point.

GUNZO: There have been cases where a robber has dropped stolen valuables, which have been traced and the fellow captured.

DOJURO: But that umbrella…

GUNZO: Saying that you forgot it at the doctor's is an obvious lie.

CHOAN: Thank you for your discrimination, Your Honor. Even so, to find the umbrella by the corpse is a blessing from the heavens.

GUNZO: As we have this evidence, Fujikake must not escape. While the court is in deliberation, you will be kept in a holding cell.

DOJURO: But then, you are punishing me for poor memory…

GUNZO: Without evidence, you cannot even claim to have a poor memory.

DOJURO: Oh no…

GUNZO: Come. Bind him.

GUARD: Yes, Your Honor.

Some commotion rises from stage right. Riyo, in modest housewife attire, enters. She has a baby in her arms.

RIYO: Please stop. Please hold, I beg you.

GUARD: Wh-who are you?

RIYO: I am the wife of Dojuro Fujikake. My name is Riyo.

GUNZO: Woman, what business have you coming to this investigation?

RIYO: I was watching from the shadows. My husband has nothing to do with the murder case.

GUNZO: The umbrella found near the corpse is ample evidence!

RIYO: Please allow me to differ, Your Honor. When my husband returned home, he said that he had forgotten his umbrella at Dr. Murai's. But as it was already past the fourth bell,[8] we decided to wait until the next day. So, we and the two children went to bed. How could my husband, who did not leave the house after that, kill somebody? Baby, don't cry, don't cry. This is an important time for your papa. Please investigate Dr. Murai. Maybe the man called Jubei borrowed the umbrella.

CHOAN: Come now, Jubei was wearing rain gear he brought from his home. Why would he need an umbrella on top of that?

RIYO: If Jubei did not use it, maybe someone else…

CHOAN: Ma'am, you are probably trying to say that I used the umbrella. Would a decent person kill his brother-in-law for money? You two are plotting to foist the blame onto me.

RIYO: You are the one who is plotting. It is doubtful that the umbrella my husband forgot can be used as evidence. You are up to something.

CHOAN: No, no, your husband is up to something.

RIYO: You are to blame, you are to blame.

CHOAN: No, no, your husband is to blame.

RIYO: No, no, it's your fault, your fault.

GUNZO: That's enough. Silence! Guards, bind Fujikake!

RIYO: Then, you will not listen?

DOJURO: Hold back. Don't get upset. Whatever you say now, without evidence nothing can be done. Take good care of little Donosuke.

RIYO: But we will lose this chance…

DOJURO: What! Stop that, woman. Get over it.

RIYO: Ahh. *(Cries loudly.)*

CHOAN: *(Sneers.)* Shameless thieves. Such expert pretense of a caring couple. Trying to win sympathy and lenience. Your ulterior motive is brazenly clear!

GUNZO: Take Fujikake to the holding cell.

GUARD: Yes, Your Honor.

The guards take Dojuro away. Music.

DOJURO: Though innocent, I must endure the notoriety of being a robber and the humiliation of imprisonment however temporary. The more I think of it, the more disgraceful it seems.

RIYO: How to combat false charges,
How to dry tears on a sad cloudy day?
There is no way on a rainy night

CHOAN: The umbrella for rainy days
Covers the body darkly

DOJURO: This world is an ethereal dream

RIYO: Its borders are like autumn colors
It changes swiftly like a watery surface
Or the shifting shadow of the moon.

DOJURO: A short life…

GUNZO: Take him away.

ALL: Aye, Your Honor.

DOJURO: Troubles, troubles…

As music plays, Dojuro is taken away.

Scene 5. Dr. Choan Murai's Kojimachi Residence

The set is the same as in Scene 1.

Soyo has an air of fatigue about her. Her disheveled hair is kept in place by a black, silk hairband. While she's drinking water from a cup, Sada is doing some housecleaning with a cloth.

SADA: Being a lodger is OK, but housecleaning does terrible things to my hands.

SOYO: Excuse me, where has my brother gone?

SADA: The doctor has gone to the baths.

SOYO: How far is it from here to Asakusa?

SADA: Almost eight kilometers.

SOYO: I can't walk that far. I want to see Oume at her new fancy workplace while I am still alive. I don't know why, but Choan won't tell me the name of the samurai in residence. He has brushed me off for two months. If you know where it is, please tell me.

SADA: Your daughter is at a house, I mean a samurai residence in Asakusa. I will ask him by and by. Being up and about won't do you any
good. Please go and rest.

SOYO: Yes, yes, of course. I want to see Oume so bad…

Soyo goes to her room.

SADA: Master is a cruel man. His sister comes all the way from Mikawa
to see her daughter. But he won't let her outside at all and has turned
her into an invalid. He knows full well she won't last long, but still
won't let her see her girl. That's not something the likes of us could
carry off.

From the hanamichi, *Choan saunters in holding a towel after his bath
and enters his house.*

CHOAN: Ahh, that was a good soak.

SADA: You're back early, Doctor.

CHOAN: Did anyone drop by during my absence?

SADA: No, no one. But your sister's been complaining about wanting to
see her girl. Once she gets well, she'll run off at full speed.

CHOAN: Whatever she says, I can't allow her to see Oume. I had better
deal with this soon. Hey, you go to the baths. On the way back, go by
the liquor store and get a big bottle of *sake*. If they kick up a fuss over
the payment, tell them I'll pay before the festival. We'll have a good
time when you return.

SADA: That's a really good idea! I'll get an eel hotpot, too.

CHOAN: Thanks.

SADA: No problem.

Sada gets a towel and goes off to the baths. Choan has a smoke.

CHOAN: While the maid's off work with a cold, Sada's filled in as a
manservant, but when it comes to cooking, it's got to be done by a
woman.

Sentaro, casually dressed in a haori, *comes to the gate.*

SENTARO: Hallo.

CHOAN: *(Coming to the front door.)* Yes, yes, who is it?

SENTARO: It's Sentaro, Doctor.

CHOAN: Oh, how about that. Come on in.

SENTARO: Thank you, Doctor.

CHOAN: What brings you all the way from Kanda today?

SENTARO: I came about the request I made yesterday.

CHOAN: What? Yesterday's request…refers to a patient?

SENTARO: No, the request I made at Kamenoo by Myojin-shita.

CHOAN: What's this? I don't remember any request.

SENTARO: Ha-ha-ha, Dr. Murai, are you teasing me? You are a joker.

CHOAN: I am a doctor and deal with life-and-death situations. Why would I crack jokes?

SENTARO: Huh? The day before yesterday, when we met at Kamenoo, you told me to come to your house today. That you'd arrange for Sayoginu to be here.

CHOAN: Well, I'll be damned. Kamenoo? Sayoginu? I don't know what the hell you're going on about!

SENTARO: Come now. When I said that I wanted to buy her out, you told me that for a client to redeem a woman, it would cost hundreds of gold coins. But if her family wanted her back, they would only have to prepare 50 gold coins, the amount they got when they sold her in the first place. I followed your advice and gave you 50 yesterday. At that time, you said you would cover for any lack in funds so that your niece could be saved quickly from the hard life imposed on her.

CHOAN: You must be ill. I can give you some medicine.

SENTARO: Then you claim to know nothing at all about this?

CHOAN: I, Choan, am not so far gone as to forget such matters.

SENTARO: Then what about the 50 gold coins, huh?

CHOAN: I know nothing of that. Nothing at all. You are making extraordinary claims. I never got 50 gold coins from you.

SENTARO: Th-that's impossible. I gave you 50.

CHOAN: Do you insist that you gave me that sum?

SENTARO: Of course.

CHOAN: Then you must have evidence.

SENTARO: At that time…

CHOAN: If you have evidence, show it.

SENTARO: When I offered to make a receipt, you said that when Sayoginu and I married, you would become my uncle. Why would a receipt be necessary among relatives? If I were to insist, you said you'd refuse to arrange the ransom. You were so upset that I decided to trust you and simply handed over the money.

CHOAN: Now, now, Sentaro, it may be foolish of me to take you on as an equal when you're young enough to be my son. But if you are picking a fight with me, I can't let it pass.

SENTARO: I'm not accusing you without charge. You lie about not accepting the money I gave you.

CHOAN: Without evidence, you are just making a false charge. Where's the evidence?

SENTARO: What?

CHOAN: What?

They continue to say "What?" at each other. Choan takes Sentaro by the collar and sits him down.

CHOAN: You brat, how dare you accuse me? *(Pushing him away.)*

SENTARO: You took my money and now feign ignorance and get violent. This is too much.

CHOAN: Too much? You claim you gave me money you never did. That's what is too much! If you won't back off, come with me.

SENTARO: Where?

CHOAN: To the local head. We will ask him to investigate the source of the 50 gold coins.

SENTARO: No. *(Backs off.)*

CHOAN: You're still living with your parents. You can't possibly have 50 gold coins of your own. Come with me.

SENTARO: Please don't take me to the local head.

CHOAN: Why not?

SENTARO: As you point out, I am still a dependent. I had to make some money secretly.

CHOAN: Did you steal?

SENTARO: As you know, I am the adopted son of one of the three best pawnbrokers in Kanda. I pawned a client's "white-dewed" dagger for 50 gold coins at another pawnbroker's without my father's knowledge. If he finds out, there will be big trouble.

CHOAN: You're a brazen bastard. I should certainly tie you up and hand you over to the local authorities.

SENTARO: No, don't do that. Please turn a blind eye.

CHOAN: Well, I'll let you off the hook. You be on your way home.

SENTARO: B-but I can't leave without my money.

CHOAN: Goddammit. Starting up again, are you?

Choan picks up a wooden sword and stands up. Sentaro makes a run for the entrance. Choan catches up, whacks him, and sends him flying.

CHOAN: For a fella with a pretty face, you're a right brazen bastard.

SENTARO: Give back my 50.

CHOAN: *(Holding the sword.)* Whaddya say?

SENTARO: Uh, nothing…

Bringing a towel to his face, Sentaro cries. Crying, he walks away sadly, occasionally looking back vengefully. Soon he runs off. Peering out from the front door, Choan watches him leave.

CHOAN: He's given up and gone. A worldly unwise young master. So incredibly naïve. Even I feel a bit guilty. But my house is just part of a rental terrace housing with a front entrance. With only five or six patients and their fees, I can't get by. Sometimes I have to resort to wild tactics. But as far as possible, I don't want to make any bad enemies.

SANJI: *(Spoken by the Choan actor.)* Are there good enemies? *(He laughs.)*

CHOAN: Who's there?

Saying this, Choan brings out a doll from his kimono. Stringless, it has a central stick to which the head and arms are attached and a kimono covers this body structure. This is Doll Sanji.

DOLL SANJI: Hi, bro.

CHOAN: Oh, it's you Sanji. Haven't seen you around for a long time.

DOLL SANJI: I lost all my cash gambling in Shinjuku. I thought I'd drop by to see you on the way home.

CHOAN: The *sake* is coming soon. Hang around for a while.

DOLL SANJI: You know, bro, I know I always say the same thing, but

I'm in a bit of a fix. When I go to the gambling joints, I lose and lose. Since the Bon Festival,[9] I've gone through 30 gold coins. Is there any work I could do?

CHOAN: There is.

DOLL SANJI: Is there?

CHOAN: Lots.

DOLL SANJI: Come on, we're not talking about a measles epidemic.

CHOAN: There's a job right now that'll bring in a tidy sum.

DOLL SANJI: That would be good.

Sada returns with a bottle of sake *and a carrying box.*

SADA: Doctor, I'm back. Oh Sanji, you're here, too.

DOLL SANJI: Well, if it isn't Sada. How're ya doing these days?

SADA: I'm taking it easy here.

CHOAN: All right, let's have a cup of cold *sake.*

DOLL SANJI: Sounds good. Thanks.

CHOAN: Try some of this, too.

DOLL SANJI: Eel hotpot. The deboned type, too. This is a treat.

CHOAN: Sada, you have some, too.

SADA: Great.

The three happily share the sake *together. From the other room, a voice is heard.*

SOYO: *(Off.)* Choan, let me see Oume. I want to see her soon. Let me see her.

CHOAN: I will, all in good time.

SOYO: *(Off.)* Let me see her while I am alive.

CHOAN: Damn it. Stop that noise. I'm telling you that you'll see her.

DOLL SANJI: Bro, who is that?

CHOAN: That...that is Jubei's wife.

DOLL SANJI: That means she's your sister.

CHOAN: That's right, Sanji. Hey, have you had a proper meal?

DOLL SANJI: Not yet.

CHOAN: Sada, go and order a thick section of eel.

SADA: With rice?

CHOAN: How else?

SADA: With a heap of pickles and hot tea?

DOLL SANJI: You got it right. Thanks for the bother.

SADA: No problem. The shop's nearby anyways.

Sada exits stage right.

CHOAN: Now Sanji, about this job I want you to do. It's bound to bring in good money. Are you ready to listen?

DOLL SANJI: I'll listen to any money-making scheme you've got.

CHOAN: What I want you to do concerns Osoyo, Jubei's wife, who clamors to see her girl. Osoyo is my sister, but this is getting complicated. The story I told you of her girl working at a samurai residence is a lie. Oume's been sold to the Clove House in the Yoshiwara pleasure quarters. There's no way I can take Osoyo there. She's sick now, but once she recovers, there'll be no stopping her. If the truth gets around, I'll become a suspect in Jubei's case. It's a bit regrettable but I want you to, you know, "take care" of her.

DOLL SANJI: I never say no when money's in the mix, but she's your sister. No, I won't do it, no way. If you wanna kill her, use drugs, not human hands.

CHOAN: Well, it's not that I haven't thought of drugs, but even powerful poison takes time to work. The victim won't die right away like they do onstage. And on top of that, the whole body changes color, complicating its disposal.

DOLL SANJI: That's why you want me to kill her.

CHOAN: I can't kill her myself, right? We're blood brothers, you and me. Help me out and get rid of her.

DOLL SANJI: I might do other things for you, but this is too much.

CHOAN: You don't get it, do you? If Oume's case goes public, I won't be the only one to get caught. You won't get away with having stamped the seal either.

DOLL SANJI: Gee, depending on the situation… *(Raising his voice.)* I'll kill after all.

CHOAN: Lower your voice, stupid.

DOLL SANJI: And so, where does the money bit come in?

At this moment, Sada returns and peeps through the entrance.

CHOAN: Remember you pawned a white-dewed dagger at the Iseya pawnbroker's in Mikawacho?

DOLL SANJI: I did, too. You knew of that, bro.

CHOAN: The young master at Iseya needed 50 gold coins. So, he pawned it for 50 at another pawnbroker's behind his father's back.

DOLL SANJI: He's a brash fella.

CHOAN: Right, now pay attention. The point is that the father doesn't know about it. Today, you go reclaim the dagger and when it turns out the article's lost, you kick up a huge fuss. That'll bring in ten or 12 gold coins.

DOLL SANJI: Juicy piece of work. Are you sure that the son took the dagger out?

CHOAN: He told me himself. You can't get closer to the truth than that.

DOLL SANJI: Let's get up a riot, huh?! We'll need something that looks like cash.

CHOAN: Oh yeah, I have just the right thing. It's a cloth-wrapped heated stone in a box. A patient brought it. I can get another box just like it and fill it with bogus coins all wrapped up. They'll look like two boxes of 25 gold coins each.

DOLL SANJI: Great, great! And if we could find someone to be the samurai owner of the dagger, that would be perfect.

SADA: *(Suddenly.)* Excuse me, excuse me.

CHOAN: What? *(Serious.)* Who's there, please?

SADA: *(Entering the house.)* I am the owner of the dagger.

CHOAN: What the fuck! That's a bad joke.

DOLL SANJI: You took me by surprise.

SADA: I overheard you from the entrance. So, I transformed into a samurai right away.

CHOAN: You're getting ahead of yourself.

DOLL SANJI: You're in your samurai element.

SADA: Ha, something I got in the old days. I'll go to the costumer and get the right outfit.

SOYO: *(Entering.)* Brother, please take me to see Oume.

DOLL SANJI: Bro, I have to go to the Isego liquor store today, so the other matter can be taken care of tomorrow, OK?

CHOAN: *(To Doll Sanji.)* We don't really have to hurry, but as she keeps going on about wanting to see Oume, the neighbors will wonder what it's all about.

SOYO: I keep seeing bad dreams and have become very fearful. I must see her, I must see her.

CHOAN: You'll see her, you'll see her. No problem.

DOLL SANJI: This is real bad!

Music.

Scene 6. The Iseya Pawnbroker's at Kanda Mikawacho

A navy blue shop curtain or a latticed counter can be used to indicate the perimeters of the pawnbroker's shop. Shop attendants Yosuke and Kiyoshichi are checking the articles against the record in the account book.

YOSUKE & KIYOSHICHI: Number 1357: The principal is two silver coins. A single Satsuma *kasuri*-woven kimono. Number 1358: The principal is one gold coin. Sixty-seven mosquito nets. Number 1359: One Mino futon.

The proprietor Gohei enters from upstage left and sneezes.

GOHEI: *(Referring to the sneezing.)* Someone is slandering me again, saying that I am greedy and stingy. Now, now, Yosuke, how long are you going to take over the accounts? Kiyoshichi, you hurry up and finish, too.

YOSUKE & KIYOSHICHI: Yes, Master. Right away, Master.

GOHEI: Whatever I say, they always come back with "Yes, Master" and nothing gets done. Hey, Yosuke, has Chosuke paid the interest?

YOSUKE: Not yet, Master.

GOHEI: *(To Chomatsu.)* Hey, you little scamp, go to Chosuke's place. Tell them that if the interest isn't paid today or tomorrow, they'll forfeit their pawned item.

CHOMATSU: Yes, yes, Master.

GOHEI: And don't waste time playing with stray dogs.

CHOMATSU: No, no, Master.

GOHEI: Tell them that if they don't pay the interest, they'll forfeit their pawned item.

CHOMATSU: Yes, yes, Master.

GOHEI: Repeat it now.

CHOMATSU: I will say, "If you pay interest, you will forfeit the pawn."

GOHEI: NO! You don't understand. Say, "If you don't pay the interest..."

CHOMATSU: If you don't pay the interest...

GOHEI: No! If you pay the interest, you will forfeit the pawn. What? I'm getting confused.

CHOMATSU: I don't understand, either.

GOHEI: You useless noodle. You waste my time. *(He picks up his pipe and is about to put the wrong end in his mouth.)*

CHOMATSU: Oh no, excuse me, Master. It's the other way around.

GOHEI: You cheeky scamp, shut up! *(He puts the hot end in his mouth.)* Ayayaya—ouch. This stupid—*(Hits the boy on the head.)*

CHOMATSU: Getting chewed out, then hit on the head... This job isn't worth it.

GOHEI: What the heck are you still doing here? Get going.

CHOMATSU: Yes, yes, Master. *(Exits.)*

Kyuhachi enters.

KYUHACHI: I am back.

GOHEI: Ahh, Kyuhachi, there you are. Were there any good items at the market?

KYUHACHI: No Master, only mediocre stuff. I didn't buy anything.

GOHEI: That is good policy. If you buy stolen goods, you lose money in the end. I appreciate having you as head clerk. In settling affairs or in perseverance, you have what I instinctively sensed in you when you were a boy. You are my favorite, Kyuhachi. In contrast, my adopted son, Sentaro, even if I take his youth into account, is restless and lazy. He's a problem.

KYUHACHI: Master, I do not notice everything, but if the young master is getting out of hand, I will warn him. Please do not worry over him too much.

GOHEI: That sets my heart at rest. I will go and have lunch, so keep an eye on the shop.

KYUHACHI: Please have a leisurely lunch, Master.

Gohei exits.

KYUHACHI: Yo, Yosuke and Kiyoshichi, the two of you go to the back room and record the forfeited items in the account book.

YOSUKE & KIYOSHICHI: *(Standing up.)* Ayee.

KYUHACHI: Make sure the Master doesn't hear you practicing love songs and mimicry.

YOSUKE & KIYOSHICHI: Ayee. We'll be careful.

The two exit.

KYUHACHI: *(Alone now.)* I must advise the young master against his visits to the Yoshiwara pleasure quarters before the master hears rumors. And, I can't find the white-dewed dagger in the stone storehouse, even though it was brought in just the other day. It's possible that the young master, pressed for money, took the article with him.

From stage right, Sentaro enters quickly, slovenly dressed.

KYUHACHI: Young master, welcome back home. Where are you heading?

SENTARO: Kyuhachi, I may die.

KYUHACHI: Are you feeling ill?

SENTARO: I'm not feeling ill but extremely mortified.

Sentaro walks hurriedly into the back of the shop.

KYUHACHI: Young master, please wait.

Kyuhachi runs after Sentaro.

Scene 7. Upstairs in Sentaro's Room

The set is changed quickly. Sentaro enters, takes a short sword, and is about to leave. Kyuhachi enters.

KYUHACHI: Young master.

SENTARO: Well, uhh, I am…

KYUHACHI: What are you going to do with that short sword?

SENTARO: Oh, this?

KYUHACHI: You intend to kill somebody and then kill yourself.

SENTARO: Why do you say that?

KYUHACHI: You were breathless when you returned and something about the way you speak tells me that someone is on your mind. Please tell me.

SENTARO: It's that hateful Choan Murai. With a great show of kindness, he deceived me of 50 gold coins. Today, he pretended to know nothing. Then he accused me of deceiving him and assaulted me. In revenge for those kicks and body blows, I thought to kill him and then commit suicide.

KYUHACHI: What's this about 50 gold coins?

SENTARO: I am ashamed to tell you, but please listen anyway.

KYUHACHI: *(Coming closer.)* Uh-huh. Uh-huh…

Piano music or cats meowing.

KYUHACHI: So that's it. I see.

SENTARO: Pheww.

KYUHACHI: In spite of your youthful ignorance of worldly matters, you're to blame for being deceived by such a female. Even if you could buy her out for 50 gold coins, do you think a prostitute can become your bride at Iseya? You must give up such thoughts.

SENTARO: The more I listen to your opinion, the more I realize my mistake. Ohh, I don't know what to do. What to do? I won't go to that house ever again.

KYUHACHI: That's what I wanted to hear.

CHOMATSU: *(Offstage voice.)* Kyuhachi, the Master is calling for you.

KYUHACHI: Ah, I will come at once.

SENTARO: My father is calling. He may have noticed that a dagger is missing from the storehouse.

KYUHACHI: Leave it to me.

CHOMATSU: *(Offstage voice.)* Kyuhachi, Kyuhachi.

KYUHACHI: Coming. What a lot of trouble.

Kyuhachi exits and Sentaro follows.

Scene 8. At the Iseya Pawnbroker's

Back at the shop. Sanji, played by the Choan actor in an identical cos-tume to that of the Doll Sanji, is puffing on his pipe. Nearby is Sada, dressed relatively casually as samurai Shibuemon and armed with a pair of swords. At the desk is Gohei.

SANJI: Excuse me, where is the dagger?
GOHEI: An attendant has gone to the storehouse to fetch it. Please have another cup of tea.

Yosuke enters from the back of the house, upstage.

YOSUKE: Master, I have checked all the shelves in the storehouse, but cannot find the dagger.
GOHEI: What's this? Look again more carefully.

Yosuke goes off in a hurry.

GOHEI: Where is Kyuhachi?
SANJI: Please hurry up.

Kyuhachi and Sentaro enter from upstage.

KYUHACHI: Can I be of any help, Master?
GOHEI: There you are, Kyuhachi. Our client has come to reclaim his dagger. But we cannot find it in the storehouse. Do you know where it is?
SENTARO: Oh, you have come…
KYUHACHI: …For the dagger.
SANJI: Are you the head attendant? Last year, on the night of August 20, I received this pawn bill from you. That dagger belongs to this samu-rai, Shibuemon Shibukawa, who asked me to pawn it. But now, he has to return suddenly to his homeland. So, I have accompanied him to make a very hurried withdrawal. As we have to go elsewhere as well, please bring it out right away.
KYUHACHI: Then sir, you are the owner of this dagger?

227

SADA: That is correct. It is my dagger and a precious heirloom. Due to circumstances beyond my power, I had to ask this man to pawn it for me. However, I must now present it as a gift to my lord. So here I am in much haste to reclaim it.

KYUHACHI: I see. The attendant has looked everywhere but cannot locate the article. Could you please wait until tomorrow?

SANJI: If the article were mine, I could wait a day or two. But this is a precious item that the samurai owner will be presenting to his lord. If word gets around that the item was pawned and lost, a worthy samurai will have to commit ritual suicide by disembowelment. You gave me a pawn bill. Now you tell me that the dagger is lost? What the hell does that mean?

KYUHACHI: We definitely did receive the article from you. So we must have it, somewhere.

SADA: The white-dewed dagger is invaluable. I must present it to my lord at once. That is why I am here in person. There is no time to waste. Sanji listen, you take care of this negotiation. Making us wait is not an option, do you hear?

SANJI: You are completely right, sire. Did you hear? Look for it right away.

GOHEI: Come on, Kyuhachi. Look for it yourself, at once.

KYUHACHI: Ye-yes, Master. *(Starts to get up.)*

SANJI: Hey, wait a moment now.

KYUHACHI: Uh, yes, sir?

SANJI: Nowadays, the sun sets early and the days are short. Cut out the crappy acting. You don't have the dagger, do you?

KYUHACHI: What?

SANJI: …You don't have it!

KYUHACHI: Why do you say that?

SANJI: A rumor's going around that your young master sold it.

SENTARO: Huh?

GOHEI: Then my son took the dagger elsewhere?

SANJI: Your son turned the dagger into cash to pay for a prostitute,

SENTARO: Wait, I can expla…

GOHEI: Sentaro, you are the worst of the worst…

KYUHACHI: Oh no, the young master didn't do that. I took it.

GOHEI: Wh-what?! Hey, Kyuhachi, why did you take a dagger that costs 50 gold coins?

KYUHACHI: I met a girl in Yoshiwara. So I borrowed five sometimes seven gold coins from the till and had to make that good. I am ashamed of myself.

CHOAN: You, the head clerk, did that? That's hard to believe.

SENTARO: Kyuhachi, you mustn't…

KYUHACHI: No, I am to blame.

GOHEI: You of all people! You have done huge damage. I am astonished. I'm at a loss for words. Do you think that 50 gold coins can be made up easily? You have to work day and night to make that much money. What are you going to do about it? This is infuriating, you are infuriating. *(He angrily pushes Kyuhachi around.)*

SANJI: You suffer a loss of 50 gold coins. We lose an article worth, uh, 200 gold coins and suffer a loss of, um, 150 gold coins. Hurry up and bring it out!

GOHEI: Kyuhachi took it, so he should pay for it. With that sum, we can buy it back and return it to you.

SANJI: Unacceptable! We can't wait that long. You must return it right now, right now, right now. Give it back! Do you understand?

KYUHACHI: I am not asking you to wait for a long time. Just until tomorrow, until tomorrow. I beg you.

SANJI: Huumph, impossible!

SENTARO: Please, it will only be a short while

SANJI: Arrgh, this is too much trouble.

KYUHACHI: But then what can be done?

SANJI: Who cares! If this is how it is, I don't need to talk with the head clerk or the young master. The item is recorded in the account book. The proprietor Gohei took the article; Gohei should return it. We've brought two boxes of cash to a total of 50 gold coins. Give back the dagger!

GOHEI: We cannot return what isn't in our keeping. You are acting like an extortionist.

SANJI: An extortionist? Oh yeah, that's fascinating. Call me an extortionist, will ya? C'mon then, turn me over to the authorities. A famous Kanda pawnbroker sold an article without the owner's consent and before the reclamation date. You'll pay for this. I'll take you down with me, Gohei Iseya. If that's what you want, c'mon now, c'mon and turn me over to the authorities.

SADA: Wait a moment, Sanji. Without the dagger, I, samurai Shibuemon

Shibukawa, will lose my life.

SANJI: Well, if you're gonna lose your life anyways, slash all these bastards to pay the boatman. Start by slaughtering this Gohei.

SADA: That is a good idea. I will start with Master Gohei and try out the sharpness of my blade. *(He stands up.)*

GOHEI: Oh my god, this has nothing to do with me.

SANJI: You won't get away…

Sanji grabs Gohei. Kyuhachi and Sentaro intervene.

KYUHACHI: I am the cause of the problem. If killing satisfies you, please kill me first.

SENTARO: No, kill me first.

SADA: Wait, if I kill those willing to die, I will lose all my samurai pride. I beg to start with our reluctant proprietor.

SANJI: Now, if you wanna live, pay up and keep your life.

SADA: If you refuse, you will lose your life. I prefer to have your life rather than the money.

GOHEI: I'll pay, I'll pay. Here's one gold coin. *(He wiggles out a gold coin from his kimono sash.)*

SANJI: The price of your life is only one gold coin? Is that all?

SADA: Will one gold coin buy forgiveness? I will cut him down, after all.

GOHEI: Ah, this is intolerable. I'll add two silver coins, which brings the total to one gold and two silver coins.

SADA: Forgiveness does not come with a few coins of chicken feed.

GOHEI: Very well then. Five gold coins. That's the limit.

SANJI: Even an adulterer is considered worth seven gold and two silver coins.

GOHEI: My life is not worth that much.

SANJI: All right, let's say the value of a man's life hangs on the weight of his head. *(Yanking Gohei's head out of his body, he feels its weight.)* Yours would be a tiny 37.5 grams of silver,[10] huh?

GOHEI: Then, then, I will pay ten gold coins to keep my head. Oh god, my life costs ten gold coins. Even I think that's too expensive. *(Pats his own head and reluctantly hands over ten gold coins.)*

SADA: Forgiveness is difficult but taking your life is shameful, too. Ten gold coins will have to do.

SANJI: *(Annoyed with Sada's easygoingness.)* Hey, he's a gutless pawn-shop owner. Even with his silly face, he'd be worth 20 to 30 gold coins. *(Sada shakes him off.)*

KYUHACHI: Master Sanji, I realize you are very upset. But could you leave for today? We will consider a separate gift of thanks to you. We depend on your mercy.

SANJI: Very well, we'll leave for today. I haven't had my full say on these matters. But out of consideration for you, I won't say anymore now.

KYUHACHI: No, no. Everything is my fault. Please give me two or three days.

SANJI: We can wait a few days.

GOHEI: In that case, there is no need for payment.

SANJI: If you want it back, I'll give it back. But instead, give me your life.

GOHEI: Oh no, that won't do.

SANJI: Well then, you have no complaints on my taking the payment, right?

GOHEI: I do and I don't.

SANJI: We leave for today. But if things aren't settled by the day after tomorrow, we'll come again.

GOHEI: Oh, I don't like that.

SANJI: Sada, let's go.

SADA: Hey… *(Trying to stand, he sits back down suddenly.)* I can't walk.

SANJI: What's the matter?

SADA: I've got pins and needles from sitting too long.

SANJI: Stupid. Put some dust on your forehead for good luck.

SADA: *(Putting dust on his forehead.)* Oh, now I can stand.

SANJI: Hey, stingy old man, we're coming the day after tomorrow. Be here.

Gohei gives an undignified squawk.

Music. The two exit.

GOHEI: Listen up, Kyuhachi, the 50 gold coins for the dagger and the ten gold coins you gave to that Sanji must be paid back to me in full by your uncle Rokuemon.

KYUHACHI: But the wages you have kept for me since I started working for you at the age of 12 comes to 35 gold coins this year. For the remainder, I could sell my clothes and clothes box. That will probably come to 14 or 15 gold coins and the total would be 50 gold coins.

GOHEI: Hold it. If you had completed your term of service with diligence, I would give you your full wages and your kimono. But you wretched girl-chaser, you don't deserve wages or anything else. I will give you nothing. Get out of here.

KYUHACHI: Well, in that case, Master, I cannot thank you enough for the long years that you have had me in your service. I am a terrible wretch costing you much trouble. Please forgive my wayward longings.

GOHEI: Cut out that fake eloquence. When you start rattling off like that, you get on my nerves.

KYUHACHI: *(To Sentaro.)* You must please take care of yourself. Take me as a negative model, and avoid becoming like me.

SENTARO: Um, Kyuhachi. I feel really bad about this. Why don't you tell my father the truth?

KYUHACHI: That will not do. Don't you understand my feelings? If you feel bad about this turn of events, please put up with it.

GOHEI: *(To Kyuhachi.)* Why are you still jabbering? *(To Sentaro.)* Son, if you get on his side, you'll catch his disloyalty and more.

SENTARO: He isn't like that.

GOHEI: Oh, he isn't? Stealing his master's articles. He's just like a thieving dog. *(To Kyuhachi.)* Get lost. Get out of here.

Gohei pushes Kyuhachi out of the front door.

SENTARO: Oh no, be careful.

Gohei pulls back Sentaro, who tries to help Kyuhachi.

GOHEI: Get out of here by tomorrow.

Gohei closes the front door with a slam.

Music. Kyuhachi exits slowly.

Scene 9. Asakusa Senzokumura District

In front of the curtain, from the hanamichi *a funeral procession appears. Rojiemon and Idoroku are heading for the crematorium carrying on a pole a very makeshift coffin (essentially just a tub) covered with a white cloth. Ichirobei enters at this moment, his kimono hem tucked up and a Yumihari lantern in one hand.*

ROJIEMON: Master Ichirobei, your deceased wife is a truly weighty *bodhisattva.*

IDOROKU: She was so big that you'd think she wouldn't die even if she were killed.

ICHIROBEI: It sounds almost stupid, but she stuffed her face with moon-viewing dumplings, and they got stuck in her throat. And that was the last of her. Such a ridiculous way to go, you know.

IDOROKU: By the way, Master Ichirobei, what is it you have in the chest fold of your kimono?

ICHIROBEI: It's the tri-colored cat my wife loved.

ROJIEMON: You're kidding. You're a really weird guy bringing a cat along on the funeral procession to the crematorium.

ICHIROBEI: What's wrong about bringing my cat?

IDOROKU: If a cat has contact with a dead person, she'll come back to life.

ROJIEMON: If my wife could rise from the dead, I would really like that to happen right now.

IDOROKU: No way. That's a really scary idea.

ICHIROBEI: Come back to life, come back to life, Nanman dabutsu, nyanmai da, nyanmai da…[11]

The procession passes and the scene changes to the Yoshiwara district. In the distance, the flickering lights of Yoshiwara can be seen. From the hanamichi *enters Sanji (played by the Choan actor), wearing a short raincoat over his kimono with its hem tucked up. He wears a short sword, and dangles an Odawara lantern from one hand. Following him is Soyo, dressed discreetly.*

SOYO: Sanji, is the residence where my daughter works still far from here?

SANJI: See on the other side of these fields? That's it.

SOYO: Then we are very close.

SANJI: Two or three more blocks, maybe.

SOYO: I really want to see her so much.

SANJI: The roads are bad here and get worse. Take this lantern and walk ahead.

SOYO: Yes certainly.

Soyo takes the lantern and steps ahead. Sanji moves back, unsheathes his blade, and raises it over his head. Soyo turns around. Sanji hurriedly hides his blade behind his back.

SOYO: Something flashed? What was that?

SANJI: Oh, just lightning.

SOYO: It's not as if it's going to rain.

SANJI: When lightning flashes without rain, it's a sure sign of a bumper crop.

SOYO: Even here, they must be busy reaping rice.

Soyo goes ahead. Sanji is looking for something and gets left behind.

SOYO: What's the matter?

SANJI: Well, I can't find my towel. I must have dropped it somewhere. Give me the lantern, will you?

Sanji takes the lantern from Soyo, pretends to search for his towel while he extinguishes the lantern light. The bell rings out the time.

SANJI: Dang, now I've dropped it.

SOYO: In this pitch-dark, I can't tell where anything is. *(She notices the lights of Yoshiwara in the distance.)* Look at the lights over there. What are they?

SANJI: Ohh, now that's the second floor where your daughter works.

Revelry is heard faintly.

SOYO: A big party must be going on.

SANJI: It's like that every night. *(He picks up his lantern, puts it in his long kimono sleeve, then raises his blade.)* See over there, that corner room is your daughter's.

SOYO: Where? Which room did you say? *(Looking back.)*

SANJI: That one over there.

Soyo looks up at the second floor. Sanji attacks her from behind. Soyo cries out and falls over. Sanji slashes her again. Soyo desperately tries to escape. Pursuing her, Sanji tries to get in another swipe.

SOYO: Why're you trying to kill me?

SANJI: I don't want to kill you. Someone told me to and I couldn't refuse.

SOYO: Who told you to?

SANJI: Oh hell. Who else but Choan!

SOYO: Y-you mean my brother?

SANJI: He fucking lied when he told you that he'd sent your girl to a samurai residence. He sold her off to a Yoshiwara house of prostitution, long ago. He even wanted me to kill you because he couldn't have you see her in a place like that. If you want to vent, spit it out at him.

SOYO: So, he sold Oume into prostitution? That monstrous brute! I'll tell him to his face what he is.

SANJI: What the hell should I know about it! If you're going to haunt the living, harass Choan. Don't you ever come to me.

SOYO: You're his accomplice in crime.

SANJI: No! Not me. It's all Choan's doing.

Sanji swings out at her again. They fight. Ichirobei, attending the makeshift coffin-tub, enters and inadvertently gets in between Sanji and Soyo. Sanji swings his blade wildly.

ICHIROBEI: Oh my god, murder, murder.

ROJIEMON & IDOROKU: *(Dropping the funeral tub and running off.)* Run, run.

Sanji chases Soyo around the makeshift coffin-tub. By mistake, Sanji cuts the rope attached to the tub. The pole that held up the tub drops. The im-

pediment removed, Sanji glares at Soyo.

SOYO: Ahh, someone help me! Murder, murder!

Music. Catching up with her, Sanji tells her.

SANJI: However much you cry and shout,
This is Nakata, a deserted rural district.
The lanterns that sometimes float in the air
May be disembodied souls.
After the Buddhist All Souls Festival,
The mourning cricket's cry,
During the sad, dry autumn night
When the ephemeral wind blows,
And becomes the crematorium's smoke
That fades away.
SOYO: Kill me if you will. I will be avenged one day.
SANJI: I'm not the one killing you. The bastard Choan is to blame.

Sanji pushes Soyo down on top of the coffin-tub, and pierces her throat. Soyo rises momentarily, clutches at air, then falls back onto the tub. Blood streams onto the white cloth covering the mouth of the tub.

SANJI: I've killed a human being for the first time in my life. It doesn't feel good.

Distastefully, Sanji pushes Soyo away from the tub. At this moment, Ichirobei enters and picks up the tub pole. Sanji and Ichirobei fight. Ichirobei jabs the tub with the pole by mistake. The tub falls over and out spills the corpse of Fumi with disheveled hair, a blood-soaked winding sheet, a sack, and leggings. Unable to defeat Sanji, Ichirobei flings away the cat and makes a run for it. Sanji pursues him. Both exit.

The hourly ringing of the bell. The sound of the wind. The cry of a cat. The corpse suddenly gets up and walks unsteadily. Sanji returns, comes face to face with the corpse, and is terrified.

SANJI: Holy shit! You are lost already and haunting me.

Sanji tries to escape but the corpse holds him back. Sanji knocks it down, slips, and sits down on his butt.

CORPSE: Vengeance is mine!
SANJI: Arggh!!

Sanji makes a great deal of commotion and runs away. At the sound of the bell, the corpse rises.

CORPSE: Moon-viewing dumplings got stuck in my throat. I died but it seems I have risen back to life.

The cry of a cat.

CORPSE: Ahh, they say, if a cat approaches a corpse, the body will start to dance. But the reason I came back to life is not because of a cat. *(A cat meows.)* Ooh, a cat, a cat!

The corpse dances and sings. The three men in the funeral procession return. They may join the song and dance.

CORPSE: I say, "A cat, a cat." But a cat would not wear clogs, hold a walking stick, nor wear a tie-dyed summer kimono. Oh-no-no-no-no-no-way.

The corpse dances on stage and exits by the hanamichi.

Scene 10. In Front of the Stage Curtain

Sentaro walks in. Behind him, a young man from the tea house enters.

YOUNG MAN: Excuse me sir, aren't you the young master from the Iseya pawnbroker's?
SENTARO: Well, if it isn't Yosuke from Yoshiwara!
YOUNG MAN: I am so glad to catch you here. Courtesan Sayoginu sent you this message.

SENTARO: What's up? *(Scanning the letter.)* She must see me soon about something? I can't go right away, but tonight I will try to visit. Please tell her that.

YOUNG MAN: Yes, young master.

The Young Man exits. Sentaro reads the letter again. Kyuhachi, shouldering a large basket of wastepaper, enters.

KYUHACHI: Young master.

SENTARO: Oh Kyuhachi, I wanted to see you.

KYUHACHI: You are the same as ever.

SENTARO: You have changed a great deal. What are you doing now?

KYUHACHI: I am staying with my uncle Rokuemon, who is a rubbish collector. I go around buying waste paper.

SENTARO: Thank you for taking on the debt of the 50 gold coins I spent, and forgive me for putting you in such a position. Also please accept this gift. *(He takes out a paper parcel, simultaneously dropping Sayoginu's letter.)*

KYUHACHI: No, I cannot accept that.

SENTARO: I cannot forgive myself unless you accept.

His uncle Rokuemon, who has been watching the two, comes over.

ROKUEMON: Now, now, Kyuhachi.

KYUHACHI: Oh, Uncle.

SENTARO: Well, you're the rubbish dealer, Rokuemon.

ROKUEMON: I was watching. You should accept the young master's gift.

KYUHACHI: Why is that?

ROKUEMON: With that as your capital, you can develop your business. That's the best way to thank him.

KYUHACHI: In that case, I would like to accept your gift.

SENTARO: I am happy to hear that.

ROKUEMON: Young master, my house is nearby. Please come by.

SENTARO: Today, I have an urgent matter to take care of. By and by, I will spend some time with you.

KYUHACHI: Young master, I look forward to seeing you again.

Sentaro exits in a hurry.

KYUHACHI: *(Opening the parcel.)* Oh, three gold coins. Uncle, please take care of this money for me.

ROKUEMON: No, you keep that. If you find any decent old clothes, buy them and make a profit.

KYUHACHI: Very well. I'll look out for a deal.

ROKUEMON: That's the spirit.

KYUHACHI: *(With a lilt.)* Wastepaper, wastepaper? Bring your wastepaper! Buying wastepaper.

Kyuhachi exits. Rokuemon gets ready to leave when he notices the letter that Sentaro dropped.

ROKUEMON: "Sentaro, please come. From Sayoginu." Oh no, this spells trouble.

Rokuemon runs after Kyuhachi. Riyo, a devoted mother, enters with her little son Minomatsu.

MINOMATSU: Mom, I'm hungry. I want something to eat.

RIYO: You have to wait a little more until your brother comes home.

Gorobei enters from the opposite side.

GOROBEI: Oh, there you are, Riyo. Today of all days, you must pay the rent.

RIYO: My son is out selling edamame but will be home soon. When he returns, I will pay as much as I can.

GOROBEI: Look now, just chuck your samurai pride and become my pretty wife.

RIYO: Landlord Gorobei, again you say such things. I've told you many times my husband was falsely charged and met a violent death. In my heart, I have become a nun and will dedicate my life to serving Buddha.

GOROBEI: Don't be so darned chaste. Just agree.

RIYO: See, always insinuating. In grief, I am always a samurai's wife.

GOROBEI: Well, in that case, pay seven months' rent right away!

RIYO: Not right away. We are mother and two boys, living from hand to mouth.

GOROBEI: If you can't, you must vacate your rooms.

RIYO: Ohh, but that is...

GOROBEI: Then become my wife.

RIYO: How dare you! I've had enough of your innuendos. Away with you and your harassment.

Riyo pushes Gorobei aside and he sits down on the ground with a bump. Minomatsu cries vigorously. Someone passes by.

GOROBEI: What the heck! Get out of my rooms.

Gorobei goes inside trying to avoid public attention. Riyo is at a loss when her elder son, Donosuke, is dragged onstage by two bully boys, Guzuichi and Hagematsu.

RIYO: There you are, my son.

DONOSUKE: Oh, Mother, I made a blunder. Please apologize for me.

GUZUICHI: We're the tough guys in this area. This shrimp dares toy with us. It's unforgivable.

RIYO: Please explain what happened.

HAGEMATSU: Yeah, I will tell you. My buddy here tells your boy to give him a pack of edamame. Your boy refuses.

GUZUICHI: I said I'd pay him tomorrow. Then he lets off that taking even one bag of beans makes me a thief. I'm gonna beat the hell out of him.

RIYO: Now please wait. It's three years since my husband died, and we are wasting away. My son is the only source of income.

RIYO & DONOSUKE: Please forgive us.

HAGEMATSU: Look, Mother, if you buy my mate a big bottle of *sake*, I'll calm him down and take him away.

RIYO: I don't have any money to buy *sake*.

HAGEMATSU: Jeez, it only costs 400 or 500 copper.

RIYO: I'm embarrassed to admit that I only have 40 or 50 coppers.

HAGEMATSU: OK, I don't care if your boy gets walloped to death. It's none of my business.

RIYO: Donosuke, how much did you make today?

DONOSUKE: About 340 or 350 coppers.

RIYO: This coin'll bring the sum up to 400. Please buy some *sake* with this.

DONOSUKE: But if you give that away, what about dinner?

HAGEMATSU: I'll give you a huge, unbelievable break and take my mate away. Come on, Guzuichi, let's go.

GUZUICHI: No, not me. I won't be satisfied with just one or two bottles.

HAGEMATSU: At this rate, you could turn 'em upside and shake hard, but nothing would come out!

GUZUICHI: Well, this is better than nothing.

HAGEMATSU: Yeah, righty-ho.

Guzunoichi and Hagematsu exit. The mother and son are at a loss as to what to do.

DONOSUKE: They've swiped our cash for buying more beans and some rice. How are we going to live, tomorrow?

RIYO: I would prefer to die than go through all this suffering. But poor, dear Minomatsu is only five years old. Also, I have continued living in the hope that I could clear my husband's name of the dreadful crime that he was accused of. Now I don't know what to do.

At that point, Kyuhachi enters with a large basket on his back.

KYUHACHI: *(Loudly.)* Wastepaper? Any wastepaper?

RIYO: Oh, wonderful, here is the rubbish collector. Could you come to the terrace housing over there?

KYUHACHI: Yes, yes. I'd be happy to.

Riyo and the boys head towards their home. Rokuemon enters in a hurry.

ROKUEMON: Kyuhachi, Kyuhachi. Where has he gone? I have to show him this letter. He has to know that the young master is still visiting the brothels.

Rokuemon passes by. Chuzo, an employment agent, enters with his two men, Hagematsu and Guzuichi.

CHUZO: So, I told you to go easy on the liquor. Is her home around here? Hurry up and find it.

HAGEMATSU: Hey, Guzuichi, go and search over there.

GUZUICHI: OK. I got drunk and went wild.

CHUZO: Hey you, Hagematsu. You go and buy a box of dried bonito or something.

HAGEMATSU: What's the box for?

CHUZO: You can't just take an empty box as a token of apology, stupid. Buy dried bonito that's packed in a box.

HAGEMATSU: Isn't that too much?

CHUZO: Shut up and just do as you're told.

Hagematsu goes off in a hurry.

CHUZO: Having stupid henchmen is a source of never-ending trouble.

Chuzo exits. Rokuemon appears from stage right calling out Kyuhachi's name. Kyuhachi himself enters with the basket still on his back. Riyo is chasing after him.

RIYO: Rubbish collector, please wait.

KYUHACHI: Tiered boxes, lidded receptacles, teacups, and other items all in a bundle for 750 copper coins. Can't pay more than that!

RIYO: *(Showing him a mirror.)* What could you give me for this?

KYUHACHI: Do you really want to sell that?

RIYO: A mirror is a woman's soul. I've come this far without selling this item. But if I can't pay the rent, I have to vacate the rooms. A bad fellow grabbed the seed money of my son's food sales and now we have no food for tomorrow. I owe everyone, everywhere. Without this money, my family will become homeless. Could you please take this for a double silver coin?

KYUHACHI: *(Bargaining her down.)* How about a silver coin and two bronzes or a silver coin and three coppers?

Donosuke comes running.

DONOSUKE: Please buy this.

KYUHACHI: This is your copybook.

242

DONOSUKE: I was going to give it to my brother.

KYUHACHI: Hm, this name written here, Donosuke Fujikake. Is that your name?

DONOSUKE: Yes, I am Donosuke, son of Dojuro.

KYUHACHI: *(Taken aback.)* Then by chance, you are the wife and the young son of Dojuro Fujikake?

MOTHER & SON: How did you know that?

KYUHACHI: Have you heard of Kyuemon, a farmer from Sunshu Ejiri?

RIYO: Oh yes, the Kyuemon couple was in the service of my husband.

KYUHACHI: Yes, I am Kyuhachi, the son of that Kyuemon. If I may ask, how did you get to be like this?

RIYO: It's a long story. The lord's dagger, we were supposed to take care of, was stolen from us on the way to the city. My husband would have had to commit ritual suicide by disembowelment, but due to the lord's mercy, he was only sent into exile.

DONOSUKE: Though it lacked an inscription, it was still a superb blade. From a dew-like marking on it, it came to be called the white-dewed dagger.

KYUHACHI: No, no, that dagger exists.

DONOSUKE: Where?

KYUHACHI: Someone pawned it for 50 gold coins at the Iseya pawnbroker's in Kanda Mikawacho.

RIYO: How wonderful! If we can get ahold of it, we can make a formal apology to the lord for my husband's failings.

DONOSUKE: Fifty gold coins is a large sum of money.

KYUHACHI: A ne'er-do-well called Sanji pawned it with his buddy, the doctor called Choan Murai, an even bigger scumbag. I came down in life because of Choan.

RIYO: Ahh Choan, yes, he is the one who had my husband imprisoned on a false charge and executed as well. The investigation could not turn up any evidence in my husband's favor.

KYUHACHI: You must be deeply disappointed. Here is something that will allow you to get some rest. I have three gold coins with me. They will come in handy for you.

RIYO: Oh, I cannot accept it. But I thank you for your kind thought.

KYUHACHI: Please accept my small gift. From now on, I will return the kindness I received from your husband with all my heart. As for today, I will leave you with your things.

Kyuhachi leaves the mirror, copybook, and other things from the basket, and goes off.

RIYO: Some gods abandon while other gods save. With this unexpected windfall, we can pay the rent that's piled up and with the rest pay the rice shop and the firewood shop. Tonight, we will be able to sleep well.

It suddenly becomes dark. Chuzo enters with Hagematsu and Guzumatsu in attendance.

CHUZO: Please excuse me, if you will.
RIYO: And who are you?
CHUZO: I am Chuzo, the boss of these two men. They have come to apologize for the disturbance they made.
HAGEMATSU: Please forgive me for what I did.
GUZUICHI: I got roaring drunk and did a stupid thing.
DONOSUKE: Look, the clouds have parted and the moon is showing its face.

The sky gets brighter.

CHUZO: *(Looking at Riyo's face.)* Are you the widow of Dojuro Fujik-ake, who lived in Kojimachi?
RIYO: And who are you that speaks?
CHUZO: I am Chuzo, an employment agent, living in Kaizuka.
RIYO: You regularly supplied our residence?
CHUZO: I serviced the Fujikake residence from the master's grandfa-ther's time. So, I knew well what the master looked like. He was treat-ed terribly.
RIYO: You lived in that area and knew what it was like.
CHUZO: The murderer was never found.
RIYO: We are still asking around day and night, but can't find any defi-nite evidence.
CHUZO: The Akabanebashi killer of farmer Jubei must have been his brother-in-law, Choan Murai.
DONOSUKE: What is your evidence?
CHUZO: I have none. But that day was the festival of Tenjin, the God of

Learning. Before the crowds descend, I always go there before dawn when birds are still silent. It had been raining since early evening the day before, and the man I passed by the back gate was Choan. I could just make out his face. He didn't have an umbrella and was drenched. He killed a dog that barked at him and then he ran off.

HAGEMATSU: They say that Choan's blood brother, Sanji, extorted 50 gold coins from a pawnbroker in Kanda.

GUZUICHI: Jubei's wife, who came from the countryside to see her daughter, was killed in Naka district. The word is that the two blood brothers were behind that, too.

RIYO: Aye, if it is Choan's doing…

DONOSUKE: Choan is the enemy of my parents.

RIYO: Son, come with me.

CHUZO: Wait a moment, where are you going all of a sudden? You are both red in the face.

RIYO: To find my husband's hated enemy, who sent him to a horrible death…

DONOSUKE: …And kill my father's enemy.

CHUZO: Come now, if you make accusations without any evidence, you will be the ones in big trouble. Calm down, calm down.

RIYO: Whatever I say, I'm only a woman. And my son is still very young.

DONOSUKE: Chuzo, please help us.

CHUZO: I am not strong but I will try to help you clear your father's name.

MOTHER & SON: Thank you for offering your assistance.

A number of people enter. Kyuhachi bumps into Rokuemon.

ROKUEMON: Found you at last, Kyuhachi. I was running around town looking for you.

KYUHACHI: Why is that? What has happened?

ROKUEMON: Sentaro is still visiting the brothels.

KYUHACHI: The young master promised me that he would never go to the brothels again.

ROKUEMON: Then what is this? The young master dropped this in the street.

KYUHACHI: *(Looking at the letter.)* Th-this is a plea for him to come tonight. Then Sentaro, you would simply go, would you? You promised me many times that you would never go again. You, you...

Kyuhachi blindly grabs Rokuemon by the collar and tightens his grip.

ROKUEMON: No, no. I am choking. Let go, let me go.
KYUHACHI: No, I will never let go.
ROKUEMON: I will d-die.
KYUHACHI: You should die, you...
ROKUEMON: Kyuhachi, it's me, it's me!
KYUHACHI: Oh my god, I got carried away in anger. Please forgive me, forgive me.

Scene 11. Nihonzutsumi Embankment

An embankment upstage. Late evening. The roofs of Yoshiwara can be seen in the distance. Midstage, Japanese pampas grass and weeping willows grow. Downstage is the marshland. Music plays throughout the scene.

Song
　　　　Yoshiwara late at night, when the lights are out
　　　　The moon is hidden in love's darkness.
　　　　In secret, leaving the red light quarters
　　　　Avoiding all eyes, along the embankment
　　　　Travel a couple of desperate lovers.

The sound of the hour bell.

Sentaro with a short sword and a towel wrapped around his head and jowl, and Sayoginu with a decorative towel over her head, come stealthily across the embankment, looking back anxiously over and over again. Sentaro groans in pain.

SAYOGINU: What is the matter?
SENTARO: I suddenly relaxed when we escaped from the quarters. Now I have a stomachache.

SAYOGINU: Oh no, I don't have any medicine on me.

SENTARO: We are going to die together, so I don't need any medicine! The trouble is the Plum Blossom Temple where we planned to commit double suicide is not close. We cannot get there quickly

SAYOGINU: If we hang around here, the posse will find us. You can imagine what they might do to us.

SENTARO: Well then, let's die here.

TOGETHER: *(Song.)*
> We view the last of this world
> Dew glistens, as we sit knee to knee.
> Our hands tremble as they entwine.
> We are each other's dream of dreams
> If this is dream, no need to waken.

SAYOGINU: Kill me quick.

SENTARO: D-do not hurry so. To die like this when we have not done our filial duty to our parents is not... We will beg forgiveness from the shadow of the grass.

The two lovers hold hands and weep. On the embankment, appears Sanji with his kimono hem tucked up and a towel wrapped around his head and jowl.

SANJI: The rumor is Sayoginu of the Clove House eloped. That idiot young master, Sentaro of Iseya, must have lured her out. I stamped the guarantor's seal when that bitch was sold to Yoshiwara. I'd better take care of this.

Sayoginu and Sentaro notice Sanji and try to run off.

SANJI: Hey, is that you Sentaro, with Sayonigu?

SENTARO & SAYONIGU: Please, please...

SANJI: Fantastic. This is a great place to meet you two

SENTARO & SAYONIGU: Please let us go.

SANJI: With someone else, I wouldn't interfere. But I was Sayonigu's guarantor. I stamped the seal. What the hell! You can't fucking take her away.

SENTARO: Please, if she and I cannot be together, we decided we had no choice but to die together. So, I've stolen her away from the house.

247

SAYOGINU: You are the blood brother of Choan, my uncle. You know I am his niece. Please turn a blind eye.

SANJI: From the viewpoint of the Clove House, they have paid a huge sum to acquire you. If you die now, they lose their total investment. They'll come after Choan and me, the guarantors. It's my lucky day in a million to find you here, and it's absolutely crazy to let you go!

SENTARO: Then you insist on capturing us?

SAYOGINU: Please, do let it pass.

SANJI: Of course not. I'll arrest you and get a good ransom.

SENTARO: Sayoginu, let's run.

SAYOGINU: Yes.

SANJI: You won't escape. If you elope with a prostitute whose term isn't up, that makes you an abductor, a criminal. Gotcha!

Sanji knocks Sentaro down. Sayoginu tries to run to Sentaro when Sanji pulls her back.

SANJI: Obey or else. Come along.

Sanji is about to drag her away. Sentaro clings to and begs Sanji, who picks up a stick and attacks him. Sentaro flees while continuing to beg, but beaten hard, he faints and collapses on the embankment.

Sayoginu tries to run to him, but Sanji stands in her way. Kyuhachi comes by.

SANJI: Oh no, a cat, a cat. *(Throws Doll Sanji.)*

KYUHACHI: *(To himself.)* …I knew that he'd gone to the tea house, but I didn't want to intrude and shame the young master in front of everyone, so I've been walking back and forth along the embankment waiting to catch him on his way back… He should be back soon. Then I'll give him an earful. *(Trips over Sentaro lying face down on the ground.)* Oh excuse me, I was preoccupied and not looking. What are you doing here at this time of day? *(Pulls him up to a sitting position.)*

Sentaro comes to and groans. The moon appears and lights up the vicinity.

KYUHACHI: Oh goodness, it's Sentaro.

SENTARO: *(Mistaking Kyuhachi for Sanji.)* Give her back. Give Sayoginu back to me.

KYUHACHI: Get a grip on yourself.

SENTARO: Who the... Oh, Kyuhachi.

KYUHACHI: Young master, what is the matter?

SENTARO: I'm really ashamed of myself... *(Tries to escape.)*

KYUHACHI: *(Grabbing Sentaro and forcing him to sit down.)* You promised never to go back to the Clove House. How dare you deceive me!

SENTARO: I never intended to deceive you. I lost my way in pleasure, and it has led to this. I am very sorry...

Sentaro draws a short sword and tries to pierce his throat.

KYUHACHI: *(Hurriedly stopping him.)* What are you doing? Oh no, you must not die now. If you die, all my years of service and loyalty go down the drain.

SENTARO: I came here tonight intending to die...

KYUHACHI: What? ...Intending to die?

SENTARO: I was unable to forget Sayoginu, my love. I cannot give her up. We agreed that if we could not live together in this world, we would commit double suicide. We escaped from her house, but Choan and Sanji caught up with us. During the argument, I was beaten and fainted. *(His voice now rises into a wail.)* Sanji took...Sayoginu away. There is no point in my living. In apology to you, I will die now. Do not stop me.

KYUHACHI: I cannot let you die.

SENTARO: Let me die, I beg you.

The two clutch at each other in their desperation and inadvertently head towards the river. Kyuhachi snatches away Sentara's short sword. Sentaro tries to retrieve it and their fight turns vicious.

KYUHACHI: If you die now, what about my pain and sorrow, my pain and sorrow?

Sentaro suddenly catches his breath and falls over backwards.

KYUHACHI: Huh, what's this? Oh no, no, no, no.

From over the embankment, Choan appears suddenly.

CHOAN: I saw what you did. Faking virtue and loyalty, you go and kill your master!

KYUHACHI: N-no, you're wrong. He…

CHOAN: You are guilty of murdering your master. Master killer. I'll deliver you to the authorities. Murderer. Come here. Come with me, you bastard.

Choan gets ahold of Kyuhachi. At that moment, Chuzo bounds in followed hard by Riyo and Donosuke.

CHUZO: Found you, Choan. You'll pay this time for your crimes of three years ago. I'll make sure you can't cover up your tracks again. I just made an appeal to the authorities. You're not getting away with it.

RIYO: Choan is my husband's worst enemy.

DONOSUKE: Despite my youth, I am the son of a samurai. I thought to destroy my father's enemy, but…

RIYO: …Chuzo advised us that the better judgment was to appeal to the authorities…

DONOSUKE: …So we have filed a suit against you.

CHUZO: I unexpectedly met Madam Riyo on the third anniversary of the Master's death. This must be due to Buddha's guidance. On that rainy day before dawn, the man I saw at the back gate of the Tenjin Shrine was you Choan.

CHUZO, RIYO & DONOSUKE: Confess your crimes.

CHOAN: Hehe, so it's Chuzo, the Kaizuka employment agent, come to save the day. Without any claims to evidence, you talk about things as if they are true and try to bury me in a deep hole. You must hold a damn serious grudge against me. Such bloodthirsty plotting. I could never come up with such a stupid accusation—going out in the rain at dawn. Listen Chuzo, you were fucking dreaming. I never did such a thing, ya sleazebag.

KYUHACHI: The reason the young master and Sayoginu eloped and decided to commit double suicide was that you tricked 50 gold coins from him. Now that you have killed my master, you must prepare to hang from a three-meter tall tree. I'm going to take you with me. Come with me.

CHOAN: What the hell?! Let me go, you fucking bastard.

Clouds pass across the moon, and the sky darkens. Choan blindly fights off Kyuhachi, Chuzo, Riyo, and Donosuke as they, just as blindly, try to capture him in the dark. At that moment, on the embankment, Gunzo and his men appear with Doll Sanji.

GUNZO: *(In the tone of a formal announcement.)* Sanji has filed an emergency appeal to the court. Speak.

DOLL SANJI: Choan offered me three gold coins to kill Osoyo, his sister by blood and the widow of Jubei, who was killed at Akabanebashi Bridge. I happened to be hard up then and nosing around for even three bronze coins. I tricked her out of the house and killed her at the Asakusa fields. It was the first time for me to kill anyone. I felt really spooked, and from that night I've been seized by shivers and pursued by Osoyo's angry spirit. On top of that, a rumor spread that I was the murderer. If I am to be executed, I'd rather own up to my crime and be punished according to the law. That way, I will make up for my wrongdoing. Also, the curse of the dead spirits will lead to Choan's arrest and his crimes will be revealed. I beg forgiveness for my evil acts and so made an emergency appeal to the court.

CHOAN: Lies, all lies! You've forgotten what you owe me, you wicked pervert. You killed my sister and now you're shamelessly trying to pass the crime onto me. You're the proverbial dog that bites its master's hand!

DOLL SANJI: At a time like this, you are turning your tail like a cowardly dog. You're faking it even to me and I know everything about you. You aren't the clever Choan anymore. If you won't spill the beans, I will—the mastermind of Jubei's murder three years ago, of the 50 gold coin extortion from the young master Sentaro at the Iseya pawnbroker's, and of Soyo's murder is Choan. You planned them all. If you added all the other crimes he's committed, he would have to die anyway. Receive the judgment of the court like a man and join me in hell!

The meowing of a cat. Will-o'-the-wisps flicker around Doll Sanji.

DOLL SANJI: Oh my god, vengeful spirits are here. The curse of the murdered is on me.

RIYO: Choan, you killed Jubei, smeared the blame on my husband, and now pretend innocence. Slicing you into pieces won't be enough to allay my vengeance.

CHOAN: Don't know nothing, nothing. Bring undeniable evidence. Without evidence, I cannot be convicted...unless I confess.

CHUZO: You still go on like that? Are you beyond fear of the authorities?

RIYO: Please your honor, execute him and grant us revenge.

GUNZO: Attend! Tie up Choan. Take him away and torture him.

The guards use ladders, large two-wheeled wagons, and rope to capture Choan. In turn, Choan attacks the guards with his sword. Hands and legs go flying, and bodies are sliced through the midriff as well. But at last, he is bound with rope and held fast.

CHOAN: Torture me if you can! Being tortured to death and being sentenced to death by confession are about the same. Even if I were sliced up, if I decide not to confess, I absolutely won't. Why should I confess to what no one knows?

DOLL SANJI: *(The Choan actor is operating it.)* Yo, Choan, life's short now. Blowing off your mouth in spite is just a sign of cowardice.

CHOAN: Fuck you and shut up. If I say I won't confess, I won't, even till I'm reduced to bone. You stupid fart. You don't have any backbone.

CHUZO: You are still spouting off about your power. Be afraid of human justice, you scumbag.

RIYO: Please, I beg you, kill this man.

CHUZO & RIYO: Execute the criminal.

GUNZO: Take them away.

CHOAN: Hey, Sanji.

DOLL SANJI: What?

GUARD: Walk straight.

CHOAN: See ya in hell! *(Spits.)*

Music comes in. Fadeout.

THE END

1 Yoshiwara was the licensed pleasure quarters of Edo. Wikipedia, s.v. "Yoshiwara," last modified December 7, 2019, 15:03, https://en.wikipedia. org/wiki/Yoshiwara.

2 A *hanamichi* is a raised walkway from the stage through the audience seating area to the back of the auditorium in *kabuki*. Wikipedia, s.v. "Hanamichi," last modified December 10, 2018, 14:27, https://en.wikipedia.org/ wiki/Hanamichi.

3 In Edo coinage, a gold coin (*ryo*) equals four silver coins (*bu*), which equals sixteen bronze coins (*shu*), which equals 4,000 copper coins (*mon*). A gold coin is estimated to be worth between ¥63,000 ($582) to ¥74,000 ($684) depending on the item, according to the Bank of Japan in 2016.

4 A seasonal time system was employed in the Edo period. This system divided a day into day and night according to the dawn and dusk. The two parts were each divided into six segments or *ittoki*, which was roughly two hours, but varied by the day and season. The method of announcing the time was by an hour-bell, and the numbering of the hour bells was complicated. Here, Choan promises to wake Jubei at the sixth dawn bell, which is struck at 6 a.m. (or thirty minutes before sunrise). "To Regular Life with 'Hour Bells,'" The Seiko Museum (website), https://museum.seiko.co.jp/en/ knowledge/relation_07/.

5 The seventh bell marks the time between 4 a.m. and 6 a.m.

6 The eighth bell marks the time between 2 a.m. and 4 a.m.

7 In the Chinese zodiac clock, the tiger takes the hours of 3 a.m. to 5 a.m.

8 10 p.m.

9 Bon Festival is held between August 13 and 15, commemorating deceased ancestors. Wikipedia, s.v. "Bon Festival," last modified December 10, 2019, 20:29, https://en.wikipedia.org/wiki/Bon_Festival.

10 The amount given is ten *monme*. *Monme* is a traditional unit of weight, equivalent to 3.75 g. "Monme," Vcalc.com, last modified October 18, 2019, 01:21, https://www.vcalc.com/wiki/jmorris/Monme+%28 Weight%2FMass%29.

11 "Nanman dabutsu" is an abbreviated form of the prayer Homage to the Amida Buddha, while "nyanmai da" is Ichirobe's own adaptation that makes it sound like a cat meowing.

Chapter 9

Kuro Tanino and *Avidya—The Dark Inn*

Kuro Tanino (b. 1976), a licensed psychiatrist turned playwright-director, is the head of the Niwa Gekidan Penino theatre company (f. 2000). He is noted for his diverse actor/character types and complex performing-objects. Tanino states that he wrote this play to showcase Mame Yamada, a short-statured actor who performs Momofuku, the master puppeteer.[1] This enigmatic character is one of the channels for conveying the uncanny, the ambiguity of individual/sociocultural identity, illusion of the vanishing, phantasm, complexity of social relationality, desire and sexuality, and Buddhist ignorance.

While storyboarding is Tanino's standard method in developing a play, with *Avidya—The Dark Inn,* he wrote a script for a change and then trimmed it down by two-thirds. For further discussion on this play, please refer to the third section of Chapter 2. (See fig. 2.7 in the color plates.)

This translation is a slightly revised version of the one published in *ENGEKI: Japanese Theatre in the New Millennium 4.*

Selected Chronology

This chronology is entirely focused on the *Avidya—The Dark Inn.* Performed fifty times domestically, it has toured to Europe and Australia.

2015
August: Premiere at Morishita Studio, Tokyo

2016
Tanino won the prestigious 60th Kishida Drama Prize.
Niwa Gekidan Penino won the ACA National Arts Festival Excellence Award.

International Performances
2016 Europe Tour
August: Theater Kampnagel, Hamburg, Germany
August: Noorderzon Performing Arts Festival, Groningen, the Netherlands
September: Aarhus Festival, Aarhus, Denmark
September: Festival d'Automne à Paris, Paris, France

2017
October: OzAsia Festival, Adelaide, Australia

2018
September: Festival d'Automne à Paris; Japonismes 2018
October: Tandem Théâtre, Douai, France

Fig. 9.1. Niwa Gekidan Penino, *Avidya—The Dark Inn*, 2016, ROHM Theatre Kyoto. Photo © Yoshikazu Inoue. Courtesy of Kyoto Experiment.

Avidya——The Dark Inn

By Kuro Tanino
Translated by Mari Boyd

This play is for Toyama, my home prefecture,
For Yatsuomachi town and the Unazuki hot springs,
For all the lives lost due to the opening of the Hokuriku Shinkansen
line,[2]
In honor of their battle.

Cast of Characters (in order of appearance)[3]
ICHIRO KURATA, 55 years old
MOMOFUKU KURATA, 82 years old
TAKIKO or **OTAKI,** 81 years old
MATSUO, 35 years old
SANSUKE, bath attendant, 47 years old
FUMIE or **FUMI,** 53 years old
IKU, 38 years old
OLD WOMAN'S VOICE

STAGE SET
An old hot spring inn. A four-sided set sits on top of a revolving stage:
Side 1: Entrance hall and restroom
Side 2: Guestrooms (men's guestroom on first floor, women's guestroom
on second floor)
Side 3: Changing room for the bath
Side 4: Open-air hot spring bath
A courtyard is at the center of the four sides, and a persimmon
tree grows there.

OLD WOMAN'S VOICE (hereafter VOICE): Japan has many places called "Hell Valley" due to the hot springs borne of abundant geothermal energy. The Hell Valley hot springs in this tale are located in the Hokuriku region of Japan. In addition to the plentiful mineral water, this place is named after the hellish-looking scenery carved out of diorite rock by the volcano that erupted about 200 years ago. Now…

The lights go on as the wall clock strikes the hour. The hour hand points to two o'clock.

VOICE: About eight kilometers from the center of the hot spring area, deep into the mountains, there is a little-known and unnamed hot spring inn. A father and son have come from Tokyo to do a job at the request of the inn's management. With autumn preparing rapidly for winter, it is a cold day and the temperature dips below 0℃. They arrive in the afternoon, three minutes after two o'clock.

Scene 1. The Front Entrance

Two o'clock on a fine day. From the front door to the entrance hall, the old wooden building has a dignified atmosphere. It displays the battle scars from many trying seasons in a deep-snow district. The plaster has peeled off the walls, the floorboards display bold cracks, and a single central pillar holds up the high ceiling.

Just inside the front door is a plain-looking lounge area equipped with a wooden bench, a freestanding ashtray, and a potbelly stove. No one is manning the unadorned reception desk. Only a string of a thousand paper cranes hanging from the ceiling gives this space some ambience.

The glass-paned front door opens with a slight trembling sound, and the cries of wild birds suddenly flood the hall.

MAN: Hello.

A man stands in the doorway. He wears a black knitted cap and a shiny down jacket. In one hand, he has a small bundle in a wrapping cloth;

with the other, he pulls a stainless steel wheeled suitcase. A 90-cm (35-in.) narrow, cowhide case for musical instruments is strapped across his shoulder.

MAN: Hello?

No one answers. Man steps into the building.

MAN: Hello!

Man exits the building once.

MAN: It is cold, so let us enter and take a rest.

An elderly figure appears. About 90 cm (30 in.) tall, this person suffers from microsomia. With a glossy, well-tended leather coat, a black knitted cap, and long, gray hair reaching down to the waist, this person's gender is not easy to discern. In fact, he is puppeteer Momofuku Kurata accompanied by his son, Ichiro. Momofuku is a little breathless after having walked up the long mountain road. He puckers up his lips to calm his breathing after the lengthy walk from the bus stop. Ichiro once again faces the depths of the inn.

ICHIRO: Hello.

There is no answer.

ICHIRO: Let's go in. See the chair over there. Please…
MOMOFUKU: Ah, yes.

Ichiro closes the front door. The cries of the wild birds fade and the ticking of the wall clock becomes louder. They take off their shoes but do not put them on the shoe rack as they do not intend to stay long. Momofuku sits down on the bench and rubs his knees tenderly. Ichiro goes to the vacant reception desk and looks around. Noticing a restroom by the desk, he knocks on the door lightly and then enters to check it.

ICHIRO: No one seems to be around. Let's wait.

MOMOFUKU: Uh-huh. That's fine.

ICHIRO: There's a toilet here.

MOMOFUKU: What's this place called?

ICHIRO: No name was given on the letter we got.

MOMOFUKU: Ahh, is that so.

ICHIRO: There's no signboard either. Old inns like this sometimes don't put any up.

MOMOFUKU: Uh-huh.

Ichiro takes out a thermos from the wrapping cloth and offers his father some tea.

MOMOFUKU: Aye, thanks. *(He sips some hot green tea.)* Mmm.

Ichiro opens a Tupperware container and offers the contents to his father.

MOMOFUKU: What's this?

ICHIRO: Dumplings smothered in sweet soy powder.

In this cold, the human body needs sugar. But, as if he has decided it is too early to consume any, Momofuku continues to have only tea. The clicking of the wall clock pendulum is loud and clear. When Ichiro is about to stand up after packing the sweets back in the wrapping cloth…

MOMOFUKU: No need to call anymore.

ICHIRO: Right.

MOMOFUKU: The letter. Have you checked it?

ICHIRO: I'll go over it again.

Ichiro kneels by his father, takes the letter out of the envelope, and reads it out loud rapidly.

ICHIRO: An Honorable Request

Dear Mr. Momofuku Kurata, Master Puppeteer,

Wafting on the wind, the season of autumn colors has arrived.
I hope this finds you enjoying days of good health.

Please excuse me for making this sudden request, but I hope you will consider it favorably... *(Skipping a line or two.)* ...and, would it be possible for you to fulfill my long-held desire for a puppet performance by your esteemed self at my inn? I take the presumption of enclosing a map with this letter. I humbly hope you will find this invitation agreeable and acceptable.

Yours Sincerely,

On a propitious October day, 2013

From further inside the inn, the sounds of someone slowly descending the stairs can be heard.

ICHIRO: Someone's coming.
MOMOFUKU: Oh really?
ICHIRO: Most likely a guest.

Momofuku finishes drinking the lukewarm tea. Right away, Ichiro pours more tea into the cup.

An old woman wearing a hood emerges from behind a curtain made of strung beads.

VOICE: This is Takiko, a villager. Those who know her call her Otaki. Her village is located about four kilometers from this spa. Over 80 years of age, she still cannot quit smoking; since her husband's death ten years ago, her daily intake has increased. She has come to this spa since childhood and now stays every year for the period between autumn and the beginning of winter. The hot spring water serves to allay her chest pains.

Otaki wears a traditional padded coat over her cotton kimono and holds a bundle, from which a small gardening sickle is visible. She is about to go out and collect some mountain vegetables.

Noticing the two men, she is startled and comes to a standstill. Ichiro

continues to pour tea. Her expression changes from surprise to caution.
He finishes pouring the tea.

ICHIRO: How do you do?

OTAKI: *(A beat.)* How do you do?

ICHIRO: I am Kurata.

OTAKI: *(A beat.)* Uh-huh.

ICHIRO: We were called from Tokyo. This evening, we are scheduled to perform.

OTAKI: Well…

ICHIRO: Is the owner of the inn away?

OTAKI: Huh? What did you say? A performance?

ICHIRO: That's right. We are looking for the inn owner.

OTAKI: I dunno. *(She shifts to the local Toyama dialect for the rest of the scene.)*

ICHIRO: Is that right. I see.

OTAKI: No one's in charge here.

ICHIRO: Huh? No one in charge?

OTAKI: Right. No one runs the inn.

ICHIRO: Where is the proprietor?

OTAKI: Proprietor? He's not here. There's no proprietor. No one like that at all.

ICHIRO: Is that so. Are you a neighbor?

OTAKI: Uh? What? Oh. Me? No, I don't live nearby.

ICHIRO: Do you come here often?

OTAKI: Aye, I do.

ICHIRO: Really.

OTAKI: *(A beat.)* Are you two sick?

ICHIRO: Huh?

OTAKI: You here to heal your sickness? Isn't that right?

ICHIRO: We only came here to perform. The proprietor asked us to.

OTAKI: So, I told you the proprietor isn't here. How many times do I have to tell you? You're lying. You two are here 'cause you're sick.

Momofuku stands up.

MOMOFUKU: She says no one's in charge.

Otaki is astounded by Momofuku's small size. She gasps.

ICHIRO: Ah, yes.
MOMOFUKU: I need to go.

Momofuku goes to the restroom. Otaki catches her breath.

OTAKI: Say, who the heck are you people?

Ichiro brings out a cigarette from his pocket and lights it. He inhales deep and then exhales the smoke slowly.

ICHIRO: Well, I do follow what you say.
OTAKI: Th-this isn't the kind of place for entertainment. We don't get travelers staying here, either. No one outside the village knows about this place. If you head farther west, towards Sanno Shrine, there's a hot spring town that has inns and such that offer entertainment. Maybe you mistook this place for one of those?
ICHIRO: I see.

The sound of Momofuku relieving himself can be heard. It is obviously a man urinating.

OTAKI: Hey, wait, wait a bit.
ICHIRO: Yes.
OTAKI: Who the heck is that man?
ICHIRO: My father.
OTAKI: Eh?
ICHIRO: He is my father.
OTAKI: Ah? What? Your fa-father?
ICHIRO: Yes.
OTAKI: Whoa, is that true?
ICHIRO: Uh-huh.
OTAKI: Your father?
ICHIRO: Yes.
OTAKI: *(Pause.)* Nahh…not true…

Momofuku emerges from the restroom.

OTAKI: *(Chants a Buddhist sutra repeatedly.)* Namandab. Namandab. Namandab, namandab… Namandab, namandab.[4]

It seems she still cannot believe him. Momofuku puts on an extra pair of straw sandals provided by the inn and goes out. When Ichiro tries to follow him, he stops his son.

MOMOFUKU: You stay. I'm going to take a look around.

Otaki continues her Buddhist chanting while Momofuku goes for a walk.

OTAKI: Haah… *(She calms down a bit.)* So, what is it? What kind of performance do you do?
ICHIRO: Puppetry.
OTAKI: Puppetry? Puppetry? I don't understand. What is that?
ICHIRO: Well, you see. To put it simply, we manipulate a puppet and make a show.
OTAKI: I don't really understand. I've never seen anything like that. Your father is an old man, enjoying a long life. He must be over 80, right?
ICHIRO: Right.
OTAKI: That's it. Same here. The poor man was brought all the way here.
ICHIRO: Yes, but this is how we make a living.
OTAKI: The bus service has ended by now.
ICHIRO: Is that so? I had better check again.
OTAKI: Never mind, you can stay tonight. Use the room down there.
ICHIRO: Uh-huh, if the buses have ended for the day, we'll have no choice but to stay.
OTAKI: Oh, the buses have all gone. Never mind, never mind. You'll meet a blind man called Matsuo in that room. People who come here are all sick.
ICHIRO: So we share a room with him. Is that right?
OTAKI: Well, there are no other rooms, so it's a squeeze.

The wind shakes the front door glass. Otaki looks out from the entrance.

OTAKI: Your father hasn't come back yet.

ICHIRO: Right.

OTAKI: What are your names? Did I ask before?

ICHIRO: I am Ichiro Kurata.

OTAKI: Ichiro, what's your father's name?

ICHIRO: Momofuku. Momofuku Kurata.

OTAKI: Momofuku? That's an unusual name. What Japanese characters does he use?

ICHIRO: The number 100 for Momo and "happiness" for fuku.

OTAKI: Wonderful. A fascinating name. I'm Takiko. Nice to meet you. After you've had a rest, please try the hot spring bath.

ICHIRO: If the buses are gone.

OTAKI: Take your luggage to your room. If you leave your bags out here, they'll get in the way. I won't be able to smoke, you know.

ICHIRO: I see.

OTAKI: You should get warmed up. *(Ichiro bows.)* Take it easy.

Ichiro ducks under the beaded curtain and heads for the guestroom. Otaki, left to herself, takes out a cigarette from her kimono sleeve. But suddenly feeling a cold draft pass over her hot body, she shivers. She decides not to smoke.

VOICE: Whether it was because of the two men's guileless appearance, or because the cold was attracted to warm bodies, or because Ichiro's eyes gleamed like a nocturnal insect's, Takiko's thoughts wandered back to her deceased husband. At her age, this was extremely unusual.

Otaki decides against mountain vegetable picking and goes back to her room. Her footsteps ascending the stairs can be heard. The central pillar in the hall also makes a low sound.

VOICE: The inn's wooden structure also trembled. At the visit of these two men, the heart of this barely known inn seemed to be shaken, too.

Blackout.

VOICE: Greetings, everyone. Thank you for coming today to see *Avidya—The Dark Inn.* Please enjoy the show.

Scene 2. Guestrooms

The two large guestrooms are on different floors: the room for men is on the first and the one for women on the second. Shared by various guests, each has the same structure—a tatami-*matted floor and a* kotatsu *table.*[5] *On the table are amenities like a thermos, teacups, teapot, and a tea canister. The second floor guestroom also has vanity mirrors and a kimono rack with two kimonos hanging. Beside them are* shamisen *instruments in paulownia box stands.*

From upstairs, a large persimmon tree can be seen standing in the courtyard with leaves past the glory of autumn colors and ripe fruit ready to drop. The tough bark that can survive hard winters distinguishes this persimmon tree from those in urban areas. To enter the spa, guests have to pass through the inner yard to reach the changing room.

Ichiro opens the sliding doors and enters the downstairs guestroom. While he is setting down the luggage, Momofuku returns from his walk. Pointing at the wheeled suitcase, he says:

MOMOFUKU: Let him stretch his arms and legs.
ICHIRO: Yes, right away.

Momofuku sits down by a window and gazes out at the scenery. Ichiro undoes the rope around the luggage. Then, he stops working on the luggage, goes to the closet, pulls out several cushions, dusts them off, and puts them on the floor by Momofuku.

ICHIRO: Please use these. Aren't you cold?
MOMOFUKU: Uh? Mm.

Ichiro prepares tea again and serves it to Momofuku with the sweet dumplings.

MOMOFUKU: Thanks.

This time he eats a dumpling as he needs the sugar to raise his energy level.

MOMOFUKU: So, what about the return bus?

ICHIRO: I don't know yet. After this, I will go check.

MOMOFUKU: Good.

Ichiro pours more tea into the cup. Momofuku looks around the room and seems to be in a daze.

MOMOFUKU: Hey, remember that time, that house we fled to? Where was it?

ICHIRO: Oh, um…

MOMOFUKU: See, that one was like this, too.

ICHIRO: I know what you mean.

MOMOFUKU: Let me see now, what was it called?

Momofuku often talks like this on his travels. Ichiro always answers in the same way.

ICHIRO: Was it Oyama?

MOMOFUKU: No, I don't think so. O…Oizumi, no, that's not it.

ICHIRO: Really.

MOMOFUKU: This is a pleasant place.

ICHIRO: Uh-huh.

MOMOFUKU: The mountains are attractive.

ICHIRO: I'll go and check the bus timetable.

MOMOFUKU: Please do.

Ichiro exits the room. Momofuku enjoys sipping tea and eating dumplings in turns.

The sun begins to set and the temperature drops. From afar, a shot from a hunting rifle is heard. The woods seem to cry out in an effort to endure the sudden change in temperature.

The changing room door opens and a man wearing glasses steps into the inner yard. He is wearing a thick sweat suit, yet it is clear that he is very thin. Though his hair has been shaved off, there are patches remaining. He is walking with care.

VOICE: This is Matsuo, from the same village as Takiko about four kilometers away. Since he damaged his eyes in an accident and lost his job, he has been staying at this spa frequently. The only clinic in the tiny village was unable to cure him. In despair, he believes that his eyesight has returned to the point that he can sense the outline of many things due to this health spa. For him, this is the last place of hope to regain his vision.

Matsuo passes through the yard and enters the guestroom. He has just left the bath and is carrying his towel over his shoulder. He sits down on the tatami *floor and starts to read a book. Momofuku gives a long yawn. Matsuo notices Momofuku for the first time.*

MATSUO: Oh, excuse me…
MOMOFUKU: How do you do?
MATSUO: *(A beat.)* I didn't realize you were here.
MOMOFUKU: Uh-huh.
MATSUO: My vision is very poor.
MOMOFUKU: Uh-huh.
MATSUO: Are you a traveler?
MOMOFUKU: Huh? Well, sort of.
MATSUO: It's unusual to have travelers here. Where are you from?
MOMOFUKU: From Tokyo.
MATSUO: Really. You must be tired. Are you alone?
MOMOFUKU: My son is with me.
MATSUO: Ohh, you're with your boy. That is commendable.
MOMOFUKU: Umm.
MATSUO: Are you here about your body?
MOMOFUKU: What do you mean? My body?
MATSUO: Well, there are hot springs farther down. No one needs to come this far up. Are you ill?
MOMOFUKU: No.
MATSUO: Oh, are you just passing by?
MOMOFUKU: That's about right.
MATSUO: Really, is that so? I am surprised you found this out-of-the-way spot.

Momofuku takes out a cigarette and smokes. He opens the window a tad to puff out the smoke.

MATSUO: Your throat is precious, you know.
MOMOFUKU: Huh? My throat is all right...
MATSUO: Ahh, but tobacco is bad for you.
MOMOFUKU: True.
MATSUO: Uh-huh, the air up here is very clean, too. Rest well and you will recover in time.

Momofuku stubs out his cigarette in the ashtray after a few more puffs as if it no longer tastes good. Matsuo continues to read his book.

MATSUO: You must consider this comical.
MOMOFUKU: What is?
MATSUO: To see a blind man reading a book.

Matsuo waits for a reply, but Momofuku shows little interest and says nothing.

MATSUO: Before, I would read Braille. But then I thought that since I couldn't see, there was no pressing need to read books.
MOMOFUKU: Ah...
MATSUO: See this, *(Showing him in high spirits.)* these are all pressed flowers. They say that if you become blind, your third eye[6] will open. But it's not that simple.
MOMOFUKU: Oh, really.
MATSUO: Being in touch with life in this way, I feel I will have an opportunity to gain such vision.
MOMOFUKU: Hmm, a third eye, you say.
MATSUO: I just mean that I am hoping for it.
MOMOFUKU: What will you see with your third eye?
MATSUO: With my third eye?
MOMOFUKU: So, with a third eye, what will you see?
MATSUO: That would be...the soul.
MOMOFUKU: Oh, really. What will you do when you see the soul?
MATSUO: *(Pause.)* Nothing. I just want to see it.
MOMOFUKU: Oh, really.

Matsuo straightens up.

MATSUO: Please excuse me. I am Matsuo. What is your name?
MOMOFUKU: Kurata.
MATSUO: Mr. Kurata, nice to meet you.
MOMOFUKU: Nice to meet you, too, Mr. Matsuo.

A pause.

MOMOFUKU: Would you like to touch?
MATSUO: Huh?

Matsuo cannot comprehend what Momofuku means and ponders over his words. As he searches hard for meaning, he has tremors from the neck up.

Ichiro returns. Matsuo suddenly moves into a defensive position and quickly looks around warily. Ichiro tells his father that he could not find anyone managing the inn and that the day's bus service has already ended.

MOMOFUKU: Yes, I see. So, we cannot return today.
ICHIRO: Exactly. The next bus leaves at 6:30 a.m.
MOMOFUKU: Yes, that will be all right.
ICHIRO: I am sorry.
MOMOFUKU: Pass me the box.

When Ichiro swings around to reach the box, he notices Matsuo.

ICHIRO: Ahh, excuse me.

Matsuo remains silent as he doesn't think Ichiro's words are directed at him.

ICHIRO: I am very sorry.
MATSUO: Uh, I, uh, yeah…

Ichiro hands Momofuku the wheeled suitcase. Momofuku opens and checks the contents. The audience should not be able to see inside the case.

ICHIRO: Mr. Matsuo, I assume. We are from Tokyo.
MATSUO: Yeah, I know. Your father told me earlier.
ICHIRO: Is that right.
MATSUO: I'm very surprised.
ICHIRO: Is something the matter?
MATSUO: No, no, I have poor eyesight, so...
ICHIRO: Oh, I see. *(Lowers his head.)*
MATSUO: No matter, no matter, you misunderstand. I can pick up on people's presence, you see...
MOMOFUKU: So, it wasn't a person just now, as you didn't feel...
MATSUO: *(Frightened.)* No, no. That's not what I mean. As you referred to your son, I was imagining a little boy...
ICHIRO: Uh-huh.

Intending to serve tea, Matsuo searches for the tea canister and teacups. Though he should be used to groping for the tea set, this time he cannot find the tea set easily.

ICHIRO: I don't need any tea, thank you.
MATSUO: Ah, uh, really? *(A beat.)* We'll be sharing this room.
ICHIRO: We're the ones intruding into your space. We'll be leaving early tomorrow morning.
MATSUO: That's unfortunate. Now that you're here, you might as well take your time.
ICHIRO: Uh-huh, we'd like to do that. But in fact, we've been conned.
MATSUO: What happened?
ICHIRO: We received a request from this inn to perform.
MATSUO: Perform?
ICHIRO: Uh-huh, we perform puppet plays, at dinner parties and so on.
MATSUO: So that's it. I thought something was strange. Even the sick don't usually come to a place like this. I see now.
ICHIRO: Uh-huh.
MATSUO: I assumed that you were here for your father's treatment. Please excuse me. A puppet show? That's unusual. And also strange.

As you can tell, this is a hot spring inn, plain and simple, without parties and entertainment. Who contacted you?

ICHIRO: An invitation arrived but without the sender's name, so… Here it is.

Ichiro offers the letter, but, naturally, Matsuo cannot read it.

MATSUO: *(A beat.)* You know… Ha-ha-ha…

ICHIRO: Oh, excuse me.

MATSUO: Never mind. But it is strange. We don't have an inn owner here.

ICHIRO: Uh-huh, we heard from the lady…

MATSUO: Ah, you mean Otaki—Takiko, the granny.

ICHIRO: At the reception by the entrance.

MATSUO: Of course, that was where the proprietor sat long ago. At that time, the surrounding villages were large, and this place was apparently quite a popular spot. With depopulation and the owner's decease, it's become open to the public and the visitors are careful of how they use the premises. The so-called visitors are basically only the regulars.

ICHIRO: I see.

MATSUO: It's not the kind of spot that would be reviewed in some tourist book.

ICHIRO: Uh-huh.

MATSUO: Ah, Sansuke might know something.

ICHIRO: Sansuke?

MATSUO: Right. He's the bath attendant. That's so unusual nowadays. Just him. But he's not employed by the inn. I don't know the details, but he's the longest resident here after Otaki.

ICHIRO: Is that so.

MATSUO: I can ask him later.

ICHIRO: Yes, please.

MATSUO: Are you in a hurry?

ICHIRO: No, no.

MATSUO: Is there anything else on your mind?

ICHIRO: Let me see.

Momofuku is already sleeping on top of the cushions with the suitcase closed. Concerned for his father, Ichiro asks:

ICHIRO: Where is the kitchen?

MATSUO: Kitchen? Of course, of course. That is a problem. There's no kitchen.

ICHIRO: As we're only staying overnight, we probably won't need to use a kitchen, but I just wanted to check.

MATSUO: Let's see. I'm about the only person who stays for long periods of time. I hardly eat at all.

ICHIRO: Uh-huh.

MATSUO: Every few days, I go to the mountains for some greens and boil them in the hot spring. Just that makes a tasty meal.

ICHIRO: Really? Spa-boiled mountain greens…

MATSUO: Sansuke and I are the only ones who've lived here long. On rainy days when the ground gets slippery, he'll gather some for both of us.

ICHIRO: That sounds like a tough life. I don't think I could bear it.

MATSUO: In the city, you can get whatever you want to eat, right?

ICHIRO: Oh yeah, for sure.

MATSUO: I'd like to go if I had the cash.

ICHIRO: Uh-huh.

MATSUO: Have you been in Tokyo all your life? Were you born there?

Momofuku is sleeping.

ICHIRO: Uh-huh.

MATSUO: *(A beat.)* Really.

The door of the changing room opens and Sansuke appears. Despite the cold weather, he is only wearing a cloth waistband, knee-length underpants, and a towel wound around his head. In contrast to Matsuo, he is large and swarthy, with a substantial belly, and generally resembles a brown bear. On his right shoulder, he has a tattoo of the Buddha of Healing and on his left, another tattoo of the Goddess of Mercy. On his wrist, he wears a gold wristwatch with diamonds embedded in the bezel. He also holds two towels to hang out to dry. Matsuo reacts to the noise Sansuke makes.

MATSUO: Ahh, that must be Sansuke.

ICHIRO: The one wearing loose white leggings?
MATSUO: Please wait while I talk with him. Could you lend me that letter?

Ichiro passes the letter to Matsuo in silence.

MATSUO: *(Taken by surprise.)* Oh-ohh, thanks.
ICHIRO: Please, see if he knows anything.
MATSUO: I'll see what he says.

Matsuo leaves the guestroom, cuts across the yard, and talks to Sansuke. Ichiro waits in the room without sitting down.

VOICE: The Japanese characters for *sansuke* are "three" and "help" lined up together. The word refers to a bath attendant who manages the bathing water supply, supervises customers, and also provides body washing and hair-combing services. A very old vocation, these attendants were paid well in the Edo period.[7] Nowadays, however, few public bathhouses hire them. This *sansuke* is a silent and hard worker. As nobody has ever heard his voice or his real name, they just call him "Sansuke."

Matsuo finishes his talk with Sansuke and returns to the room.

MATSUO: He doesn't seem to know anything. Thank you for this. *(He returns the letter.)*
ICHIRO: Thank you very much.

Sansuke enters the room.

MATSUO: This is Sansuke.
ICHIRO: *(Politely.)* I am Kurata. My father and I will be staying overnight. Thank you for your services.

Sansuke looks at the sleeping Momofuku and prepares the bedding.

ICHIRO: Please do not bother.

Sansuke disregards Ichiro and continues working.

Upstairs, Otaki gets up. She was lying down but was not asleep. Moving to the window, she sits and ruminates over the father-son pair below.

ICHIRO: Thank you for talking with him. It's a great help to us.

MATSUO: I am sorry I couldn't find anything out.

ICHIRO: Oh no, not at all. Thank you very much, anyway.

MATSUO: He's the silent type. Very silent… *(Lowering his voice.)* He's probably dumb. Ha-ha-ha.

ICHIRO: Oh no, don't say that.

Sansuke picks up Momofuku and carefully lays him down on the futon. Sansuke is breathing hard. Beads of sweat form on his brow.

ICHIRO: Oh, I will do that…

Sansuke does not stop working. Ichiro keeps a strict eye on him.

MATSUO: Is something bothering you?

ICHIRO: *(A beat.)* No…

MATSUO: Uh-oh, has your father fallen asleep? Oh yeah, he's asleep.

Ichiro stares at Sansuke without replying to Matsuo's question. Sansuke puts Momofuku to bed and then moves on to preparing Ichiro's futon.

ICHIRO: I will do my own.

Sansuke stops working and exits.

MATSUO: Did he do something weird?

ICHIRO: No.

Matsuo has tremors from the neck up. Ichiro takes off his knitted cap and down jacket. He folds them up carefully and places them on the tatami floor. Matsuo reacts to the sound of a zipper being lowered.

MATSUO: You can open the window if you like.

ICHIRO: Oh, I'm not hot.
MATSUO: Are you feeling cold?
ICHIRO: No, neither.

Ichiro takes cigarettes and a lighter out of his pocket and places them on top of his folded jacket. Listening to the sound of that sequence of actions, Matsuo speaks.

MATSUO: If you want to smoke, don't worry about me. There's an ashtray somewhere around here...
ICHIRO: Thank you.

Ichiro sits down on the tatami *floor. A while later, he stands up, and Matsuo immediately speaks up.*

MATSUO: If you are looking for a cushion…
ICHIRO: I need to go.
MATSUO: There's a toilet beyond the reception at the end of the hall on the left.
ICHIRO: Thanks.

Ichiro exits the room.

Momofuku's breathing can be heard clearly. Matsuo approaches the soundly sleeping figure. Ascertaining that he is truly in a deep sleep, Matsuo touches Momofuku through the bedding. He finds that this man's body is abnormally small. Matsuo startles at the sound of women's voices coming from the changing room, withdraws his hands, and returns to the kotatsu *table. In the process, he knocks over a teacup. He is deeply upset.*

Two women in cotton kimonos come out from the changing room. Without any makeup on, their faces glow pink from the heat of the spa.

VOICE: Eight kilometers east of this inn lies a rustic hot spring town. These two women, Fumie and Iku, are geisha working there.

Fumie speaks the Toyama dialect. She tries hard to use standard Japa-

nese with her customers, but her pronunciation is a bit off. Iku is younger, so her accent is not as strong. The two climb the stairs, open the sliding door, and enter the upstairs room.

IKU: *(Noticing Otaki.)* Wow, surprise, surprise!
FUMIE: Huh? Oh, Otaki? You didn't go mountain veggie gathering after all?
OTAKI: No, I didn't.
FUMIE: Really.

Downstairs, Matsuo begins to rifle through Momofuku and Ichiro's belongings. His hands keep trembling.

OTAKI: Fumi, Fumi, Fumi, hey.
FUMIE: Uh?
OTAKI: Did you see the strange father-son pair downstairs?
FUMIE: Father-son? No. Are they guests? How unusual, at a place like this.
OTAKI: Well, they are parent-child, but close to our age. I hear they came from Tokyo.
IKU: Wow, from Tokyo?
FUMIE: Tokyo?
OTAKI: They came here to perform—to do a puppet show.
FUMIE: A puppet show? Oh my, at which place? Iku, did you hear about it?
IKU: No way.
OTAKI: Right here.
IKU: Huh?
FUMIE: Here?!
OTAKI: Yeah, that's what they said. I was dumbfounded.

Fumie and Iku exchange glances and laugh.

FUMIE: You're kidding us. How 'bout some tea?
IKU: You sure are kidding.
OTAKI: You two think I've gone senile. I'm telling the truth.
FUMIE: But this place isn't for dinner parties. *(Offering tea to Iku.)* How 'bout you?

IKU: Oh, thank you. Looks good.
OTAKI: Then go downstairs and ask them.

Pressured by Otaki's earnestness, Fumie and Iku look at each other again. Fumie puts down the teapot.

FUMIE: Really?
IKU: You're kidding.
FUMIE: Someone hired them?
IKU: What? Who would do that?
OTAKI: Aye, they had an invitation letter.
FUMIE: Huh?
OTAKI: Aye, and a map.
IKU: Of what? Of this place?
OTAKI: Aye.
FUMIE: It's a prank.
OTAKI: It's true!
FUMIE: That sounds spooky.
IKU: You know… *(She thinks.)* I know, it's Sansuke's doing.
FUMIE: No way. How could he? He can't even talk.
IKU: You're right. He can't write either.
FUMIE: I agree. It's a mistake, a mistake. Some kind of misunderstanding. Tonight, another inn is short two performers.
OTAKI: *(Suddenly lowers her voice.)* Like the *shamisen*, the dad is. About that much.
IKU: What is?
OTAKI: *(Pointing at the* shamisen.*)* His height.
FUMIE: Eh?
IKU: Oh yeah, he's short?
OTAKI: Aye.
FUMIE: *(Pause.)* Well, so, you know… There are people like that.
IKU: What?
OTAKI: Nah, there aren't. I've never seen one before.
FUMIE: Must be. Some are born like that.

The sound of Ichiro pulling on the toilet roll can be heard. Matsuo stills his hand for a moment but then continues rummaging through the luggage. He finds Ichiro's down jacket and tries it on.

OTAKI: Now, the son is…
FUMIE: What, there's more?
IKU: Is also short?
OTAKI: Nah, he's normal height. He's normal, but when you look at him, you'll feel butterflies in your stomach. Mmm.
FUMIE: What, what d'ya mean by butterflies?
OTAKI: *(A beat.)* Nah, never mind, never mind.
FUMIE: What's got into you?
OTAKI: Never mind. It's bedtime, bedtime.

Otaki disappears deep into the futon.

IKU: What was that about? Having butterflies?

The faint sound of a toilet flushing is heard. Matsuo feels something in the wrapping cloth.

MATSUO: Hm? Diapers? *(Has tremors from the neck up.)*
FUMIE: Well, that's enough. Otaki, Iku and me have to practice. *(Otaki doesn't answer.)*
IKU: Will the people below mind?
FUMIE: No, they won't.
OTAKI: How should I know? Go ask them.
FUMIE: Never mind. This is that kind of place.
IKU: Bravo, sis!
OTAKI: Don't blame me.
FUMIE: We won't. OK, Iku, here we go.
IKU: Ready.

Fumie and Iku tune their two shamisen *together.*

VOICE: Age-wise, Fumie and Iku are like mother and daughter. Fumie, who is childless, treats Iku like a dear daughter, and Iku involuntarily recalls her own mother when she looks at Fumie's short, knobbly fingers.

Otaki, protruding her head from the futon, watches the two women quiet-

ly.

VOICE: It was the usual kind of evening. Yet tonight seemed different. Thinking so, Otaki felt butterflies again.

The two musicians finish their tuning.

FUMIE: All right, let's go over what we did last night.
IKU: Yes.

The shamisen *practice begins.*

Downstairs, Ichiro returns to the guestroom. Matsuo hurriedly gets to the low table.

MATSUO: Wo-would you like some tea?
ICHIRO: Huh? No thanks.

Ichiro tidies his father's crumpled futon and then sits by the window and looks outside. Taking out a cigarette, he begins to smoke. He looks just like his father at this moment. When he opens the window a tad, the shamisen *music becomes audible.*

MATSUO: *(In a high-pitched voice.)* It sounds good.
ICHIRO: It certainly does.
MATSUO: They are geisha.
ICHIRO: Oh really.
MATSUO: They come here often. They live in a dormitory in the hot spring town but come here so they can practice whenever they want.
ICHIRO: Indeed.
MATSUO: They are stupendous drinkers—they can drink any of the men here under the table.
ICHIRO: Really.
MATSUO: They're also cheerful and kind. Uhh.

For a while, Matsuo feels uncomfortable.

ICHIRO: Just like family.

MATSUO: Oh, family? Ha-ha-ha. I guess so. But during winter, what with the heavy snow, we can't use this place. We all go our different ways. When it warms up and the snow decreases, we meet again here. But each reunion is a totally new meeting of strangers, as if nothing had happened before. Ha-haha.

Matsuo grows chatty.

ICHIRO: And that too melts away.
MATSUO: Um, ha-haha. Uh-huh, like the snow as you say.
ICHIRO: Uh-huh.

Matsuo has tremors from the neck up.

MATSUO: Is your father always...
ICHIRO: *(Looking at Matsuo.)* Uh-huh?
MATSUO: *(Conscious of being watched.)* ...With you?
ICHIRO: Uh-huh.

The shamisen *practice comes to an end.*

FUMIE: That's good enough for today.
IKU: Thank you very much. Oh, Otaki's fallen asleep.
FUMIE: Oh my.

The two put away their instruments. Iku heads for the window and, looking outside, massages and stretches her stiff back.

IKU: Ah, the mountaintops are covered with snow. It really is winter.
FUMIE: Is it? Seems a little early, you know.
IKU: Let me see… Oh, I can't recall any of them. Really, I can't remember their darn names.
FUMIE: You mean that one? That's Mount Hoten. You don't need to know.
IKU: But how many years have I been here already?
FUMIE: Don't count! Here. *(Offers tea.)*
IKU: Ah, thanks.

They drink hot green tea.

FUMIE: Do you see that white temporary building? Construction is about to begin. Next summer, a railroad will be laid down here.
IKU: Is that really going to happen? I heard about it.

Otaki sits up.

OTAKI: Hey, is that true?
FUMIE: Big sis, I didn't know you were awake.
OTAKI: Is it true?
FUMIE: One of my customers has an important position in a construction company and he told me. The new bullet train will pass through this area, though the hot spring town farther down won't be affected.
OTAKI: Is that real? What about here? What's gonna happen to this place?
FUMIE: I don't know the details.
IKU: It might vanish…
FUMIE: It's hard to tell. But if the demolition team comes here, this building will be the first to go.
IKU: *(A beat.)* Without the owner, that's inevitable.
OTAKI: That is so sad. I wanted to die here.
FUMIE: Now, don't get like that, brrr.
IKU: This place has been so convenient. Having a soak, practicing, performing at parties, getting drunk, staying here whenever we please. No fear of bumping into customers!
FUMIE: Right you are.
OTAKI: What a shame…
IKU: *(A beat.)* Just another year would help…
OTAKI: Why another year?
IKU: It's going to be winter very soon.
FUMIE: Without this place, Sansuke will leave. Iku will turn 39 next year, you know.

Iku doesn't speak.

OTAKI: Oh, so that's what it's about.
FUMIE: It's tremendously important.

OTAKI: Iku, what's your husband doing?

IKU: Oh, Kozo's on a business trip to Hokkaido. But he'll return soon. He's got my back. For his sake, too, I want to have a baby before I turn 40.

OTAKI: You've got to work on it.

FUMIE: Come on. You'll do fine. No problem.

OTAKI: Ahh, but it'll be lonely here.

Otaki and Iku quietly end their conversation while Fumie ponders over something. Downstairs...

MATSUO: May I have one?

ICHIRO: Uh, a cigarette?

MATSUO: Is that OK?

ICHIRO: Of course.

Ichiro balances a cigarette between Matsuo's fingertips.

MATSUO: Could you light it for me, too?

Ichiro uses his lighter. Matsuo, unused to smoking, starts coughing right away.

ICHIRO: Are you all right?

MATSUO: *(Pause.)* Uh-huh...

Upstairs...

The sunset deepens and the persimmons add their orange blush to the flaming red of the room. Fumie gets up softly and stands by the window overlooking the yard.

FUMIE: Look over here.

Otaki looks toward Fumie.

FUMIE: So ripe and good to eat.

OTAKI: Hm? Oh, the persimmons?

FUMIE: I wondered why the sunset seemed so red. Now I know. The fruit is ready to be harvested.

OTAKI: You think so? They look a tad on the brown side. When they ripen that much, they are spoilt.

FUMIE: A touch of brown brings out their best.

OTAKI: Then try some.

FUMIE: I will later. Don't fuss. Come on, Iku, get ready. Our contact will arrive soon to pick us up.

OTAKI: Are you two going already?

FUMIE: Today's an early performance. Iku?

IKU: *(A beat.)* I'm coming. Right away.

OTAKI: Are you both busy?

FUMIE: Not at all. This time today is unusual. I wonder if there'll be more work when the bullet train comes through.

OTAKI: With the new railroad, you'll lose your jobs to the young women moving in.

FUMIE: *(Reprimanding her.)* Otaki!

OTAKI: What?

FUMIE: Don't talk like that.

To deflect Fumie's aggressive attitude, Otaki gives a huge yawn.

OTAKI: I'll take a nap and then another soak in the spa. Ahh, what a shame. *(Chants a sutra.)* Namandab, namandab…

FUMIE: Make sure you really sleep.

Fumie and Iku start on their professional makeup in front of the vanity mirrors.

Otaki gazes outside for a while before falling asleep.

Downstairs…

MATSUO: Let me show you the bath.

ICHIRO: Uh-huh.

MATSUO: Are you sure you don't need to wake up your father?

ICHIRO: No, not at all.

MATSUO: You see, I want to see your bodies. Do you think it's strange for me to say that?

ICHIRO: Well, why do you?

MATSUO: Not many men come around here. They are unusual.

ICHIRO: Is that so?

MATSUO: This is a very unusual opportunity and what's more...

ICHIRO: Yes...

MATSUO: ...I said I was startled at your appearance because I thought you'd be a little boy. Maybe, maybe that wasn't the only reason.

ICHIRO: Well, my body's hardly for display, you know. Please go ahead. I'll have another smoke.

MATSUO: I'll wait for you.

Ichiro lights another cigarette.

MATSUO: Your father is sleeping well.

Upstairs...

FUMIE: Oh, Otaki, do you want me to bring something back for you?

OTAKI: How about some leafy pickles?

FUMIE: Sure thing...

Downstairs...

Momofuku wakes up and leaves the room. Matsuo is so excited that he doesn't notice Momofuku has left.

The stage revolves quietly. The setting sun casts shifting shadows on the six characters' faces.

Scene 3. The Changing Room at the Bath

Sunset. The rays of the setting sun enter through the ventilation duct, giving the changing room enough light. The electric fan on the wall is on but rattles from old age, humidity, and overuse. Arranged around the room are scales, a wooden bench, and shelves lined with baskets. The sound of hot spring water flowing into the bathtub in the bathing area can be heard.

Sansuke is cleaning the changing room with zest. He is going after each spot that needs attention. The door of the changing room opens and Momofuku enters. Sansuke stiffens and stands at attention.

MOMOFUKU: Oh, so you are Sansuke. How curious.

Sansuke nods eagerly, like a rat devouring bait. As Momofuku undresses, his puny, aged, naked body is revealed. Sansuke is absolutely thrilled and almost paralyzed with joy.

MOMOFUKU: Here. *(Throws small change into a small bamboo basket on the floor.)*

Sansuke bows deeply.

MOMOFUKU: I'll have a soak first.

Momofuku opens the sliding door to the bathing area and disappears into the clouds of steam. Sounds are heard of Momofuku pouring hot spring water over himself, followed by lighter, snappier sounds of the wood basin being handled.

Sansuke presses himself against the glass door and peers in at Momofuku in the bathing area. Liquid oozes from Sansuke's nose. He wipes it away with his finger. A nosebleed. He tries sniffing many times, but the bleeding won't stop. He shoves some tissue paper hard up his nose. A distant temple bell rings faintly. Sansuke looks at his gold wristwatch. It is just about five o'clock.

Sansuke feels something happening between his legs. His penis is erect and throbbing vigorously. He is astonished by this reaction and tries to repress it by blowing on or hitting himself.

The changing room door opens and Ichiro and Matsuo enter. Sansuke hurriedly tries to stand up but cannot stand upright.

MATSUO: You can undress here.

ICHIRO: Thank you.

MATSUO: You probably don't have a hand towel. Sansuke can provide you with one.

Putting down his own towel, Ichiro begins to undress. Matsuo "watches" him spellbound. Taking ¥20,000[8] from his wallet, Ichiro places the banknotes in the bamboo basket. Sansuke's eyes open wide in surprise.

ICHIRO: I'll go ahead.

MATSUO: Oh...sure.

Matsuo removes his clothes hurriedly. He is so thin, he could grate a radish on his protruding rib cage, and his legs are like driftwood that has floated around for years. He has no body hair and his skin is a dazzling white. Sansuke stops Matsuo, who is about to enter the bathing area, and removes his eyeglasses for him.

MATSUO: I am shaking. Let me rest a bit.

Matsuo sits down heavily on the bench to rest for a while. Sansuke gently pats him on the head.

VOICE: What is it that the blind Matsuo wants to see? What can there be for him?

MATSUO: Thanks. Now I'm ready.

Sansuke takes Matsuo's hand and leads him to the bathing area.

VOICE: Now, let us enter the bathing area.

The stage set revolves.

Scene 4. The Bathing Area

From evening into night. An open-air rock bath comes into view. Many candles have been placed in an offhand manner on the stone ledge of the bathtub. The melted wax has hardened and become the base for the next candle. With the repetition of this process, the rock bath offers the ambience of a limestone cave. A few of these candles are lit.

At the end of the bathtub, large matchboxes and new candles are placed in a vinyl bag to keep out the damp. The sunset provides sufficient light, but when the area dims, more candles will be lit.

The sound of the continual waves of bubbling hot water makes one aware of the submerged power of the mountains, the formidable pulsation of nature.

Momofuku and Ichiro are already soaking in the rock bath. Due to the high temperature of the hot spring water, both men have bright red faces and large beads of sweat on their foreheads. Sansuke and Matsuo enter the bathing area.

MATSUO: *(To Sansuke.)* I'm feeling all right now.

Passing his hand over the stony surface of the tub, Matsuo walks along the bath. With practiced motions, he pours hot spring water over himself twice and then enters the bathtub. He does not allow his attention to waver from Ichiro, who is on the other side of the misty steam.

Momofuku rises from the tub.

MOMOFUKU: *(To Sansuke.)* Hey.

Matsuo is surprised.

MATSUO: Oh, Mr. Kurata…you were here after all.

Sansuke comes running from the changing room to the bathing area. He washes Momofuku's back delicately and then massages his shoulders; after which, taking a tortoiseshell comb, he styles Momofuku's long gray hair.

MOMOFUKU: Good job. Thanks.

Red-faced, Sansuke gives a huge smile of joy.

MOMOFUKU: Your turn now.
ICHIRO: Thanks.

When Ichiro steps out of the tub, Matsuo reacts sensitively to his movements.

ICHIRO: My turn, please.

Sansuke gives Ichiro's back a wash. Moving on to massaging his back, Sansuke feels his thick biceps begin to quiver.

MOMOFUKU: The blind do look younger than others. Don't you think?
MATSUO: Uh, I can't tell.
ICHIRO: Touch yourself and you'll see. Use those fingertips you pride
    yourself on. Go on, go on.
MATSUO: You're an interesting character...
MOMOFUKU: Are your fingers only for pressing flowers?
MATSUO: How about you, Mr. Kurata? What's it like?
MOMOFUKU: What is?
MATSUO: How is your body?
MOMOFUKU: It's hideous. Do you want to touch it?

Momofuku tenderly strokes Matsuo's cheek. Matsuo jumps away in surprise.

MATSUO: ...Um, I didn't mean to be rude...
MOMOFUKU: That's too bad.

Sansuke is red in the face, struggling to massage Ichiro's extraordinarily stiff body.

MATSUO: What about your son?
MOMOFUKU: Ichiro? He's in a worse state.
MATSUO: *(A beat.)* Is that so?

Momofuku smiles.

MATSUO: I don't understand.
MOMOFUKU: Well, there's no need to be so tense.

Sansuke finishes washing Ichiro and goes back to the changing room. Ichiro returns to the bathtub. Matsuo stiffens his body and tries to sense where Ichiro is.

Silence continues for a while. Only the sound of the flowing spring water is heard.

Momofuku puts his head against the edge of the bathtub and falls asleep. The faint sound of his breathing reaches Matsuo's ears. Trying not to disturb the father, Matsuo approaches the son, Ichiro.

MATSUO: He must be tired.
ICHIRO: Has he fallen asleep?
MATSUO: I talked too much. But not to worry. The spring waters here are gentle and pleasing.
ICHIRO: Uh-huh, I can feel that.
MATSUO: I'm just a blind man, you know. But your father is eccentric. I can tell from what he says. That makes him very interesting. Uh…
ICHIRO: I see.
MATSUO: Excuse me.
ICHIRO: Not at all.
MATSUO: *(Wiping sweat from his brow.)* I'd like to see your puppet show.
ICHIRO: Well, it is unlikely that we will perform.
MATSUO: Of course, I wouldn't be able to see it anyway.
ICHIRO: Ah.
MATSUO: What kind of puppet is it?
ICHIRO: What kind?
MATSUO: Um, the shape. What does it represent?
ICHIRO: My father made it, so…
MATSUO: Is it like a ventriloquist show?
ICHIRO: Oh no.
MATSUO: Really. If it's OK by you, could I touch the puppet later?

ICHIRO: No, you can't.

MATSUO: Why not?

ICHIRO: No one can touch it. Not even me.

MATSUO: *(A beat.)* I see. Excuse me for asking.

VOICE: At this moment, Matsuo felt that Ichiro's heart was at the bottom of "eternal night." He felt darkness swell and ripple like a fully-fed snake's belly and come after him. Where was the darkness rising from? How profound was it? For the first time since he became blind, Matsuo experienced an overwhelming desire. He wanted to see with his own eyes. To see. To see.

MATSUO: Ichiro…

MOMOFUKU: *(With his eyes closed.)* Mr. Matsuo.

MATSUO: Wha—? Oh, yes.

MOMOFUKU: What you are searching for, the soul… It doesn't exist. Not anywhere. Not in me nor in you.

The flowing hot spring water suddenly surges.

MATSUO: Oh, it's hot—

As if escaping, Matsuo crawls out of the bathtub but quickly collapses on the floor. His lean, emaciated body heaves with irregular breaths.

The thin glass shakes hard as the bath door is opened. Otaki enters the bathing area. With her hair done up in a bun, she looks somewhat younger than before.

OTAKI: Excuse me. Oh my, what are you doing here? Are you all right?

MATSUO: *(As if on his last breath.)* Excuse me. *(He exits the bathing area.)*

OTAKI: Well, well. That's a strange one.

Otaki pours hot spring water over herself twice and steps into the rock tub.

OTAKI: The hot water feels weird today, eh.

Looking at Momofuku and Ichiro in turns, Otaki expels the discomfort in her chest by huffing out her breath.

OTAKI: Humph… *(Gets out of the tub.)* Yoohoo, over here!

Sansuke enters the bathing area.

OTAKI: The usual, OK.

Sansuke gives Otaki the standard wash, but the extra pressure he had to use when he was massaging Ichiro remains in his touch.

OTAKI: Ow, oww! Too strong! What're you doing to me?!

Otaki hits him on the head.

OTAKI: I gave you plenty of money. Now do your job.

Sansuke restrains himself and gets on with the usual treatment.

OTAKI: That's it, that's right. You know, the girls will be back early to-night from their party duty. *(Looking at Sansuke in the face.)* Take care of Iku tonight, OK? Hey, did you hear me? *(Grabs his crotch.)* That's enough. Finish up, finish up. You don't need to do my hair.

Sansuke goes back to the changing room, and Otaki steps into the bath.

OTAKI: Ahh, that was good. Thank god.

Momofuku wakes up.

MOMOFUKU: Excuse me.
OTAKI: Go ahead.

Momofuku goes to the changing room. Ichiro also readies to leave.

OTAKI: Isn't your father tired?
ICHIRO: Oh, well, maybe.
OTAKI: The spring water is pleasant here.

ICHIRO: Yes, it is.
OTAKI: You can't get this in Tokyo, right?
ICHIRO: You're right.
OTAKI: Aren't you glad you stayed?
ICHIRO: Yes, to be sure.
OTAKI: I knew it.

Otaki is beaming triumphantly. Ichiro is about to leave, but Otaki keeps on talking.

OTAKI: What about your mother? Isn't she about my age?
ICHIRO: She's gone.
OTAKI: Really? Did she pass away?
ICHIRO: Uh-huh, right after she gave birth to me.
OTAKI: Right after your birth? Oh, what a shame. Are you married?
ICHIRO: No.
OTAKI: Not even once?
ICHIRO: No.
OTAKI: No lovers?
ICHIRO: None.
OTAKI: Oh my, that's terrible. In junior high, you must've had a sweetheart. Do you remember?
ICHIRO: I didn't go to school.
OTAKI: What, you didn't go to junior high?
ICHIRO: No.
OTAKI: How about elementary school?
ICHIRO: No.
OTAKI: *(A beat.)* What were you doing then?
ICHIRO: I helped my father.
OTAKI: With the puppets?
ICHIRO: Uh-huh.
OTAKI: All the time?
ICHIRO: Yes.
OTAKI: But…why did you?
ICHIRO: That was my father's decision. Excuse me. Got to go.

Ichiro leaves the bathing area.

OTAKI: Namandab, namandab, namandab...
VOICE: The sun has set completely.

The stage revolves.

Scene 5. At the Guestrooms

Nighttime. It is a little after six o'clock in the evening, but it is already completely dark outside. The shaded incandescent light above the changing room door brightens up the immediate area. After his bath, Momofuku is in the yard looking up at the persimmon tree. Matsuo is in the downstairs guestroom, but the room light is not on. Momofuku returns to the room.

MOMOFUKU: Darn, it's dark in here.

Momofuku gets up on the low table, pulls the dangling pull string, and lights up the room.

MOMOFUKU: Ahhh! You were here after all.
MATSUO: I'm going for a walk.
MOMOFUKU: Oh? Isn't it dangerous at night?
MATSUO: I'll take care.
MOMOFUKU: You'll take care? Isn't it better to stay inside?

Matsuo exits. Momofuku sits by a window and smokes. He looks lonely. Ichiro returns.

ICHIRO: Excuse me, I got held up.
MOMOFUKU: Anything to eat?
ICHIRO: Only rice balls. I'm sorry. *(Brings out the food from the backpack.)*
MOMOFUKU: And some tea, too.
ICHIRO: Certainly.
MOMOFUKU: It's strange, isn't it?
ICHIRO: Uh-huh.
MOMOFUKU: Are we such a curiosity?

ICHIRO: Not really. They just want to think so.
MOMOFUKU: Well, I look utterly miserable.
ICHIRO: If that's what you want to think, Father.
MOMOFUKU: Hm, I do.

The sound of the front door of the inn being opened roughly. At the same time, Fumie and Iku's strident voices reverberate. They have returned from work. Both are drunk, especially Fumie. They are bad-mouthing their customers and boasting of how they escaped from having to help out in the kitchen.

MOMOFUKU: Hear that. The wild beasts have arrived to grace our table.

Ichiro grows tense.

MOMOFUKU: They can be both quiet and active, you know?
ICHIRO: Uh-huh, they know how to prey on you.
MOMOFUKU: Afraid? Aren't you afraid? They've come to devour you.

Ichiro does not speak.

MOMOFUKU: Women are terrifying!

On their way to their room upstairs, Fumie and Iku crash into walls, trip on the stairs, but suddenly the sound of their footsteps subsides.

MOMOFUKU: Hush. Here they come.

After a while, the door of the first floor guestroom is opened. Pushed to it by Fumie, Iku peeks in first.

IKU: Oh! Uh, good evening…
FUMIE: Good evening.
IKU: Good evening.
FUMIE: No kidding…you're father and son?!
IKU: Shh!

Momofuku draws out a cigarette.

IKU: Yikes! He moved! He moved, really moved!

FUMIE: That thing. Is it a puppet?

IKU: No way. That's the man who handles the puppet.

FUMIE: A puppet man?

IKU: What d'ya mean by "puppet man"? He looks like a puppet, right?

FUMIE: I'm totally confused.

IKU: Why?

FUMIE: You mean there's a puppet that moves the puppets?

IKU: Just stop it. They can hear us!

FUMIE: Close the door. Just close it!

They close the door. Momofuku puts his cigarette away.

IKU: Let's be proper.

FUMIE: I agree. I totally understand.

They open the door again with professional geisha mien.

FUMIE: Good evening. I'm Fumie.

IKU: And I'm Iku. We are geisha at the hot spring town.

They show the men the shamisen *strapped on their backs. Fumie plays air-*shamisen.

FUMIE: Ping, PING!

IKU: Shh…

ICHIRO: Good evening. We're from Tokyo and have arranged to stay overnight. The name's Kurata.

FUMIE: That's quite all right. Mr. Kurata, please have an enjoyable stay.

IKU: Oh man, don't act as if you own this place, sis!

Fumie and Iku share a huge laugh.

FUMIE: We've finished for the day.

IKU: Completely finished. *(Politely.)* Mr. Kurata, would you like some *sake*?

Iku brings out a large bottle of sake[9] *from her wrapping cloth.*

IKU: I snitched it from the dinner party.
FUMIE: *(With a lilt.)* Aha! Bad girl!
IKU: You said it'd be all right, sis!

Again, they burst out into laughter. Ichiro sits still without any change in facial expression.

IKU: Let's have a drink!
FUMIE: That's the spirit. Drink, drink!

Otaki comes out of the changing room.

FUMIE: Oh, Otaki! It's Otaki for crying out loud.
OTAKI: Aha, you girls back already?
FUMIE: That's right. Wanna join us?
OTAKI: Uh-uh.
FUMIE: Too bad. What a loss. Let the grinch go and let's have some fun!
OTAKI: Stop bugging me.

Otaki starts going upstairs. On hearing her footsteps, Fumie bursts out—

FUMIE: Piss off, ya bitch!

Fumie alone gives a huge guffaw.

Upstairs, Otaki hangs up her towel and sits by a window to cool down. With an ashtray in one hand, she smokes. When she opens the window, the sound of boisterous voices rises up.

OTAKI: Shut the fuck up, you dumbasses.

Downstairs, Fumie and Iku are serving sake. *They pour it generously into the teacups. Fumie turns to Momofuku.*

FUMIE: Would the master care for some?
ICHIRO: *(Speaking for his father.)* No, thank you. My father doesn't

drink.

IKU: Aw, what a shame. *(To Ichiro.)* This is for you.

FUMIE: Welcome to our part of the world.

ICHIRO: I'll take just this one.

While Ichiro only wets his lips, Iku and Fumie do bottoms up.

FUMIE: Ahh, great *sake*.

Fumie unobtrusively wipes lipstick off her teacup.

IKU: *(To Fumie.)* Ready? Here's another.

Iku takes note of Ichiro's reaction as she speaks.

IKU: Tokyo's my dream. It's an ideal place. I wanna go there.

FUMIE: You're citizens from an ideal city with stone-paved roads and rows of red brick buildings.

IKU: Yay, yay!

FUMIE: Everyone eats outside.

IKU: Outside?!

FUMIE: You didn't know? They take their table and chairs outside.

IKU: And they drink wine!

FUMIE: They don't eat rice. Not cool, you know. They eat potatoes. Potatoes. Mashed potatoes. See?

IKU: Yeah, and drink delicious wine. Not this smelly, old *sake*.

FUMIE: Shoot, I almost forgot.

Fumie brings out some pickles.

IKU: Didn't you get that for Otaki?

FUMIE: Who cares? She won't want it anyway. *(Offering some to Ichiro.)* Here you go.

ICHIRO: No, thanks.

FUMIE: Aw, come on. Don't hold back.

IKU: It's very tasty.

Fumie takes a pinch.

IKU: I want some, too. *(Opens her mouth wide.)* In here, ahh.

The two eat noisily, then swallow slowly.

FUMIE: I hear you guys do puppetry.
ICHIRO: *(A beat.)* Uh-huh.
IKU: Wow!
FUMIE: What kind? Like traditional *joruri* puppetry?[10] Or like the rod
    puppets in that old TV show *Romance of the Three Kingdoms*? Oh, I
    know, that's it. What's it called—the kind with strings?
IKU: What kind do you use?
ICHIRO: No, it's not like that.
FUMIE: Well then, what is it like?
ICHIRO: Well, let me see…

Momofuku begins to smoke. Fumie doesn't wait for Ichiro's answer.

FUMIE: I'd love to see your show.
IKU: Wanna see. Wanna see. Wanna see.
ICHIRO: But not today…
FUMIE: Please, oh please.

Fumie slides across the tatami *floor to where Ichiro is. She pushes her
firm breasts against his arm.*

ICHIRO: Oh no, that's not…
FUMIE: We beg you, please.
ICHIRO: Even so, it's not possible.

Fumie and Iku exchange looks.

FUMIE: In that case, we'll go first, and you go next, OK.
IKU: We go first. You're next.
FUMIE: All righty, what's the music?
IKU: Whatever you like, sis, is fine with me.
FUMIE: Anything goes, huh? We're so drunk, everything will sound the
    same!

The two take up their shamisen.

IKU: Let's see, what would... Oh, now... What 'bout this? Or something else?
FUMIE: "Echigo Lion"? That's depressing. Let's do something livelier.
IKU: I know! How's this?

The shamisen *performance begins. The players are well matched and play with a savage intensity that shakes the small inn. Their music reveals wild female energy. Fumie's kimono neckline becomes disheveled and reveals her deep cleavage. Iku's kimono hem becomes disarrayed, and her milky-white thighs are partially exposed. Her smooth legs are soft and inviting as if nourished by the gentle spring water.*

Upstairs, Otaki spits out her venom.

OTAKI: Shut the fuck up!

Otaki, about to go down and interrupt the shamisen *performance, changes her mind. A cigarette dangling from her mouth, she sits quietly in front of a vanity mirror, which she rarely uses, and loosens her hair to comb it.*

VOICE: As a young woman, Otaki learned how to play the *shamisen* but soon gave it up. She did not become a geisha partly because of the war, but mostly it was because she knew she wasn't beautiful. She was jealous of Fumie and Iku but also supportive. She wanted to be like family with them. Usually, she pretended not to pay attention to their *shamisen* strumming.
However, the sound of their music, rising from downstairs, clutched at her woman's heart. Her jealousy was ignited. She had dreamed of herself as a geisha—with a beautiful figure, love with patrons, the gaze of construction workers on her ample breasts. Her memories and dreams intermingled, floated, and then were chased by the strong tone of the music into evaporating.

Otaki closes the vanity mirror and descends to the first floor. Entering the guestroom, she glares at Fumie and Iku but does not interrupt them. She does not want to stop them. The session ends.

OTAKI: You're the pits.
FUMIE: Aw, Otaki, come join us.
OTAKI: Join you? You're so noisy, I can't sleep.
FUMIE: You wanted to join us, right?
OTAKI: What the hell…
IKU: Aw, come on.
OTAKI: No, this is no good! This isn't a dinner party. How dare you play so loud. Ping, ping, ping!
FUMIE: I know.
OTAKI: You can't use this place as you like.
FUMIE: I know that. What're you so grumpy 'bout?
OTAKI: Fumi! Just cut it out, will you!
FUMIE: I'm done. It's over. It's over.

Otaki goes over and fixes the two women's disheveled clothing.

OTAKI: You behave yourselves in front of the guests!
FUMIE: My kimono just got a bit messed up.
IKU: Otaki, the Kurata father and son's puppet performance is about to start now.
OTAKI: What's that?
FUMIE: Time for entertainment, quality entertainment.
OTAKI: No, these guests are tired and need their sleep.
IKU: Stay and watch, Otaki.
OTAKI: Don't be ridiculous! Get up now and go upstairs.

Otaki seizes Fumie and Iku by the hand and tries to lead them out of the room. Suddenly, Momofuku stands up.

MOMOFUKU: Hey.
ICHIRO: Uh?
MOMOFUKU: We'll do a short piece.
ICHIRO: Yes, sir.
FUMIE: What, really?
IKU: Yay! You guys are the best!
FUMIE: Wowee! Fantastic! There you go!

Ichiro places the suitcase in front of Momofuku. After that, he opens a black leather hard case and takes out a musical instrument.

IKU: What's that instrument? I've never seen it before.
FUMIE: It's a *kokyu*, a Japanese fiddle.
IKU: A fiddle?

Suddenly, Sansuke charges into the room.

IKU: Oh, Sansuke.

Sansuke puts away the cups and pot and turns the top board over to the mahjong side. He wipes down the board with his hand towel and goes rushing out again.

FUMIE: Sansuke? Huh?
IKU: What? What was that about?
OTAKI: Hush! It's beginning.

Ichiro closes his eyes and begins to play. It is a sound his audience has never heard before.

The Ecchu Owara Wind Lantern Festival has been held in Yatsuomachi, Toyama City in Toyama Prefecture for 300 years. Everyone dances quietly and continuously for two weeks, including the eve of the festival. Whether day or night, someone is always dancing in town. One of the many musical instruments that accompanies this dancing is the Japanese fiddle. Its melancholic music matches well the shadowy street corners of this town and raises a mournful tone that seems to contribute to a mystical power, making the very boundary between this world and the next pulsate.

To Ichiro's Japanese fiddle, Momofuku opens the suitcase and takes out the puppet. It has a very large face in ratio to its small body. Its arms are thin, but the five fingers of each hand are big and long, especially the thumb. Totally naked, the puppet displays a large penis. Dr. Wilder Penfield, a Canadian neurosurgeon, made this model called a homunculus to indicate the relationship between the cerebral cortex motor field, the so-matosensory cortex, and various body parts in a heightened way.

Holding this puppet, Momofuku gets on top of the low table. The puppet seems to cuddle up to him, as if he were its father, and stays close to him. Momofuku gazes back gently at the puppet and speaks to him in a soft voice.

MOMOFUKU: Good boy. Yes, that's it. Just move as you like. Move as you always do. Don't be embarrassed. Just try it.

The timbre of the fiddle changes and the key modulates easily in the middle of the piece. Momofuku dances with his puppet.

MOMOFUKU: That's it. You've got the rhythm.

Gradually, the puppet livens up.

MOMOFUKU: Excellent! You're doing a fantastic job.

The puppet is dancing as if on its own.

It begins to snow. No one notices the snowfall.

Momofuku, in a trancelike state, is dancing with the puppet. Ichiro's eyes open. The fiddle's tone grows wilder and more violent. It gradually loses its musicality. The performance ends. Momofuku makes the puppet sit down and take a bow. In a flurry, Otaki, Fumie, and Iku all bow. Ichiro also puts both hands on the tatami *floor and bows deeply. Then he puts away the fiddle. Silence pervades.*

FUMIE: Ohh… Um…
IKU: Uhh…
FUMIE: Ahh, well…let's see.
IKU: Fantastic… It was…
FUMIE: Yeah, right, that's it. Th-thank you very much.
IKU: Thank you very much.
ICHIRO: Thank you for the *shamisen* performance.

FUMIE: Oh, not at all…

Momofuku, continuing to talk gently to the puppet, puts him back in the suitcase.

MOMOFUKU: You did very well today. Tomorrow, we'll start early. Let's get some sleep. We have to take the early bird bus back to Tokyo.

Otaki, Fumie, and Iku watch this interaction for a while. They cannot fathom what they had seen or what had happened.

Momofuku gets into his futon and falls asleep.

Sansuke is standing in the courtyard. A thin layer of snow is forming on his head and shoulders.

IKU: I fink…I'm wasted…
FUMIE: Uh-huh, me too. Let's go back up?
IKU: Yeah…
FUMIE: Good night.
IKU: Good night everyone.
OTAKI: You girls are such brats.

Iku opens the door and finds an exhausted Matsuo standing right in front of her.

IKU: Oh my god! You totally spooked me… Matsuo, were you here all the time?

Matsuo gives no response. Fumie and Iku run up the stairs, undress, and hang up their kimonos on the clothes rack. They get in their respective futon with their long white undergarments still on. The pair do not share any thoughts.

Downstairs…

OTAKI: Thank you so much. It was a fabulous performance. Well, good night now. Take care not to catch cold. Thanks again.

ICHIRO: Otaki, thank you very much.

Otaki leaves the room. At the top of the stairs, she turns off the light the two women had left on.

OTAKI: Good night.

Otaki gets into her futon. Lying on her back, she raises one arm and moves her fingers. She isn't trying to mimic the puppetry but to confirm that she is alive. She wants to touch life itself.

Iku stretches her hand from the futon, finds her smartphone on the low table, and phones her husband, who is on a business trip. As there is no reply, she emails instead.

Fumie is wrapped up in her futon and does not move.

Sansuke is still standing outside. He is sobbing loudly and large tears are running down his face. Ichiro opens the window.

ICHIRO: The show's over. It's all right now. You'll catch cold out there.

Sansuke is immobile.

ICHIRO: Excuse me…

Matsuo enters the room. He faces the inner yard.

MATSUO: Sansuke?
ICHIRO: Look Sansuke, it's over…

Sansuke makes no effort to move. Ichiro slams the window shut.

ICHIRO: He's gone back inside.

Sansuke remains in the yard. His tears continue to flow.

MATSUO: Sansuke…you know…

ICHIRO: He's gone.
MATSUO: That's not—
ICHIRO: *(Interrupts.)* Mr. Matsuo, let it go.

Matsuo falls silent.

ICHIRO: I'm going to bed.
MATSUO: Uh…uh-huh, I see your point.
ICHIRO: May I turn off the light?
MATSUO: Please don't worry about me. Go ahead and turn it off.
ICHIRO: Thank you.
MATSUO: It doesn't matter to me either way.

Ichiro turns off the electric light. Matsuo also tries to turn it off but has difficulty finding the pull string. Ichiro grabs Matsuo's arm.

MATSUO: Argh!

Ichiro makes Matsuo grasp the pull string.

MATSUO: *(A beat.)* I never turn the light on…so I'm not used to finding the cord...

The whole inn is now in darkness. Only the small incandescent light by the changing room shines—on large flakes of snow.

Sansuke bows deeply and returns to the changing room. Matsuo, still standing, takes off his dark glasses with trembling hands. Revealed are two holes where his eyeballs would be.

MATSUO: No one uses it anymore, but a very long time ago…
ICHIRO: Uh-huh.
MATSUO: …This place was called Avidya Inn.
ICHIRO: Really…
MATSUO: Avidya means "ignorance" and is one of the twelve *nidanas* in Buddhism. Are you familiar with them?
ICHIRO: Uh-uh.
MATSUO: The twelve *nidanas* are the twelve linked doctrines that de-

scribe causes of human pain. The first one is Ignorance, which means "not knowing."

ICHIRO: Indeed.

MATSUO: It begins with Ignorance, then Constructing Activities, Consciousness, Name-and-Form, Six Senses, Contact, Feeling, Love, Clinging, Becoming, Birth, and Aging-and-Death. They are considered the primary causal relationships between the connected links. Humans are naturally in anguish of mostly everything and that is what we call life. Understanding these doctrines and their relationships would truly lead to—spiritual awakening in Buddhahood.

ICHIRO: Is that right.

MATSUO: It is intriguing that in Buddhism, love is considered a cause of suffering.

ICHIRO: Uh-huh.

MATSUO: Please excuse me. The blind are blabbermouths. *(A beat.)* Mr. Kurata?

ICHIRO: Yes?

MATSUO: Do you have any anxieties?

ICHIRO: Well, don't we all?

MATSUO: Do you have someone to love?

ICHIRO: Mr. Matsuo.

MATSUO: ...If I may ask.

Looking at his sleeping father, Ichiro speaks in a quiet but forceful tone.

ICHIRO: That's enough.

Sounds of Sansuke cleaning the bath and changing room with a scrub brush and such.

Iku shuts off her smartphone, gets out of her futon, and leaves the room on tiptoe. But when Iku's warm body passes through, the icy-cold wooden inn creaks loudly. She silently begs, "Quiet, oh please..." as she descends the stairs. Iku reaches the courtyard. In her long white undergarment, she spreads a hand towel over her hair to keep it from getting wet from the snow. She knocks on the changing room door, but there is no answer. It is cold. She knocks again, but Sansuke doesn't hear.

Looking down, she spots a ripe persimmon fallen on the snowy ground. She picks it up, blows on it, and brushes the snow off. The surface snow melts and a fully ripe orange persimmon glows in the palm of her hand. The changing room door opens slowly, and Sansuke's face appears.

IKU: Sansuke, could you give me a wash?

Sansuke nods and invites her in. The sound of coins dropping into the bamboo basket.

Upstairs...

OTAKI: Fumi, are you awake?

FUMIE: Umm, I can't sleep.

OTAKI: Me neither.

FUMIE: That puppet show… It scared me. I kept my face down 'cause it was too much for me. You know what I mean?

OTAKI: Uh-huh.

FUMIE: Yeah, that puppet was creepy.

OTAKI: Really weird city people. I didn't understand them, but that dad was working his butt off.

FUMIE: That was his son, his eternal baby who never grows up.

OTAKI: What are you going on about? I don't get it.

FUMIE: Remember, I couldn't have a baby?

OTAKI: What? What happened?

FUMIE: Remember?

OTAKI: *(A beat.)* And so?

FUMIE: No, so you see…I don't know. *(Otaki is silent.)* I feel something, something'll slip away.

OTAKI: *(A beat.)* Got to get more sleep.

FUMIE: I get a fluttering… Don't you?

OTAKI: Shut it. You are different from them.

FUMIE: No, no. That's not the point!

OTAKI: You're weird. I just went blank.

FUMIE: She was staring.

OTAKI: Huh?

FUMIE: Iku was staring hard.

Otaki heaves a big sigh.

FUMIE: Iku, I hope it goes well this time. Sansuke, go for it!
OTAKI: Fumi…
FUMIE: This time you're bound to succeed, for me, too. What is it?
OTAKI: Never mind.

Otaki gets out of her futon and puts on her coat.

FUMIE: What's the matter, Otaki?
OTAKI: I'm going for a smoke.
FUMIE: Why don't you quit? It'll kill you, you know.
OTAKI: Your *shamisen* playing has improved. The sound was attractive.
  Iku's got so much better, too. It's sad that we might not be able to en-
  joy your performance from next year.

Otaki leaves the room.

FUMIE: Aw, shit!

Otaki s descending footsteps echo weakly.

FUMIE: Cut it out.

Fumie gets up and pursues Otaki.

Iku's panting can be heard from the changing room.

Downstairs in the men's guestroom…

MATSUO: Ichiro?

*Ichiro doesn't answer. Matsuo assumes that Ichiro has fallen asleep and
searches for the suitcase. Practically crawling around the room quietly
in the darkness, he eventually finds it. Ichiro is alert and watches Matsuo's every move.*

Matsuo opens the suitcase and raises up the puppet. Face, hands, body, legs—all the puppet's body parts Matsuo touches are abnormal. For a blind person, a homunculus drawn in the imagination from the sense of touch alone is a horrendous monster. Matsuo freezes up.

MATSUO: *(Inner voice.)* Aaaaaargh.

His cry of horror is almost vocalized, and when he tries to cover his mouth with his hand, the mechanism by the puppet's mouth is released and its huge tongue flaps out. It hits Matsuo right in the face.

MATSUO: AAAAAAAAAARRRGH!

Deeply upset, he runs out of the room, cuts across the yard, and opens the changing room door.

IKU: What! Mr. Matsuo. What's going on?!

Matsuo pays no mind and enters the changing room; then, leaving the door open, he goes straight to the bathing area.

IKU: Why don't you close the door, stupid!

Ichiro and Momofuku are left in the guestroom. Ichiro sits by a window and lights a cigarette. By opening the window, a crack, he can hear many voices and sounds; from the changing room comes Iku's moans; from the entrance hall, Fumie's weeping; from the bathing area, Matsuo's voice fraught with anguish and pain. These sounds intermix and shake the small hot spring inn. Or maybe the inn itself trembles.

Ichiro puts out his cigarette, closes the window, and leaves the room. In the yard, he looks up at the sky. The snowfall is getting heavier. He enters the changing room.

From this point, the stage leisurely begins and continues to revolve.

Sansuke and Iku are in an embrace in the changing room. Iku is on top of him and kissing his neck over and over again. She is in ecstasy and doesn't notice Ichiro. He watches for a while, then moves to the bathing area, where all the candles are lit. Matsuo has his mouth directly on the spout from which the hot spring water flows and drinks the hot water in desperation. Ichiro watches for a while, then moves out of the bathing area. In the entrance hall, Otaki is smoking. Next to her, Fumie is standing and crying. Ichiro watches for a while, then moves back to his room. Momofuku is asleep with the puppet in his arms. Ichiro sits nearby.

The stage continues to rotate.

In the changing room, Iku is astride Sansuke and moving her hips energetically. Eventually, with a huge convulsion, they both climax. In the bathing area, Matsuo is still frantically swallowing the spring water. His stomach looks swollen like a pregnant woman's from the large amount of spring water he has drunk. In the entrance hall, Fumie is crying with her face against Otaki's bosom. Holding on tight with both hands to Otaki's cotton kimono, she is crying like a child.

The stage comes to a stop when the entrance hall faces downstage and the audience.

With a cigarette dangling from his mouth, Ichiro enters the entrance hall and hurries to the restroom. His left hand is hovering over his fly.

OTAKI: Excuse me…
ICHIRO: Yes?
OTAKI: Excuse me, but it's pitch-dark in there.

Ichiro enters the toilet. The sound of Ichiro relieving himself.

VOICE: As his father was afflicted with microsomia, Ichiro had no choice in life. That was all. Observing his pee run weakly, he thinks, "Oh, how I've aged…" Looking up at the ceiling, he notices that the remains of a moth caught in a spider's web are swinging in the draft.

The eastern sky brightens.

VOICE: The new day, early in the morning.

The stage revolves quietly. It stops at the point where the changing room and the bathing area can be seen simultaneously by the audience.

Scene 6. The Changing Room and the Bathing Area

Early morning. At six o'clock, silvery-white rays of sunlight penetrate the changing room and the bathing area. On a day like this, the cries of the wild birds that have just awakened in the woods and the sounds in the bathing area blend beautifully.

Sansuke and Iku are sleeping cuddled up together in the changing room. Soon they wake up. Iku goes for a soak, and Sansuke returns to his usual work. When Iku opens the door to the bath area, cold air flows in.

IKU: Yikes, it's chilly!

In the bathing area, Matsuo is sitting on the edge of the rock bathtub and weakly resting his back against the wall.

IKU: Oh, Mr. Matsuo? Good morning. Um…have you been here this whole time?

Matsuo neither answers nor moves.

IKU: What's happened? Are you all right?

Fumie enters the changing room.

FUMIE: *(To Sansuke.)* Good morning.

She undresses and moves to the bathing area.

IKU: Yoo-hoo, sis. Good morning.
FUMIE: Good morning.
IKU: You fell asleep right away last night, yeah?
FUMIE: Oh, um, yeah…

Otaki enters the bathing area.

IKU: *(Yawning.)* Morning.
FUMIE: *(A beat. In a low voice.)* Morning.
OTAKI: Good morning.

As usual, Otaki carefully pours hot spring water over herself twice and gets in the rock bath. The three women are now soaking in the tub in the morning light. Their white skin and three pairs of breasts loosely hanging in various ways blend with the slick spring water and present an upbeat portrait of humanity.

Fumie recalls what happened the night before and puts some distance between herself and Otaki. Iku is doing air-shamisen.

IKU: Big sis, how does the rest go? *(Fumie doesn't respond.)* Big sis?
FUMIE: Huh? What's up?
IKU: Come on. You were just totally spaced out.
FUMIE: Sorry, what is it?
IKU: So, I'd like you to show me how to play the tune after this part.
FUMIE: Oh, that goes like this. Whoops, was it up pick or down pick? I can't remember.
IKU: All right!
OTAKI: It's gotta be down pick.
IKU: Huh?
OTAKI: It's down pick.
IKU: Really?
FUMIE: Big sister Otaki, you're the one.
OTAKI: Anyone would know how to play that tune.
FUMIE: Then could you help Iku with the rest of it?
OTAKI: Wha—?
IKU: Yay, Otaki, this is the bit I don't get.
OTAKI: Like this, this. No, no. This way.
IKU: Chinchiri chirichiri, chinchiri chirichiri…
OTAKI: Fumi, I can't remember the rest.
FUMIE: Hehehe, OK.

Fumie moves closer to Otaki. The three cover for each other as they con-

nect the tune by humming it.

VOICE: Now, now, now; now, now, now; now, now, now…

Suddenly the bathing area door opens.

MOMOFUKU: Good mooorning!

Momofuku and Ichiro come into the bathing area in street clothes and with their luggage. Momofuku is holding the puppet.

MOMOFUKU: Here we are. Good mooorning, everyone!
VOICE: Now, now, now…
MOMOFUKU: Do the cleansing ritual.

Ichiro takes a basin, scoops up some hot spring water, and pours it over the puppet.

VOICE: Now, now, now; now, now, now…
MOMOFUKU: *(To the puppet.)* Yes, very good. Now, let's take a bath.

Momofuku picks up the puppet lovingly in his arms and gently, carefully, washes him, just as if he were bathing a real baby.

MOMOFUKU: Is it too hot? Are you OK?

Otaki, Fumie, and Iku do not understand what is happening.

VOICE: Hehehe, now, now, now, eeheehee, now, now, eeheehee, now…

Ichiro is laughing. A ray of sunlight cuts straight through the clear air and reaches the back of Ichiro's head, making an eclipse effect. The details of Ichiro's facial expression cannot be discerned, but it is definite that he is laughing.

VOICE: For Matsuo alone, the overnight ordeal is not over.

Seeing Ichiro's facial expression, Matsuo is petrified and then throws up.

A hefty amount of vomit splashes onto the bathroom floor. He repeats this vomiting many times. The spring water he drank last night to purify himself has burst out.

VOICE: After this incident, Matsuo left the inn for good.

Blackout.

The Old Woman's Voice is heard during the blackout.

VOICE: Momofuku and Ichiro depart for their next performance venue. As the whole country has gone insane and is craving blood, Momofuku's dwarfish figure and puppetry were in much demand. People want to see misery, overwhelming misery.

Quietude.

VOICE: Time at this inn was different from ordinary time. On the way down, Momofuku and Ichiro exchanged glances and smiled. This was not because they recalled the gold wristwatch and the generous payment. It was simply a familiar smile between father and son.

The sound of the hot spring gushing.

VOICE: Several days later, as if dropping through a crack in the sky, the hard winter season set in. Every year, snow becomes two to two-and-a-half meters deep in this settlement of villages. Few visitors come and the villagers stay indoors. Due to a shortage of workers, the hot spring inns all close down. This inn is no exception.

The sound of the hot spring begins to fade.

VOICE: The hot spring water alone continues to gush out and wait for the snow to thaw. This year in particular, the hot spring sounded sad, as if shivering. It seems afraid of the roar of heavy machinery arriving to lay the rails for the new bullet train.

The sound of the hot spring has thinned out and echoes plaintively. Then comes the violent noise of heavy machinery erasing the hot spring sounds.

Quietude returns.

After a while, the buzzing of cicadas is heard.

VOICE: Ten months pass and summer comes around again. The trees are spreading their fleshy leaves and displaying the fertility of nature. Below them, cicadas are competing for their lives.
So, what has happened to the little-known and unnamed hot spring inn at Hell Valley?

Scene 7. The Women's Guestroom

Summer, daytime. In the courtyard, the persimmon tree is spreading its deep green leaves wide. Morning glories are colorfully curled around its trunk. The inn sparkles in the midsummer sun.

A baby is crying. Upstairs, Iku awakens and cuddles her baby. She brings out one of her breasts and nurses her babe. The baby sucks on the large dark nipple.

VOICE: We look forward to seeing you again.

The sound of the bullet train passing through can be heard in the distance.

A gust of wind rings the wind chime. A cicada, startled by the sound, flies up and away, the buzz of its wings fading slowly in the distance.

Blackout.

THE END

Supplementary Materials Provided by the Author

1. Sansuke

Fertility spas called *kodakara no yu*, where childless women are believed to be cured of their infertility, exist all over Japan. In the Edo period, the bathhouse attendants called *sansuke* were thought to impregnate their female clients. When the cause of childlessness was on the husband's side, there was a chance for the wife to become pregnant.

It is said that many *sansuke* hailed from the snow-heavy areas of Echizen, Ecchu, and Echigo, and the good-looking ones among them were popular with their women customers. Edo people had a different ethical code of conduct from that of present times; furthermore, it was imperative that they maintained their family line. Parents-in-law of a childless daughter-in-law would persuade her to visit the curative hot springs and the husband, even if he were to suspect that something was going on, could not refuse her such visits.

2. The Twelve Nidanas

The twelve *nidanas* are from Buddhist teachings. Aging-and-death is not simply a biological phenomenon; it is a serious fact of life and so is life itself. From aging-and-death, suffering arises, and even in living, suffering arises. By observing oneself wander in transient suffering, one realizes the fragility of happiness based on joy and ease and that transient suffering is the nature of human existence itself. Living also is not simply a biological phenomenon, but the root of transient suffering. Life and aging-and-death are suffering; the whole cycle of human life is suffering. Why should life and aging-and-death be suffering? Daily living is such that we cannot help feeling that life and aging-and-death are all about suffering. Life from that perspective is called "becoming." We feel that becoming is suffering because we are always prone to attachment. In particular, we are attached to our self and our possessions. Life is a becoming through attachment. That attachment arises from love. There are three kinds of love: craving for becoming, for death, and for stimuli (sensations and self-generated stimuli like ideas, images, etc.).

References: Entries on the "twelve *nidanas*" of the online Japanese and English Wikipedia.

1 Mame Yamada (b. 1965), a performer of diminutive height, can evoke an uncanny presence on stage and in film. A comedian in the 1960s and a magician in the 1970s, he became an actor from the 1980s. Yamada appeared in three of director Yukio Ninagawa's productions—*Water Magician* (Shiraito no taki, by Juro Kara, 1989/2000), *Hamlet* (2001), and *Poison Boy* (Shintokumaru, by Shuji Terayama, 2002)—as well as in Tanino's productions, such as *Tanino and the Dwarfs' Homage to Tadeusz Kantor* (Tanino to dowafu-tachi ni yoru Kantoru ni sasageru omaji, 2015) and *MOON* (2017). Yamada's website is http://hccweb5.bai.ne.jp/~hdl03601/.

2 The Hokuriku Shinkansen is part of a plan to connect Tokyo and Osaka by bullet train via the Hokuriku region of Toyama, Kanazawa, Fukui, and other cities. Construction was begun in 1997 and the line is to be completed in the 2020s.

3 Concerning the characters' speech, the two puppeteers speak standard Japanese; Sansuke never speaks. The others are locals and can speak both standard Japanese and the local Toyama dialect. No attempt, however, has been made to reproduce the local language in translation.

4 "Namandab" is a truncated form of the Japanese pronunciation of the Amida sutra, a Mahayana Buddhist sutra. It means "Hail Amitabha Buddha."

5 A *kotatsu* is a low table with a heat source underneath and a coverlet placed between the table frame and tabletop.

6 The third eye, or *Ajna chakra,* is the sixth primary *chakra* in the body according to Hinduism. It is believed to reveal insights about the future.

7 Edo period: 1603–1867.

8 The amount is approximately $200.

9 A large bottle of *sake* holds 1.8 L (60.9 fl. oz.) of liquor.

10 *Joruri* puppetry, popularly known as *bunraku* puppetry, refers to traditional three-person puppetry with narrator and *shamisen* accompaniment.

Appendix

As the Sparrows Wended in a Windless Winter
(abbr. *The Sparrows Wended*)

1. Cast of Characters
NURSING HOME STAFF

DOCTOR, around sixty-three, uncle to Shaolin, medical director at the Nursing Home, approaching retirement.

FEMALE CAREGIVER 1, too interested in the Old Lady's treasure box, dies young.

FEMALE CAREGIVER 2, a bully who appears in Li Tokusei's dream.

SHAOLIN (played by a male actor), a new caregiver, just released from prison.

RESIDENTS & THEIR RELATIVES

OLD LADY, nineties, deaf, the oldest and healthiest resident, loves her son but not her daughter. An epitome of avarice.

DAUGHTER OF OLD LADY, obsessive regarding rights of inheritance.

LI TOKUSEI, aged seventy-five, widower, has a daughter, wants to marry Shimei.

DAUGHTER OF LI TOKUSEI, is computer-literate, impatient with her father.

SHIMEI, around sixty-eight, widow, has a son, is Li Tokusei's girlfriend, healthy, used to nursing home life.

YOZEI, a retired military man, suffers from a hernia and cancer, attempts suicide by hanging, gas, and electric drill; married to Sujen, jealous of Tokusei and Shimei's romance.

SUJEN, around sixty-five, unhappily married to Yozei, voluptuous, obsessed with beautification, Shimei's rival for Tokusei's attention.

CHILIRENKA, a thirteen-year-old delusionary girl, abandoned by her father, settles down at the Home.

FATHER OF CHILIRENKA, leaves his daughter at the Nursing Home, wants to believe it is a mental hospital.

YOUNGER VERSIONS of Li Tokusei, Shimei, Yozei, Sujen, and Shaolin as well as miscellaneous residents at the Home who are between seventy-five and eighty-five years of age.

OTHERS
AHON, a celebrant of multi-faith services.

2. Ethnography of the devising of *The Sparrows Wended*

The Sparrows Wended is a relatively new work unknown to many, so I have added an ethnographic study of its making to illustrate how the co-creative process was carried out through devising, workshops, and rehearsals.

As "devising" and "workshopping" are common terms used in performing arts literature, often with little elaboration, some may be puzzled as to what is actually conducted in those activities. Neither term strays away greatly from their dictionary definitions in such sources as the *Oxford English Dictionary* and *Random House Unabridged Dictionary* (Dictionary.com). Devising generally means "to contrive, plan, or elaborate; invent from ideas" and workshopping refers to a group activity "that emphasizes exchange of ideas and the demonstration and application of techniques, skills, etc." In contemporary Japanese theatre, workshopping, as in the West, assumes de-emphasis of written scripts, interest in more egalitarian sharing of ideas among the participants, and engagement in training, theatre games, and études as part of co-creation—although the director usually makes the final decisions.

With *The Sparrows Wended* production at the Za-Koenji Public Theatre scheduled for late November to early December of 2017, three workshops and a major rehearsal were conducted over a period of sixteen months beforehand. The first workshop was a three-day session in September 2016 led by Wang; the next two were six-day sessions in 2017—one in February and the other in August—both co-led by Wang and Zhao. The main rehearsal period—from October 6 to November 26, with a break from October 17 to October 29—was led by Wang. All sessions were held at the Youkiza Studio in Koganei City, Tokyo.

Conceptualization of the play and its evolution

Zhao's tester for the first workshop was a three-scene English draft with the working title "Farewell Party," which was about a private nursing home somewhere in East Asia for relatively healthy, wealthy, and fashionable elders with their various desires and phobias. His introduction follows:

We see repetitively on the news that old people are killed in nursing homes by their caregivers. This has become an international phenomenon. They appear to be hate-crimes. But what are the REAL intentions of killing the weak? This play focuses on one nursing home. The nursing home lobby is divided into left and right halves. The right half is in normal size; the left half is in small size for the puppets. There are five elderly people (performed by puppets) living in the nursing home. They are okay with the small-sized part of the lobby, but when they move into the normal, human-sized part, it becomes so difficult for them to reach the chair, the table, and the doorknob. They cannot talk. They can only utter small sounds as they are too old. There is a young man (played by a male actor) working for them. He is the only one who can speak. He helps them and listens to their life stories told by gestures and photos. He looks huge and capable; they look so small and incapable. He loves these beautiful old people. Then why does he kill them in the end? (Email correspondence, September 2016. Emphasis added.)

Director Wang's "note" echoes similar concerns:

[The aging of the world is] a poignant issue in theatre. We will all soon be aged. The art of puppetry is also going to be aged. What does it mean to be old and weak? How can we understand the very people who built this world as they are too weak to act or speak? What can we learn from the relationship? Is it possible to communicate? And how to kill a person you love? I wish to answer these questions in the play. (Ibid. Emphasis added.)

With an established reputation as an innovative director in Chinese New Wave theatre, Wang took an explorative approach to the first workshop. He continued:

The purpose of the workshop is to generate new ideas on string-objects and live video. [...] Besides the idea of having a separate narrator, I am also interested in the possibility of creating an old silent film with music and intertitles. When the characters have to say something, they don't say it out loud. Instead, we read the lines on intertitles. This approach needs a very visual story and very few "spoken" words. (Ibid. Emphasis added.)

As this was Zhao's first time to write for the material theatre and Wang's second time to direct a performing-object play, their general unfamiliarity with the potential of Youkiza's string-objects in terms of mobility, manipulation, size (about 70–80 cm, or 27.6–31 in., tall), and material art had to be addressed. Wang wanted to discuss more, but workshopping for the manipulators meant being able to test the dramatic content in action by practicing their art. As none of the new string-objects were yet available for trial runs, the participants dipped into the company's stock, which did not necessarily help formulate the right image for the character or staging.

The conceptualization of the play and directing was complex while the script itself was still short with sketchy scenes. This period was fruitful in that the manipulators had to learn right away what integration or entanglement of medial processes required of them in terms of devising. The absolute conditions of the staging were the string-object size and the video camera frame dimensions. The entanglement with the video medium disrupted their usual relations with their string-figures.

The string-objects had to be positioned within the video camera/monitor frame without fear of "decapitation," while the manipulators could not invade the performing-figures' space with their disproportionally large hands and arms. Furthermore, as they had to peer at the monitor vigilantly to see how the string-figures were framed, they experienced some difficulty in sustaining their usual perspective of looking through the strings for a view of their performing-object from behind. During rehearsal, they were compelled to glance back and forth until they became acclimatized to the stage affordances. The framing also led them to curb their accelerated stylistic of almost swinging their string-objects swiftly across stage. They were caught in-between the video camera's lens and their own string-objects.

Aside from devising adjustments to the framing, they also switched to wearing slit-less black outfits that did not flap inadvertently when the video camera panned over them and requested the director devise alternative business for such hand movements as grasping or clicking that were difficult for string-objects without articulated fingers.

Wang, on his part, could share his live video technique while getting to know the string-figures' capacity for action and the manipulator-actors' range in acting ability. He found he had to spend excessive time training some of the manipulators to act and emote, to such an extent that he eventually withdrew from developing a diegetic layer to the manipulators' relations in their fictional private lives. Thus, the manipulators became the designated shadow manipulators of the string-objects without any character elaboration or dramaturgical development of their own. This was a major reduction of the original vision.

Apart from this loss, the first short workshop generally stayed at the level of sharing expertise rather than generating new ideas or imaginative territory. Working in the three languages of Chinese, English, and Japanese was taxing for Wang, so Youkiza decided to find a Chinese-Japanese interpreter for future sessions.

By the second workshop five months later, the working title had grown to *As the Sparrows Wended in a Windless Winter—A Collage of Nursing Home Wash Paintings in Solitude.* Zhao's draft was now a ten-scene script that retained the satirical opening scene from the "Farewell Party" about a "dying lady who will not die." The characters increased from five to twenty-nine, and their situations and stories were revealed through interactions among themselves and with two younger newcomers to the institution.

Zhao identified his conceptual specifications as follows:

1. All the young/non-elderly characters are played by the same actor. The aged are played by performing-objects.
2. The actor speaks, acts, and moves around just like in any other play, while the nursing-home residents speak in a puppet's tone, which should be different, as an indication of the residents' isolation from the "normal" world.
3. Silences and pauses spread all over the play—if this counts as a play—since all of the characters speak little, the words they do say should stand out.
4. This is a comedy, for sure. But if anyone finds it sad and tear-jerking, it's fine, too.
5. Scene changes are essential in any phase of the rehearsals. Try to keep them as short as possible to have control over the pace.
6. It is okay to change the order of the scenes, as it's not a linear

story.
(Zhao 2017a. Emphasis added.)

The general characteristics of Wang's staging directions at that time, according to researcher Tarryn Li-Min Chun, were using multiple sets in one space, bringing cameras on stage, switching cameras, and employing real-time editing and live projection. Wang switches between different perspectives to indicate that various and equally valid versions are possible. Chun also clarifies that Wang's objective is to disrupt continuity as an "attack on the constructedness of art and theatre [...] and as a specific attack on the desire to maintain aesthetic and interpretative consistency of the conventional way of mounting a performance" (2016, 254–57).

Wang and Zhao worked closely together and quickly discerned the limitations of their collaboration with Youkiza. Although Wang and Zhao wanted to introduce more variety, specifically by having a very large puppet, different platform heights, and more emotive acting, Youkiza as a professional group evinced little inclination to add non-string-objects or stagger the height of the performance areas, which would require frequent adjustment of the string length, or to allocate precious time to actor training. These compromises effectively led to a wide, open staging with miniature props easily rolled in and out enabling frequent scene changes rather than the packed stage picture that Chun had indicated as the norm for Wang.

By the third workshop, Zhao had prepared a twenty-six-scene revision and Wang's objectives as director had crystallized into a desire:

to capture the power relations through the video cam lens and film how the objects/actor/characters respond sensitively to the verbal exchanges in the play [...] he identified three perspectives[:] the object level, the human level as seen in Shaolin, and the camera level, which is also the manipulator's level. Shaolin can shoot from his own perspective and also from other perspectives. As for the structure, the puppets and Shaolin are central to the play and the manipulators are separate. The cameramen are separate from Shaolin. Different perspective. (Email correspondence, August 2017)

The main rehearsal period generated two more drafts with twenty-three and twenty scenes respectively. The last became the final performance script. Only five scenes from the early ten-scene workshop draft survived the rewriting. Zhao discarded many of his earlier, conceptual specifications cited above. Age specificity was not carried out in the assignment of performing-object to character. The single character performed by an actor was the new male caregiver, Shaolin.

Zhao also abandoned the division in types of speech between the object characters and the human character perhaps because it would be difficult to convey the complexity of the characters' background and present relations without verbal exchanges of private stories and self-expression of internal states. The deaf Old Lady was the one object character who retained her own "speech" of ear-piercing ejaculations. The other characters also became more verbal, so that pauses and silences did not seem prominent. Comedic aspects developed around the love rivalry between Sujen/Shumei over Li Tokusei and also the hybrid celebrant Ahon, but the emphasis grew increasingly on the residents' stark alienation from each other as well as from the external society.

Thanks to Wang's expertise with the mise en scène, hardly any extra time was spent solely on scene changes. At the very end of the rehearsal, Wang excised a couple of scenes for brevity's sake. The performance was successfully kept under two hours, though this was still quite long for a performing-object play.

As for the participants' response to the workshops and rehearsals, the manipulators at first felt unfree and manipulated as they were constantly being told to adjust to the video camera lens. This injunction required them to stand sometimes at awkward angles to their string-object or reach over a prop or another manipulator to animate their character. Their discomfort can be considered a symptom of the "interpenetration" process of intermedial theatre. However, by the rehearsal period, they had adapted to prioritizing the "framing" of their objects.

The sole actor, Atsushi Sakamoto,[1] who joined from the second workshop, had to work at floor level with the performing-objects much of the time and also stay within the frame. He adapted without much difficulty, telling this writer that he had experience in multimedia theatre and did not feel constrained, but that he could tell this performance was somehow more demanding than the usual multimedia collaboration he was used to. Although he did not articulate what that difference was, his tangling with the incontinent Yozei, weaving around other string-objects, using props that varied in scale, and simultaneously being framed at the performing-object scale as well as at his own height seemed a sufficiently disorienting experience.

While the single male caregiver's laborious services may ironically suggest the burden on the younger generation of the former Chinese one-child policy in caring for parents and grandparents, this nursing home is nonetheless consistently portrayed as one for affluent elderly residents, whose concerns arise from an awareness of the loss of self-determination as well as fear of solitude and death, rather than financial matters. Their own attempts at regaining self-determination seem insufficient in answering the question of how to live in the face of imminent death.

I will now address the abuse of the elderly in terms of this loss of self-determination. Zhao chose this topic as it is a major issue in recent nursing homes in both China and Japan as well as other parts of the world. The real-life incident that captured his attention was the 2016 Sagamihara incident at the Yamayurien nursing home for the mentally disabled in Kanagawa Prefecture. A former male caretaker, twenty-six-year-old Satoshi Uematsu, killed nineteen patients and wounded twenty-five others in a mass knife attack. He wanted people with disabilities to "disappear." In a letter to a politician threatening to kill hundreds of disabled people, he urged the revision of laws to enable euthanasia of the severely disabled.

Recent studies indicate that abuse at nursing homes is mainly by the employed caregivers and is generally known to take five forms: physical abuse, sexual abuse, psychological abuse (emotional, verbal, non-verbal), financial exploitation, and neglect. The following chart (fig. A.1.), adapted from Karl Pillemer's well-known Theoretical Model of Patient Maltreatment, identifies the main players and factors in the human and environmental dynamics of abuse.[2]

The three main intrinsic needs in self-determination are competence, autonomy, and relatedness. Competence is the need that makes one seek to manage, control, and display mastery. Autonomy is the drive to gain free agency in accordance with one's self-image or values, and relatedness is the urge to connect with others and share safety, happiness, and confirmation through a network of relations. Aging often involves the unwilling diminishment of these needs/qualities and is accompanied by physiological, emotional, or mental deterioration. The awareness of decline in self-determination can lead the resident into a power play to raise

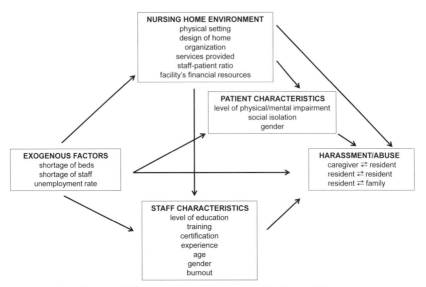

Fig. A.1. Adapted Version of Karl Pillemer's Theoretical Model of Patient Maltreatment.

a sense of personal competence and autonomy, if not relatedness. This, combined with the caregiver's relatively low social position and income as well as with the extremely demanding nature of the work, can trigger hostile/antagonistic situations.

The types of abuse addressed in this play are physical, psychological, sexual, and financial. The play opens with physical abuse arising from an attempt at monetary exploitation. A female caregiver attempts to steal the precious treasure box of the presumably dead Old Lady, and is drawn into an extremely violent battle with her. While in real criminal cases, the resident is sometimes killed, the playwright, given to satire, rather has the caregiver die when she knocks her head hard against the bed railing.

Regarding psychological abuse, one example is Li Tokusei's nightmarish fantasy of a kindergarten assistant verbally bullying him as a little boy about not being able to defecate on command. Another more complex case occurs between Yozei and Shaolin. Yozei had identified with the military and depended on it for regulation and recognition. Through retirement, he lost social status and a sense of self-determination. Desperately seeking confirmation of competence, he exploits his resident status and demands that Shaolin carry him around the large common room in what becomes an absurd Sisyphean dance. However, his whimsical commands, unsupported by any systematic design, are meaningless so that his attempt to regain autonomy and flaunt competence makes no positive impression on Shaolin. This exercise is humiliating for Shaolin, for unlike Yozei, his incarceration in prison has taught him to despise meaninglessness. Later on, when Yozei develops difficulty in passing water, Shaolin finds an opportunity to return in kind by pulling him about the same room mockingly to see if he can help Yozei find a good place to urinate.

Zhao's treatment of sexual harassment is milder than that of the other types of abuse. In this area, he finds his best outlet for the comedic. Su-jen, Yozei's wife, is the cougar in the final script. Yozei, an adulterer in the past but now incapacitated by a hernia, is unable to keep her satisfied. She trails hungrily after Li Tokusei and flashes her flabby wares at the Doctor in hope of getting plastic surgery. She is consistent in her attitude to men and would prey on Shaolin if he did not taunt her mercilessly. She is a tremendous source of comedy in this painful narrative, and it is a pity that Scene 5, "Married Life," had to be omitted due to the constraints of performance time.

Concerning Chilirenka, the "exclusive" reasons clarified by the girl herself indicate that she does not fit into this framework of self-determination. She was only just beginning to relate positively to others and the result was a disaster when viewed from within the social system. She cannot be made sense of as society excludes her in order to justify its own organization.

Here ends the documentation of the process of devising, workshopping, and rehearsal. The initial conceptual aspects and how they were carried forth or were discarded during the physicalization of the diegesis have been identified. Also discussed was the visceral sense of entanglement the manipulators and, to a lesser extent, the human actor felt in adjusting to the extra-diegetic intermediality.

1 Atsushi Sakamoto is actor and co-founder of the Onsen Dragon theatre company (f. 2010), which produces hard-boiled plays about life and death.
2 Pillemer himself chose to categorize nursing home abuse into three kinds: physical violence, verbal aggression, and neglect (Pillemer 1988, 229).

Selected Bibliography

Adachi, Barbara. 1985. *Backstage at Bunraku.* New York: Weatherhill.

Advanced Telecommunications Research Institute International. 2006. *Understanding the Mechanism of* Sonzai-Kan. http://www.geminoid. jp/projects/kibans/Data/panel-20060719-mod2-eOnly.pdf.

Alternative & Material Theatre Project 2000. n.d. Alternative & Material Theatre Project 2000 (website). Accessed October 2, 2019. http:// www.puppetpark.com/2000/video1.html.

Amano, Tengai. 2004. *Heitaro no bakemono nikki* [Heitaro's *Yokai* Diary]. Tokyo: Hokuto Publisher.

———. 2007. "Special on I.T.O. Project *Heitaro's Yokai Diary.*" *Theater Guide.* http://www.theaterguide.co.jp/feature/ito/page4.html (site discontinued).

———. 2018a. "Artist Interview." Interview by Jun Kobori. *Performing Artists Network Japan,* September 18, 2018. https://www.performingarts. jp/E/art_interview/1808/1.html.

———. 2018b. *Heitaro bakemono nikki* [Heitaro's *Yokai* Diary], DVD. I.T.O. Project.

Amano, Tengai, and Toshihiko Yamada. 2018a. "Amano Tengai & Yamada Toshihiko ga kataru, ITO purojekuto *Takaoka shinno kokaiki* (supeshiaru rensai Vol. 1)" [Tengai Amano and Toshihiko Yamada Speak on the I.T.O. Project *The Voyage of Imperial Prince Takaoka* (Special Issue Part 1)]. *Spice,* February 28, 2018. https://spice.eplus.jp/articles/ 175124.

———. 2018b. "ITO purojekuto *Takaoka shinno kokaiki,* ito-ayatsuri ningyo no sosaku to sosa no himitsu ni semaru (supeshiaru rensai Vol. 2)" [I.T.O. Project *The Voyage of Imperial Prince Takaoka*: Zooming in on the Secret Teachings of Creating and Manipulating Stringobjects (Special Issue Part 2)]. *Spice,* March 26, 2018. https://spice. eplus.jp/articles/179455.

Anderson, Ryan. 2016. "The Taste of Nostalgia: Vanishing Flavors from the Ancestral Japanese Village." *Savage Minds,* October 18, 2016. https:// savageminds.org/2016/10/18/the-taste-of-nostalgia-vanishing-flavors-from-the-ancestral-japanese-village/.

ARICA, Theatre Company. 2020. *KIOSK* pamphlet, distributed at BankART Station, Yokohama.

ART Prometheus, o.s. n.d. "Who We Are." ART Prometheus.cz. Accessed November 20, 2019. https://www.artprometheus.cz/en/who-we-are/.

Bay-Cheng, Sarah, Chiel Kattenbelt, Andy Lavender, and Robin Nelson, eds. 2010. *Mapping Intermediality in Performance.* Amsterdam: Amsterdam University Press.

Bell, John. 1997. "Puppets and Performing Objects in the Twentieth Century." *Performing Arts Journal* 19, no. 2: 29–46. https://www.jstor.org/stable/3245861.

———. 2014. "Playing with the Eternal Uncanny: The Persistent Life of Lifeless Objects." In Posner, Orenstein, and Bell, eds., *Routledge Companion to Puppetry and Material Performance,* 43–52.

Bennett, Jane. 2010. *Vibrant Matter: A Political Ecology of Things.* Durham, NC: Duke University Press.

Berger, Laurent P. 2011. Tokyo Arts and Space (website). Updated May 1, 2011. https//www.tokyoartsandspace.jp/en/creator/index/B/107.html.

———. n.d. "Biography." Berger&Berger (website). Accessed August 28, 2019. http://www.berger-berger.com/bio.

Bidgood, Jeremy. 2015. "The Problem of Bunraku: A practice-led investigation into contemporary uses and misuses of *ningyo-joruri.*" PhD diss., Royal Holloway, University of London. http://www.takey.com/.

Bird-David, Nurit. 1999. "Animism Revisited: Personhood, Environment, and Relational Epistemology." *Current Anthropology* 40: 67–79.

Boenisch, Peter. M. 2006a. "Aesthetic Art to Aisthetic Act: Theatre, Media, Intermedial Performance." In Chapple and Kattenbelt, eds., *Intermediality in Theatre and Performance,* 103–16.

———. 2006b. "Mediation Unfinished: Choreographing Intermediality in Contemporary Dance Performance." In Chapple and Kattenbelt, eds., *Intermediality in Theatre and Performance,* 151–66.

Bolter, Jay David, and Richard Grusin. 2000. *Remediation: Understanding New Media.* Boston: MIT Press.

Bono, Mayumi, Oriza Hirata, Hiroshi Ishikawa, and Yuichiro Yoshikawa. 2014. "The Meaning of Robot/Android-Human Theatre from the Perspectives of Engineering, Science and Arts." *Fundamentals Review* 7, no. 4: 326–35. http://www.ieice.org/ess/ESS/Fundam-Review.html.

Boyd, Mari. 2006. *Aesthetics of Quietude: Ota Shogo and the Theatre of*

Divestiture. Tokyo: Sophia University Press.

———. 2009. "Surviving and Succeeding: The Story of the Yukiza Marionette Theatre Company." In *Rising from the Flames: The Rebirth of Theater in Occupied Japan, 1945–1952,* edited by Samuel Leiter, 217–30. Lexington: Lexington Books.

———. 2010. Review of *Yaburegasa Choan: Choan and the Ripped Umbrella,* by Kiyokazu Yamamoto. *Puppetry International* 27: 30–31.

Braidotti, Rosi. 2011. *Nomadic Theory: Portable Rosi Braidotti.* New York: Columbia University Press.

Brandesky, Joseph. 2007. "Sources of the Czech Design Legacy." In *Czech Theatre Design in the 20th Century: Metaphor and Irony Revisited,* edited by Joseph Brandesky. Iowa City: University of Iowa Press.

———. 2013. "Strings Attached: The Living Tradition of Czech Puppets." In *Strings Attached: The Living Tradition of Czech Puppets,* edited by Joseph Brandesky, Beth Kettelman, Nina Malikova, and Lenka Saldova. Columbus, Ohio: Columbus Museum of Art.

Center for the Study of Communication Design at the Osaka University, ed. 2010. *Robotto engeki* [Robot Theatre]. Osaka: Osaka University Press.

Chapple, Freda, and Chiel Kattenbelt, eds. 2006. *Intermediality in Theatre and Performance.* Amsterdam and New York: Rodopi Press.

Cicchelli, Vincenzo, Sylvie Octobre, and Viviane Riegel. "Global Culture and Aesthetic Cosmopolitanism International Conference – Sao Paulo, October 2016."

Chong, Wishing. 2007a. "Artist Interview." Interview by Jun Kobori. *Performing Arts Network Japan,* December 28, 2007. https://performingarts.jp/E/art_interview/0711/1.html.

———. 2007b. "Doll Town." Unpublished play script.

Chun, Tarryn Li-Min. 2016. "Stage Technology in Modern China: The Media of Revolution and Resistance." PhD diss., Harvard University.

Dale, Joshua Paul. 2016. "Cute Studies: an Emerging Field." *East Asian Journal of Popular Culture* 2, no. 1: 5–13.

Dixon, Steve. 2007. *Digital Performance: A History of New Media in Theatre, Dance, Performance Art and Installation.* Cambridge, Massachusetts; London: MIT Press.

Dolar, Mladen. 1991. "'I Shall Be with You on Your Wedding-Night':

Lacan and the Uncanny." *October* 58 (Autumn 1991): 5–23.

———. 2005. "Nothing has changed." *Filozofski vestnik* 26, no. 2: 147–60.

———. 2006. *A Voice and Nothing More.* Cambridge, Massachusetts: MIT Press.

Down, Mark. n.d. "Shunkin." Blind Summit Theatre (website). Accessed December 9, 2018. https://www.blindsummit.com/shunkin.

Dubuska, Alice, Jan Novak, Nina Malikova, and Marie Zdenkova. 2006. *Czech Puppet Theatre—Yesterday and Today.* Translated by Don Nixon. Prague: Theatre Institute in Prague.

Eckersall, Peter, Helena Grehan, and Edward Sheer. 2015. "New Media Dramaturgy." In *The Routledge Companion to Dramaturgy,* edited by Magda Romanska, 375–81. New York and London: Routledge.

Edo Marionette Theatre Youkiza. 2008. *Heisei nozoki karakuri yaburegasa Choan* [Choan and the Ripped Umbrella], DVD. Tokyo, NHK: 2008.

———. 2010. *Descendants of the Eunuch Admiral.* Performance program.

Eguchi, Katsuhiko. 2007. *Inobe-ke no ichinichi* [One Day in the Life of the Inobe Family]. Tokyo: PHP Institute.

Feltham, Oliver. 2008. *Alain Badiou: Live Theory.* London and New York: Continuum.

Francis, Penny. 2012. *Puppetry: A Reader in Theatre Practice.* Basingstoke, UK: Palgrave Macmillan.

Freud, Sigmund. (1919) 1988. *The Uncanny.* Translated by R. Hingley. New York, New York: Penguin Books.

Fukada, Koji. 2015. "Feature Film *Sayonara* Production Project. Film Version of Android Theatre by Hirata Oriza x Ishiguro Hiroshi Research Team!" Motion Gallery. https://motion-gallery.net/projects/sayonara.

Harrison, Oliver. 2014. *Revolutionary Subjectivity in Post-Marxist Thought: Laclau, Negri, Badiou.* London: Routledge.

Harvey, Graham. 2013. *The Handbook of Contemporary Animism.* Durham: Acumen Publishing.

Hirata, Oriza. 1998. *Engeki nyumon* [Introduction to Theatre]. Tokyo: Kodansha Gendai Shinsho.

———. 2012a. "About Our Robot/Android Theatre." Translated by Kei Hibino. *Comparative Theatre Review* 11, no. 1: 1. https://www.jstage.

jst.go.jp/article/ctr/11/1/11_1_29/_article/-char/en.

———. 2012b. "Three Sisters, Android Version." Translated by Hiroko Matsuda and M. Cody Poulton. Unpublished play script.

———. 2019a. *I, Worker.* In *Citizens of Tokyo: Six Plays,* edited by M. Cody Poulton. New York: Seagull Books.

———. 2019b. *Sayonara.* In *Citizens of Tokyo: Six Plays.*

Hozumi, Ikan. (1738) 1955. *Naniwa miyage.* In *The Anthology of Japanese Literature: From the Earliest Era to the Mid-Nineteenth Century,* compiled and edited by Donald Keene, 386–90. New York: Grove Press.

Ichihara, Satoko. 2019a. *Favonia's Fruitless Fable.* Translated by Aya Ogawa. In *ENGEKI: Japanese Theatre in the New Millennium 4,* edited by Japan Playwrights Association, 117–51. Tokyo: Japan Playwrights Association.

———. 2019b. Profile. In *ENGEKI: Japanese Theatre in the New Millennium 4,* edited by Japan Playwrights Association, 154. Tokyo: Japan Playwrights Association.

Iida Puppet Festa. http://en.iida-puppet.com/.

Imai, Yoichi. n.d. "Usuitakai no tetsugaku: Taruho Inagaki" [The Philosophy of the Thin Sheets Dimension: Taruho Inagaki]. Accessed November 11, 2019. http://www.geocities.jp/maomao_mac/hakubankai.html (site discontinued).

Inagaki, Taruho. 1969. *Senichibyo monogatari* [One-Thousand-and-One Second Stories]. Tokyo: Shincho Bunko.

Ishiguro, Hiroshi. 2007. *Andoroido saiensu: Ningen o shiru tame no robotto kenkyu* [Android Science: Robotics Research for Human Understanding]. Tokyo: Asahi Communications.

———. n.d. ISHIGURO Symbiotic Human-Robot Interaction Project (website). Accessed November 11, 2019. https://www.jst.go.jp/erato/ishiguro/en/index.html.

Ishii, Tatsuro. 2004. "Introduction to Terayama Shuji's *La Marie-Vison*." Translated by Carol Fisher Sorgenfrei. In *Half a Century of Japanese Theater VI, 1960s Part 1,* edited by Japan Playwrights Association, 22–26. Tokyo: Kinokuniya Publishers.

Ivy, Marilyn. 1995. *Discourses of the Vanishing: Modernity, Phantasm, Japan.* Chicago: University of Chicago Press.

———. 2010. "Art of Cute Little Things; Nara Yoshitomo's Parapolitics," *Mechademia* 5: 3–29. https://muse.jhu.edu/article/400548/pdf.

Iwaki, Kyoko. 2011. *Tokyo Theatre Today—Conversations with Eight Emerging Theatre Artists.* London: Hublet Publishing.

Japan Council of Performers Rights & Performing Arts Organizations (Geidankyo). 2016. *Annual Report 2016.* https://www.geidankyo.or.jp/img/disclosure/2016annual-report.pdf.

Japan Foundation. 2007. "Presenter Topics: Avignon Festival 2007 line-up (July 6–27, 2007)." *Performing Arts Network Japan,* June 30, 2007. https://performingarts.jp/E/topics/archive/2007/p20070603.html.

Japan Puppet Theater Conference (Zenninkyo). n.d. Accessed December 12, 2019. http://www.zenninkyo.jp/.

Jensen, Casper Bruun, and Andrey Blok. 2013. *Techno-animism in Japan: Shinto Cosmograms, Actor-network Theory, and the Enabling Powers of Non-human Agencies.* SAGE Publications.

Jentsch, Ernest. (1906) 2008. "On the Psychology of the Uncanny." In *Uncanny Modernity,* edited by Jo Collins and John Jervis. 216–28. London: Palgrave Macmillan.

Jones, Basil. 2014. "Puppetry, Authorship, and the Ur-Narrative". In *The Routledge Companion to Puppetry and Material Performance,* edited by Dassia N. Posner, Claudia Orenstein, and John Bell, 61–69. New York: Routledge.

Jurkowski, Henryk. (1988) 2013. *Aspects of Puppet Theatre.* 2nd ed. Translated by Penny Francis. New York: Palgrave Macmillan.

———. 1990. *Chiteki boken toshite no ningyo geki: Obujekuto shiata e* [Aspects of the Puppet Theatre]. Translated by Akiko Kato. Tokyo: Shinjusha.

———. 2012. "Puppetry Aesthetics at the Start of the Twenty-first Century." In *Puppetry: A Reader in Theatre Practice,* edited by Penny Francis, 126–32. London: Palgrave Macmillan.

———. 2015. "Ningyogeki to sono jikkokachi" [Puppetry and Its Performing Value]. "Sonzaiteki geki ningyo no himitsu" [Ontological Puppet Secrets]. Translated and edited by UNIMA-Japan. In *The Yearbook of Japanese Puppetry '15.* Tokyo: UNIMA-Japan.

Kato, Akiko. 2007. *Nippon no ningyo engeki 1867–2007* [The History of Japanese Material Performance, 1867–2007]. Tokyo: Hosei University Press.

Katsuno, Hirofumi. 2015. "Branding Humanoid Japan." In *Assembling Japan: Modernity, Technology and Global Culture,* edited by Griseldis Kirsch, Dolores P. Martinez, and Merry White. Oxford, UK: Peter Lang.

Kattenbelt, Chiel. 2008. "Intermediality in Theatre and Performance: Definitions, Perceptions and Medial Relationships." *Cultura, Lenguaje y Representación / Culture, Language And Representation* 6: 19–29.

Kawajiri, Taiji. 1984. *A History of the Puppet Theatre PUK 1929–1984.* Tokyo: Miraisha.

———. 1986. *Nihon ningyo hattatsushi-ko* [Thoughts on the Development of Japanese Puppetry]. Tokyo: Bansei Shobo.

Kawatake, Mokuami. (1862) 1968. *Kanzen choaku nozoki karakuri* [Poetic Justice Peep Show]. In *Meisaku kabuki zenshu* [Collection of Famous Kabuki Plays] Vol. 10, edited by Toshio Kawatake et al., 210–336. Tokyo: Sogen-shinsha.

Kennedy, Dennis, and Yong Li Lan, eds. 2010. *Shakespeare in Asia: Contemporary Performance.* Cambridge, UK: Cambridge University Press.

Kimura, Yoko. 2017. "Robot Theatre by Oriza Hirata. Case Study of Literary Adaptation as a Creative Source." *Mejiro Journal of Humanities* 13: 1–15.

Klich, Rosemary, and Edward Scheer. 2012. *Multimedia Performance.* Basingstoke, UK: Palgrave Macmillan.

Knowles, Ric. 2004. *Reading the Material Theatre.* Cambridge, UK: Cambridge University Press.

———. 2010. *Theatre & Interculturalism.* Basingstoke, UK: Palgrave Macmillan.

Kuo Pao Kun. (1995) 2003. *Descendants of the Eunuch Admiral.* In *Two Plays by Kuo Pao Kun: Descendants of the Eunuch Admiral & The Spirits Play,* edited by C. J. Wan-ling Wee and Chee Keng Lee. Singapore: SNP Editions.

Kurotani, Miyako. 2004. "Cover Interview: Miyako Kurotani, the Kugutsume." *Doll Forum Japan* 42 (September):18–33.

Kyburz, Josef. A. 1997. "Magical Thought at the Interface of Nature and Culture." In *Japanese Images of Nature: Cultural Perspectives,* edited by Pamela Asquith and Arne Kalland, 257–79. Surrey: Curzon Press.

Latour, Bruno. 1991. *We Have Never Been Modern.* Translated by Catherine Porter. Boston: Harvard University Press.

————. 2004. *Politics of Nature: How to Bring the Sciences into Democracy.* Translated by Catherine Porter. Cambridge, Massachusetts: Harvard University Press.

Law, Jane Marie. 1997. *Puppets of Nostalgia: The Life, Death, and Rebirth of the Japanese Awaji Ningyo Tradition.* Princeton, New Jersey: Princeton University Press.

Lin Ke Huan. 2003. "Spiritual Wanderings and Confessions of the Soul." Translated by Teo Han Wue. In Kuo Pao Kun, *Two Plays by Kuo Pao Kun,* 130–41.

Lo, Jacqueline, and Helen Gilbert. 2002. "Toward a Topography of Cross-Cultural Theatre." *TDR/The Drama Review* 46, no. 3: 31–53.

Lo, Jacqueline, Tseen Khoo, and Helen Gilbert. 2000. *Diaspora: Negotiating Asian-Australia.* St. Lucia, Queensland: University of Queensland Press.

Macpherson, Ian, and Teri Jane Bryant. 2018. "Softening Power: Cuteness as Organizational Communication Strategy in Japan and the West." *Journal of International and Advanced Japanese Studies* 10: 39–55.

Martin, Carol. 2013. *Theatre of the Real.* Basingstoke, UK: Palgrave Macmillan.

May, Simon. 2019. *Power of Cute.* New York: Princeton University Press.

McBurney, Simon. 2011. "How We Met: Simon McBurney & Kathryn Hunter." Interview by Adam Jacques. *Independent,* September 4, 2011. https://www.independent.co.uk/news/people/profiles/how-we-met-simon-mcburney-amp-kathryn-hunter-2347009.html.

McConachie, Bruce, Tobin Nellhaus, Carol Fisher Sorgenfrei, and Tamara Underiner. 2016. *Theatre Histories: An Introduction.* 3rd ed. New York: Routledge.

Merleau-Ponty, Maurice. 1968. *The Visible and the Invisible, Followed by Working Notes.* Translated by Alphonso Lingis. Evanston: Northwestern University Press.

Minami, Ryuta, Ian Carruthers, and John Gilles, eds. 2001. *Performing Shakespeare in Japan.* Cambridge, UK: Cambridge University Press.

Minister, Stephen. 2005. "Forging Identities and Respecting Otherness: Levinas, Badiou, and the Ethics of Commitment." *Symposium* 9, no. 2: 267–87.

Ministry of Justice. 2018. *Homusho zairyu gaikokujin tokei 2018 nenpo*

[Resident Foreigners Statistics Report 2018].
http://www.moj.go.jp/housei/toukei/housei05_00032.html.
Mitani, Koki. 2012. *Sorenari shinju* [Much Ado About Love Suicides],
DVD. Tokyo: Parco Publishers.
———. 2014. "Puppet Entertainment Sherlock Holmes." NHK Archives. https://www2.nhk.or.jp/archives/tv60bin/detail/index.cgi?das_
id=D0009040449_00000.
Mori, Masahiro. 1970. "Bukimi no tani" [The Uncanny Valley]. *Energy
Magazine* 7, no. 4: 33–35.
———. 2005. "The Uncanny Valley Revisited." Paper presented at the
14th IEEE International Workshop on Robots and Human Interactive
Communication, Nashville, USA, August 2005. https://doi.org/10.1109/
ROMAN.2005.1513772.
———. 2012. "The Uncanny Valley (From the Field)." Translated by
Karl F. MacDorman and Norri Kageki. *IEEE Robotics & Automation
Magazine* (June). https://doi.org/10.1109/MRA.2012.2192811.
NHK (Japan Broadcasting Corporation). 2009. "Backstage Interview on
Puppetry: Higashi Sato (Studio Nova) on *The Three Musketeers*."
NHK Archives. https://www2.nhk.or.jp/archives/search/special/detail/
?d=backstage 008.
Nittono, Hiroshi, Michiko Fukushima, Akihiro Yano, and Hiroki Moriya.
2012. "The Power of *Kawaii*: Viewing Cute Images Promotes a Careful
Behavior and Narrows Attentional Focus." *PLoS ONE* 7, no. 9. https://
journals.plos.org/plosone/article?id=10.1371/journal.pone.0046362.
———. 2016. "The two-layer model of 'kawaii': A behavioural science
framework for understanding kawaii and cuteness." *East Asian Journal of Popular Culture* 2, no. 1: 79–95. https://doi.org/10.1386/
eapc.2.1.79_1.
———. 2019. *Kawaii no chikara: Jikken de saguru sono shinri* [The
Power of Cute: Experiments in its Psychology]. Tokyo: Dojin Sensho.
Object Performance Theater. n.d. "Object Performance Theater towa"
[What is Object Performance Theater?]. Object Performance Theater
(website). Accessed December 15, 2019. http://www.page.sannet.ne.
jp/nag-maki/opttoppage.htm.
———. n.d. OPT profile page. CoRich Butai Geijutsu. Accessed December 15, 2019. https://stage.corich.jp/troupe/5271.
Odin, Steve. 2001. *Artistic Detachment in Japan and the West: Psychic
Distance in Comparative Aesthetics.* Honolulu: University of Hawaii

Press.

Otmazgin, Nissim. 2014. "Anime in the US: The entrepreneurial dimensions of globalized culture." *Pacific Affairs,* 87, no. 1: 53–69. https://doi.org/10.5509/201487153.

Pierterse, Jan Nederveen. 2019. *Globalization and Culture: Global Mélange.* 4th ed. Maryland: Rowman & Littlefield.

Pillemer, Karl. 1988 "Maltreatment of Patients in Nursing Homes: Overview and Research Agenda." *Journal of Health and Social Behavior* 29, no. 3: 227–38. https://www.jstor.org/stable/2137034.

Pluta, Izabella. 2016. "Theater and Robotics: Hiroshi Ishiguro's Androids as Staged by Oriza Hirata." *Art Research Journal* 3, no. 1: 65–79.

Pluth, Ed. 2010. *Alain Badiou: A Philosophy of the New.* Cambridge, UK; Maiden, Mass: Polity.

Posner, Dassia N., Claudia Orenstein, and John Bell, eds. 2014. *The Routledge Companion to Puppetry and Material Performance.* London: Routledge.

Prime Minister of Japan and His Cabinet. 2007a. *Innovation 25.* February 26, 2007. https://japan.kantei.go.jp/innovation/interimbody_e.html.

———. 2007b. *Long-term Strategic Guidelines of Innovation 25.* June 1, 2007. https://japan.kantei.go.jp/innovation/innovation_final.pdf.

———. 2015. "Robot Revolution Realization Council." Kantei.go.jp. January 23, 2015. https://japan.kantei.go.jp/97_abe/actions/201501/23 article3.html.

———. n.d. "Innovation." Kantei.go.jp. Accessed December 8, 2019. https://japan.kantei.go.jp/innovation/okotae2e.html (site discontinued).

Ravid, Ofer. 2014. "Presentness: Developing Presence Through Psychophysical Actor-Training." PhD diss., York University.

Rebellato, Dan. 2009. *Theatre & Globalization.* Basingstoke, UK: Palgrave Macmillan.

Reilly, Kara. 2011. *Automata and Mimesis on the Stage of Theatre History.* Basingstoke, UK: Palgrave Macmillan.

Research Resources: Multicultural Japan. n.d. "Korean People in Japan." Chuo University (website). Accessed September 10, 2019. http://c-faculty.chuo-u.ac.jp/~mikenix1/jms/Koreans.html (site discontinued).

Robinson, Andrew. 2014. "An A to Z of Theory | Alain Badiou: Event." *Ceasefire,* December 15, 2014. https://ceasefiremagazine.co.uk/

alain-badiou-event/.

Rosner, Krisztina. 2018. "The Gaze of The Robot: Oriza Hirata's Robot Theatre." *The Theatre Times,* March 11, 2018. https://thetheatretimes. com/the-gaze-of-the-robot/.

Robertson, Jennifer. 2018. *Robo-Sapiens Japanicus: Robots, Gender, Family, and the Japanese Nation.* Oakland, California: University of California Press.

Rahimi, Sadeq. 2013. "The ego, the ocular, and the uncanny: Why are metaphors of vision central in accounts of the uncanny?" *The International Journal of Psychoanalysis* 94, no. 3: 453–76. https://doi. org/10.1111/j.1745-8315.2012.00660.x.

Sankei News. 2018. "Gakucho ni sakka no Hirata Oriza-shi, Hyogo Toyooka ni yonen-sei no kenritsu senmonshoku daigaku ga kaiko e" [Writer Oriza Hirata Becomes President, to Open a Prefectural Fouryear Vocational College in Toyooka, Hyogo], August 24, 2018. https://www.sankei.com/west/news/180824/wst1808240089-n1.html.

Sawa, Noriyuki. 2008a. "Artist Database." *Performing Arts Network Japan.* https://www.performingarts.jp/e/data_art/theater/p-10470. html.

———. 2008b. "Artist Interview." Interview by Chiemi Tsukada. *Performing Arts Network Japan,* July 22, 2008. https://www.performingarts. jp/J/art_interview/0807/1.html.

———. n.d. "Nori Sawa's Puppet Gallery." Puppet House (website). Accessed September 21, 2019. https://www.puppet-house.co.jp/nori/ puppet.htm.

Seiko Museum, The. n.d. "To Regular Life with 'Hour Bells.'" The Seiko Museum (website). Accessed December 14, 2019. https://museum.seiko. co.jp/en/knowledge/relation_07/.

Seinendan. n.d. Seinendan.org. Accessed December 6, 2019. http://www. seinendan.org/eng/.

Seinendan Agora Project and Theatre Television. 2013. *Three Sisters, Android Version,* DVD. Tokyo: Theatre Television.

Senda, Yasuko. 2012. *KARAKURI NINGYO JAPANESE AUTOMATA.* Translated by Tom Slemmons. Nagoya: Senda Yasuko Publishing.

Setagaya Public Theatre. 2008. *Shun-kin.* Performance program.

Shuzui, Kenji. 1962. *Naniwa miyage hottan.* In *Koten nihon bungaku zenshu* 36 [Classical Japanese Literature Complete Works 36]. Tokyo: Chikuma Shobo.

Sone, Yuji. 2017. *Japanese Robot Culture: Performance, Imagination, and Modernity*. London: Palgrave Macmillan.

Stuever, Hank. 2000. "What Would Godzilla Say?" *Washington Post*, February 14, 2000. https://www.washingtonpost.com/wp-srv/WPcap/2000-02/14/001r-021400-idx.html.

Sugimoto, Hiroshi. 2012. *Sugimoto bunraku Sonezaki shinju tsuketari Kannon meguri* [Sonezaki Shinju Kannon Pilgrimage], DVD. Tokyo: NHK Enterprise.

———. 2014. "Inochi no nai ki no ningyo ni nihonjin no tamashii o fukikomu Sugimoto bunraku, to iu atarashii dento" [Sugimoto *Bunraku*, the New Tradition, Breathes Soulful Life into Wooden Puppets]. *Wochi Kochi Magazine*, January 2014. https://www.wochikochi.jp/topstory/2014/01/sugimotobunraku.php.

Taira, Jo. 2014. *La Marie-Vison*, DVD. Tokyo: Horipro Inc.

Tanino, Kuro. 2011. "Artist Interview." Interview by Kyoko Iwaki. *Performing Arts Network Japan*, August 9, 2011. https://performingarts.jp/E/art_interview/1106/1.html.

———. 2014. "Penino Envy: Kuro Tanino on the Architecture of the Inner Life." Interview by Abigail Sebaly. *The Walker Reader*, January 13, 2014. https://walkerart.org/magazine/kuro-tanino-phallic-symbols-penino.

———. 2016. *Jigokudani onsen Mumyo no yado* [Avidya—The Dark Inn]. Tokyo: Hakusuisha.

———. 2017. "Niwa gekidan penino *Jigokudani onsen Mumyo no yado*. Saishu koen o shusai Tanino Kuro ga kataru: 'Tada hadaka ni natte yu ni tsukaru, onsen ijo ni fueana basho wa nai.'" [Tanino Kuro, the Company Head of Niwa Gekidan Penino, Speaks on the Final Production of *Avidya—The Dark Inn*: "No Place Is As Conducive to Honesty Than a Hot Spring, Where You Can Skinny-dip Together"]. Interview by Koichi Imai. *Spice*, October 28, 2017. https://spice.eplus.jp/articles/154255.

———. 2019a. *Avidya—The Dark Inn*. Translated by Mari Boyd. In *ENGEKI: Japanese Theatre in the New Millennium 4*, edited by Japan Playwrights Association, 55–116. Tokyo: Japan Playwrights Association.

———. 2019b. Profile. In *ENGEKI: Japanese Theatre in the New Millennium 4*, edited by Japan Playwrights Association, 155. Tokyo: Japan Playwrights Association.

Tanizaki, Junichiro. (1933) 2008. *Shunkin-sho.* In *Chikuma Japanese Literature 014 Tanizaki Junichiro.* Tokyo: Chikuma Shobo.

Tillis, Steve. 1992. *Towards an Aesthetics of the Puppet: Puppetry as a Theatrical Art.* New York: Greenwood Press.

Toyotake, Rosetayu. 2013. "Artist Interview." Interview by Kazumi Narabe. *Performing Arts Network Japan,* September 30, 2013. https://performingarts.jp/E/art_interview/1308/1.html.

Unita, Momiichi. 2010. "Shonen-Ojakan aruiwa 'michi' no hohojosetsu" ["Discourse on the Shonen-Ojakan's Methodology or Its 'Unknown'"]. *1001 (Ichizero zeroichi)* performance program. Tokyo: New National Theatre, Tokyo.

UNIMA-Japan. 2015–2019. *The Yearbook of Japanese Puppetry '15– '18.* Tokyo: UNIMA-Japan.

Uzaki, Ryudo. 2002. *Bunraku ningyo Sonezaki shinju rock,* DVD. Tokyo: TV Tokyo/RU Office.

Walsh, Aylwyn. 2012. Review of *Theatre & Globalization, Theatre & Interculturalism, and Theatre & Prison,* by Dan Rebellato, Ric Knowles, and Caoimhe McAvinche. *Theatre Topics* 22, no. 1: 110–12. https://doi.org/10.1353/tt.2012.0008.

Wagner, Meike. 2006. "Of Other Bodies: The Intermedial Gaze." In Chapple and Kattenbelt, eds., *Intermediality in Theatre and Performance,* 125–36.

Watum, Marc. 2017. "Huntington, Said, and Pieterse: The Great Clash of Perceptions." *The Erudite,* October 27, 2017. https://www.eruditejournal.com.

White, Gareth. 2013. *Audience Participation in Theatre: Aesthetics of the Invitation.* London: Palgrave Macmillan.

World Encyclopedia of Puppetry Arts. n.d. s.v. "Object theatre." Accessed April 4, 2018. https://wepa.unima.org/en/object-theatre/.

Yamaguchi, Masao. 2002. "*Karakuri*: the ludic relationship between man and machine in Tokugawa Japan." In *Japan at Play: The Ludic and the Logic of Power,* edited by Joy Hendry and Massimo Raveri, 72–83. London: Routledge.

Yamamoto, Kiyokazu. 2011. "Heisei nozoki karakuri yaburegasa Choan" [Choan and the Ripped Umbrella: Heisei Trick Peep Show]. Unpublished play script.

Yamamura, Akiyoshi. 2018. *Nihonjin wa naze gaikokujin ni shinto o setsumei dekinai no ka* [Why the Japanese Cannot Explain Shinto to

Foreigners]. Tokyo: Bestsellers.

Zhao Binghao. 2017a. "As the Sparrows Wended in a Windless Winter—A Collage of Nursing Home Wash Paintings in Solitude" (ten-scene draft). Translated from English to Japanese by Saori Isogai. Unpublished play script.

———. 2017b. "Chechydonrai" [*Suzume sarite fuyu kitari*; As the Sparrows Wended in a Windless Winter]. Translated from Chinese into Japanese by Akiko Nobue. Unpublished play script.

Index

ボイド眞理子（Mari BOYD）

上智大学名誉教授。研究分野は現代日本演劇、特に静か系演劇、人形演劇、インターカルチュラル・パフォーマンス。ミッションは上質の日本のコンテンポラリ・パフォーミング・アーツを海外に英語で発信することにある。研究書には『静けさの美学―太田省吾と裸形の演劇』（上智大学出版 2006）のほか、共著『20世紀の戯曲Ⅲ：現代戯曲の変貌』（社会評論社 2005）、『戦火から甦る：占領下の日本演劇の復興1945-52年』（レクシングトンブックス 2009）、『コロンビア日本戯曲集』（コロンビア大学出版 2014）、『ケンブリッジ日本演劇史』（ケンブリッジ大学出版 2016）等がある。英訳編集には日本劇作家協会編『現代日本の劇作』10巻（紀伊國屋書店 1999-2008）、『長谷川孝治戯曲集：弘前劇場の二つの場所』（太田出版 2002）、『エンゲキ： 新世紀の日本演劇』1-5巻（日本劇作家協会 2016-2020）。

Mari Boyd

Professor Emeritus at Sophia University, Tokyo. Her mission is to make high-quality contemporary Japanese performing arts available to the English-speaking world. Her overlapping research foci are modern Japanese theatre, performing-object theatre, and intercultural theatre. Author of *The Aesthetics of Quietude: Ota Shogo and the Theatre of Divestiture* (Sophia University Press, 2006), she contributed to *Drama in the Twentieth Century III* (Shakaihyoronsha, 2005), *Rising From the Flames: The Rebirth of Theatre in Occupied Japan, 1945–1952* (Lexington Books, 2009), *Columbia Anthology of Modern Japanese Drama* (Columbia University Press, 2014), and *A History of Japanese Theatre* (Cambridge University Press, 2016). She is also a translation editor of and contributor to *Half a Century of Japanese Theater* (Kinokuniya Publishers, 1999–2008), *Koji Hasegawa's Plays: The Two Worlds of Hirosaki Theater* (Ohta Publishers, 2002), and *ENGEKI: Japanese Theatre in the New Millennium* (Japan Playwrights Association, 2016–2020).

Japanese Contemporary Objects,
Manipulators, and Actors in Performance

人形演劇の現在
モノ、モノ遣い、アクター

2020年9月10日　第1版第1刷発行

著　者：ボイド　眞理子
発行者：佐久間　勤
発　行：Sophia University Press
　　　　上　智　大　学　出　版

〒102-8554　東京都千代田区紀尾井町7-1
URL：https://www.sophia.ac.jp/

制作・発売　㈱ぎょうせい

〒136-8575　東京都江東区新木場1-18-11
TEL 03-6892-6666　FAX 03-6892-6925
フリーコール　0120-953-431

〈検印省略〉　　　URL：https://gyosei.jp

印刷・製本　ぎょうせいデジタル㈱
ISBN978-4-324-10829-1
(5300303-00-000)
［略号：（上智）人形演劇］

Sophia University Press

　上智大学は、その基本理念の一つとして、
「本学は、その特色を活かして、キリスト教とその文化を
研究する機会を提供する。これと同時に、思想の多様性を
認め、各種の思想の学問的研究を奨励する」と謳っている。
　大学は、この学問的成果を学術書として発表する「独自
の場」を保有することが望まれる。どのような学問的成果
を世に発信しうるかは、その大学の学問的水準・評価と深
く関わりを持つ。
　上智大学は、⑴　高度な水準にある学術書、⑵　キリス
ト教ヒューマニズムに関連する優れた作品、⑶　啓蒙的問
題提起の書、⑷　学問研究への導入となる特色ある教科書
等、個人の研究のみならず、共同の研究成果を刊行するこ
とによって、文化の創造に寄与し、大学の発展とその歴史
に貢献する。